# FISH CREEK VOICES

## An Oral History
## of A Door County Village

Martha Hochmeister Cherry, a Fish Creek "resorter," living it up on vacation in the summer of 1918.

# FISH CREEK VOICES
## An Oral History of A Door County Village

*edited by*

*Edward & Lois Schreiber*

**Wm CAXTON LTD**
Sister Bay, Wisconsin

Published by

Wm Caxton Ltd
Box 709 – Smith Drive & Hwy 57
Sister Bay, WI 54234

(414) 854-2955

Printed in the United States of America.

10  9  8  7  6  5  4  3  2  1

**Library of Congress Cataloging-in-Publication Data**

Fish creek voices : an oral history of a Door County village / Edward & Lois
Schreiber.
    p.    cm.
    ISBN  0-940473-15-1 (alk. paper) :  $20.00 -- ISBN 0-940473-16-X (pbk. : alk.
paper)  $9.95
    1. Fish Creek (Wis.)--Social life and customs. 2. Fish Creek (Wis.)--Biography.
3. Oral history.   I. Schreiber, Edward, 1914-   .  II. Schreiber, Lois, 1910-1990.
F589.F616F57  1990
977.5'63--dc20                                                            90-38035
                                                                              CIP


ISBN#  0-940473-15-1   (hardcover)
ISBN#  0-940473-16-X   (paperback)

This book is set in a version of Times Roman type chosen for its readability and attractiveness; it is printed on acid-neutral paper bound in sewn signatures and is intended to provide a very long useful life.

This book is dedicated to the memory of my wife Lois Schreiber, who helped in many ways to organize the information and suggest the form of the material included here. She eagerly awaited the day it would be published, and she shared every step forward with me. It is my sincere hope that her expectations will be fulfilled.

*Edward Schreiber*

Church of the Atonement

# Table of Contents

Preface
    by *Edward Schreiber* and *Lois Schreiber*     ix
Before The First Man
    by *Duncan Thorp*     1

## The Village

Fish Creek Then and Now
    by *Edward Schreiber*     5
A Talk At The Women's Club (1975)
    by *Harry Schuyler*     42
Cottage Row – Fact or Fiction?
    by *Archibald G. Douglass, Jr.*     62
First Impressions
    by *Lois Schreiber*     71
My Years With the Fish Creek Post Office
    by *Anita Schulz*     75

## Growing Up In Fish Creek

Fish Creek Memories
    by *Allen Schreiber*     81
The Seasons In Fish Creek
    by *Helen Schreiber Allen*     98
The *Hackley* Tragedy
    by *Richard J. Boyd* and *Michael J. Burda*     126
Notes From A Conversation with Elsa Bartelda Carl
    by *Erna Carl Gilliam*     138
Growing Up in Fish Creek
    by *Duncan Thorp*     143

## Families and Personalities

The Hill Family and Steamboat Line
    by *Harwood William Hill*     153
Martin Kinsey
    by *Ann Thorp*     170

The Ingham Kinsey Family
  by *Roy Kinsey* and *Virginia Kinsey*    174
The Herr Doktor
  by *Ann Thorp*    178
The Duclon Family
  by *Vivian Duclon Shine, Grace Duclon Lefebvre,*
    *Lucille Duclon Hays,* and *Clyde J. Duclon*  183
The Thorp Family
  by *Duncan Thorp*    189
Ferdinand Hotz
  by *G. Leonard Apfelbach, MD*    202
Sketches From Life: Fish Creek Voices
  by *Duncan Thorp*    205
Vlad W. Rousseff –Depression Artist
  by *Duncan Thorp*    230
Ella Weborg's Travels
  by *Duncan Thorp*    232

**Places and Institutions**

The Peninsula Players Theatre-In-A-Garden
  by *Tom Connors*    237
Chambers Island
  by *Joel Blahnik*    240
How We Were Almost Killed by An Icelandic Cod, and
  Other Tales of the Heritage Ensemble
  by *Gerald Pelrine*    249
The Peninsula Players
  by *Tom Birmingham*    258

Index    269

# Preface

The idea for *Fish Creek Voices* presented itself to us one day as we were discussing the fact that there really is no history of Fish Creek other than one chapter in Hjalmar Holand's *Old Peninsula Days*. Our generation, which gradually is being depleted, has memories and experiences which may be of interest to future generations. We felt that what we know of Fish Creek's past should be organized and written down, and we began to plan the project.

Very early on, we solicited the opinion and aid of Duncan Thorp, a member of one of Fish Creek's founding families, and of Harwood Hill, who knows a great deal about the history of the Hill family and about steamboats and transportation generally in the town's early years. Both were enthusiastic. Both contributed manuscripts within a short time. Suddenly we had the beginnings of a book on Fish Creek, and we decided to seek out others to contribute chapters on different aspects of Fish Creek's past. Everyone we spoke with was enthusiastic, and, almost before we knew it, the project had grown to the size presented in this volume.

We were very fortunate to obtain the photographs and maps included here, almost all of which were supplied by Bill Guenzel, who has copied and preserved a great deal of graphic material relating to the history of Door County. Bill's collection was dramatically expanded and improved by work he did under a grant from Madeline Tourtelot through the Artists-In-Residence Program at the Peninsula School of Art in 1975. A great many people have allowed him to make photographic copies of old photographs and maps, and his collection is of great historical value. Bill is always interested in additional material, and anyone who has old photographs or maps that might be copied and added to the collection is urged to contact him. When we spoke to him about our project, he generously made his collection available to us.

The following people contributed photos or maps that were included or offered for use in this volume: Alice Hotz Apfelbach, Josh Bell, James Brown, Elsa Carl, Martha Hochmeister Cherry, Eunice Clark, Archibald Douglass, Jr., Skip Fairchild, Mrs. Alfred Franke, Wilmer Gartman, Alice Paepcke Guenzel, Betsy and Paul Guenzel, Ferdinand L. Hotz, Dr. Gertrude Howe, Mrs. Caa McGee, Foster Olson, Rose Pelke, Vivian Duclon Shine, Harold Thorp, Merle Thorp, Ralph Von Briessen, Hudson Van Vorous, and Alma Lundberg Waldo. We thank them all for their generosity.

We are also indebted to Linda Silvasi Kelly for line drawings which appear in several places in the book.

It has been our intention in this book to record in a more or less informal way the beginnings of the village of Fish Creek, its people, and its development from a small Wisconsin fishing and lumbering village to a popular resort area. We have been as precise as memories will allow, and we beg our readers' indulgence for any inaccuracies or discrepancies. We feel that we have presented a well-rounded picture of Fish Creek as it existed during the early part of the century, and we hope that you enjoy reading it as much as we have enjoyed bringing it to you.

The royalties from the sale of this book will benefit the Gibraltar Historical Association.

*Edward Schreiber*
*Lois Schreiber*
Fish Creek, January 1990

# Before the First Man
by
*Duncan Thorp*

In the beginning was the greatest wall of ice the Earth had ever seen. It devastated two-thirds of Europe and the top half of North America, where it was called the Wisconsin or Algonquin Glacier. It reached south beyond Chicago, and it melted into mighty rivers. It was a blue-steel plow that rent the land at random, or bent it into vast valleys with its enormous weight. Where the basins of Lakes Michigan and Huron join near the Straits of Mackinac, a plow of ice split off from the great Lake Michigan lobe and plowed a deep trench with sub-mountains on one side and limestone cliffs on the other. This became an arm of the lake that was named *Baiee Vert* (Green Bay) by early French explorers. The riven splinter of land is the hundred-mile-long finger of cliff and forest, sequined with water and a jeweled archipelago of islands, now known as the Door County Peninsula, though it was named Cape Townsend for a few years. The bluffs of Door County are part of the Niagara Escarpment, extending east to Niagara Falls.

The peninsula was one of those wondrous nooks that explorers were always discovering as they prowled across the new lands. It was an Eden of waters, fish, nests and game for the settler, with acres of soil for husbandmen with plow and seed, and trees for lumbermen with saw and axe.

Before European settlers found it, red men prized the Cape and fought bloody wars here. On one occasion, so they told the first Europeans they met, the last of the original Cape Indians were driven to the tip of the Cape, and most of their fighting men established themselves on the islands just north of Land's End. Determined to recover their homeland in one last great battle, the Indians on the islands sent ashore two spies to seek out the enemy camp, with instructions to build a small signal fire on the beach where it was possible to land a raiding party at night. The two spies were captured and "persuaded" to reveal their mission. On a stormy night the enemies built the signal fire when the waves smashed against the crags, and the entire flotilla of canoes set forth and were wrecked in the night and the storm. A handful managed to climb the low cliff and were promptly tomahawked for their pains. Never again was the Cape the exclusive grounds of the Potowatami, and the strait at the tip of the Cape became known in French histories as *Port des Mortes* - Door of the Dead. The strait eventually was called "The Door" and the peninsula, Door County.

White men prized it as much as red men, though their affection was demonstrated first with axes and later with bulldozers and billboards. Only a few of those who came arrived in time to understand what the Indians found on the Cape worth fighting about. One of these was a New England veteran of the War of 1812 and a descendant of Robert McClathlan, an immigrant from Argyleshire, Scotland, though the name had been pruned to Clafflin after six generations in Massachusetts. Increase Clafflin married a Cleveland widow named Mary Ann Walker and trekked west into the forests as a fur buyer. After trying to settle in three different places, he set off north over the ice of Green Bay in mid-winter with a team of horses, bobsled, and furniture. He selected an obscure cove under a beetling cliff and named it Fish Creek, as the stream that flowed into it was fairly squirming with fish. The Clafflins settled down in a stout log cabin with a big fireplace of granite boulders, and his trusty muzzle-loader to keep the growing family in meat. One of his daughters, Maria, would marry Jacob Thorp, father of Roy Thorp, my grandfather.

✛ ✛ ✛

# The Village

# Fish Creek Then and Now
by
*Edward Schreiber*

Fish Creek was already a well-established village when my parents moved here from Peshtigo, Wisconsin in 1916, though it was in many ways much different than now. Some of the early families still lived along the waterfront in Fish Creek around the turn of the century, including the McSweeneys, the McCummins, the Rockendorf brothers, the Roy Thorps, the Grahams (who had a sawmill), John Brown (who had a cooper's shed), the Sellicks (who owned a sawmill), the Gus Baxters, and the Churches.

The village was founded as a fishing and lumbering center, and these two industries developed and prospered on the strength of local timber supplies and a fine harbor. Early pictures I have seen show that one of the two sawmills was located at the foot of the main pier. Many fish-packing sheds dotted the shoreline, and there was also a cooperage where coopers made the barrel-like containers in which each day's catch was packed, salted, and made ready for shipment to the larger cities.

Land transportation was practically nonexistent in those days, and the packed fish were loaded for shipment onto one of the many boats that served Fish Creek. Several ships of the Goodrich Line out of Chicago took port here, and smaller boats sailed the Green Bay waters, stopping at Green Bay, Marinette, Menominee, and other cities of the upper Michigan peninsula. Several of the boats that plied Green Bay were built and fitted with steam engines by the Hill family in Fish Creek. Among these were the *Cecelia Hill* and the *W.W. Hill*, both fairly good-sized boats capable of transporting heavy cargoes over the waters of the bay. Fish Creek was not the only village to export fish, as several other Door County towns also had fishing industries.

Lumber from the sawmills also was loaded onto ships and sent on its way to the cities. In this way many of the townsfolk made their living and were able to establish homes of their own in the area.

Farming in the surrounding countryside also began to take hold, as people cleared the land and began to raise cattle and plant crops and orchards. Early on, it was discovered that the underlying strata of limestone in Door County were just what cherry trees needed to thrive, and thus was born the now-extensive cherry industry.

I was rather young when the commercial fishing industry thrived in Fish Creek, but I've heard many interesting stories concerning it. Packing and salting the day's catch was a social function much enjoyed by the townsfolk. It took on an air of partying and relieved some of the pressures of a hard day's work. One old woman who didn't approve of such merriment stormed into the midst of a fish-packing session one night, waving her broom and shouting at the merrymakers to stop their jigging and drinking before singling out her husband and leading him out of the shed and on home. But, the task of preparing the fish for shipment had to be done, and the townspeople dealt with it the easiest way they could.

With the plentiful supply of fresh whitefish and trout in the waters of Green Bay and Lake Michigan, fish inevitably became an important part of our diet. In the early 1930s, someone came up with the concept of boiling freshly cut steaks of fish in a large kettle over an outdoor fire. Thus began what we know as a "fish boil," an extremely popular meal now served by many restaurants in the county during the summer season. One of the first fish boils was instituted by the Community Church of Fish Creek as a social event to raise money for the church. Its popularity was immediate, and eating places throughout the county shortly afterwards were offering fish boils every night of the week. As far as I know, the popularity of fish boils is confined to Door County.

About fifty years ago small fish known as smelt started entering the small creeks and brooks of the county each spring in great numbers. When the smelt were running, townsfolk lined the banks of the creeks every night, armed with nets, tubs, baskets, and anything else they could use to dip into the water to gather in the little fish. Smelt were so thick that one could reach into the water with one's bare hands and take out several pounds in a few minutes.

A Fish Creek dock scene in about 1900, with fish sheds and warehouse buildings; the building with a smokestack on the shore behind and to the right of the building on the dock was a sawmill.

Some of the more enterprising fishermen used large nets strung across the creek, and, by working in groups, they could catch several tons in an evening. The smelt were then packed into boxes and shipped by truck to Chicago and Milwaukee the following day.

It's hard to describe the mood that prevailed on those dark, still nights. Voices spoke in hushed tones as fishermen moved about, flashing their lanterns and flashlights into the dark swirling waters along the grassy banks of the creek. The smelt mysteriously ceased to run in Fish Creek after a few springs. I've heard of smelt runs in other parts of the county in later years, but they have never returned to Fish Creek.

✛ ✛ ✛

One of the first families to settle in Fish Creek was the Asa Thorp family. Asa Thorp was responsible for the Asa Thorp Plat which appears on old maps as the first platting of the village. Asa's son Edgar and Edgar's wife Matilda owned one of the first major hotels in Fish Creek in the early part of the century. Edgar and Matilda had four children who grew up to learn the operation of the business and who later took over running the hotel when the elder Thorps retired. Leland, the younger of their two sons, eventually took over management of the hotel and served as its genial host for many years. The hotel offered supervised fishing parties, cab and horse transportation, and telephone and telegraph service in a day when telephones were few. It was also known for its fine cuisine.

Many hotel guests arrived each year around Memorial Day on the ships of the Goodrich Steamship Line and stayed until Labor Day, enjoying a full season of the hotel's hospitality. They came from Chicago, St. Louis, and many other places. Many of the hotel's patrons later bought properties on Cottage Row and established summer homes there, some of which are still owned by descendants of the original owners.

When the old Thorp Hotel was sold to a group of investors there was a general feeling of loss and sadness in the community. It was the end of an important era for the town. Early one morning in February of 1984, after the sale, the village was awakened to the sound of sirens and the smell of smoke. The main lodge of the hotel was engulfed in flames, and the fire threatened to spread to the surrounding cottages. The fire departments from several villages responded, but the best they could do was to keep the fire from spreading. The old Thorp Hotel burned to the ground. Shortly afterwards, the new owners built another building strongly resembling the original. It is now operated as part of the Founder's Square complex.

The other major hotel in Fish Creek was the Welcker Resort, which included extensive properties in town. The Casino, which is now the Whistling Swan, was moved across the ice from Marinette in sections, and served as the hub of social events at the resort during the season. Concerts and literary programs, usually put on by local artists, were on the agenda there several times a month, and the Casino also boasted game rooms and a library for the enjoyment of guests.

Across the street from the Casino was the hotel's large dining room. One could set one's watch by the outdoor dinner bell which rang to call guests for meals morning, noon, and evening. Dr. Welcker, the German gentleman who owned the resort, was a stickler for punctuality, and his hotel ran like a tight ship. He personally took charge of the exercise program, which consisted of scheduled hikes resembling military marches. They were not for the weak at heart.

The other properties of the resort consisted mostly of the block behind the Casino and most of the block below it, including the hotel's laundry on the shore. What is now the White Gull Inn housed guests, as did several adjacent cottages. American plan meals were the rule at both hotels.

Several other hotels and rooming houses figured in the village activities. My grandfather, Edward Schreiber, and my step grandmother, whom we called Aunt Lottie, owned and operated a hotel called "The Nook," which stood on the corner now occupied by Bunda's Hutch. The hotel had a large veranda which extended across

# GOODRICH BOATS

## On LAKE MICHIGAN and GREEN BAY

## TOURIST ROUTES and RATES

### VIA LAKE and RAIL

Meals and berth included in rate where star ★ is shown.

To Agents:—In drawing orders for tickets via routes shown below, do not fail to show route number and rate from Chicago on order. Special routes and rates furnished on application.

R. C. DAVIS, Gen. Pass. Agt., Foot Michigan Ave., Chicago.

| Local Passenger Fares | | From Chicago | | From Milwaukee | |
|---|---|---|---|---|---|
| | | One Way | Round Trip | One Way | Round Trip |
| Chicago . . . . . . . . . . . . . .Ill. | | . . . . . . . . . | . . . . . . . . . | $ 1.00 | $ 1.50 |
| Ephraim . . . . . . . . . . . .Wis. | | ★ $8.00 | ★ $15.00 | ★ 7.00 | ★ 13.00 |
| Escanaba . . . . . . . . . . .Mich. | | ★ 8.00 | ★ 15.00 | ★ 7.00 | ★ 13.00 |
| Fish Creek . . . . . . . . . . .Wis. | | ★ 8.00 | ★ 15.00 | ★ 7.00 | ★ 13.00 |
| Green Bay . . . . . . . . . . .Wis. | | ★ 8.00 | ★ 15.00 | ★ 7.00 | ★ 13.00 |
| Grand Haven . . . . . . . . .Mich. | | 1.50 | 2.75 | . . . . . . . . | . . . . . . . . |
| Grand Rapids . . . . . . . . .Mich. | | 2 00 | 3 75 | . . . . . . . . | . . . . . . . . |
| Kewaunee . . . . . . . . . . .Wis. | | 3.25 | 5.50 | 3.25 | 4.00 |
| Lake Harbor (Hotel) . . .Mich. | | Sell | to Muske | gon | |
| Mackinac Island . . . . . . .Mich. | | ★ 10.00 | ★ 18.00 | ★ 10.00 | ★ 18.00 |
| Manitowoc . . . . . . . . . . .Wis. | | 2.25 | 3.75 | 1.25 | 2.25 |
| Marinette . . . . . . . . . . .Wis. | | ★ 8.00 | ★ 15.00 | 7.00 | ★ 13.00 |
| Menominee . . . . . . . . . .Mich. | | ★ 8.00 | ★ 15.00 | 7.00 | ★ 13.00 |
| Milwaukee . . . . . . . . . . .Wis. | | 1.00 | 1.50 | . . . . . . . . | . . . . . . . . |
| Milwaukee { Good only on S. S. "Columbus," going and returning same day. | | . . . . . . . . | 1.00 | . . . . . . . . | . . . . . . . . |
| Muskegon . . . . . . . . . . .Mich. | | 1.50 | 2.75 | . . . . . . . . | . . . . . . . . |
| Racine . . . . . . . . . . . . .Wis. | | 1.00 | 1 50 | .25 | .50 |
| Sheboygan . . . . . . . . . . .Wis. | | 2.00 | 3.25 | 1.00 | 1.75 |
| Sister Bay . . . . . . . . . . .Wis. | | ★ 8.00 | ★ 15.00 | ★ 7.00 | ★ 13.00 |
| Sturgeon Bay . . . . . . . . .Wis. | | ★ 6.50 | ★ 12.00 | ★ 5.00 | ★ 9.50 |
| Washington Island . . . . .Wis. | | ★ 8.00 | ★ 15.00 | ★ 7.00 | ★ 13.00 |
| White Hall (White Lake)Mich. | | 1.75 | 3.00 | . . . . . . . . | . . . . . . . . |

ROUTE 1.

Buffalo
New York
{ ★ Goodrich Transit Co . . . . . . . .to Mackinac Island
Detroit & Cleveland Nav. Co..to Detroit
Detroit & Buffalo S. B. Co..to Buffalo
From Chicago or Milwaukee, $18.00.
Round Trip, $32.50.

Tourist Routes and Rates of the Goodrich Transportation Company on Lake Michigan and Green Bay in 1908.

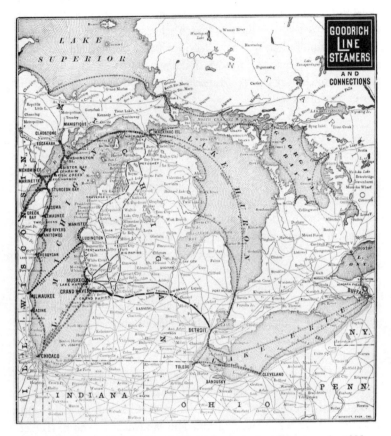

Steamer Routes of the Goodrich Transportation Company in 1908.

the front and around one side. It was a common sight to see guests sitting on swings and rocking chairs watching the street traffic pass.

Ed and Lottie ran this hotel for many years with the help of Ethel, Goldie, and Hollis, my dad's two sisters and brother. My grandparents owned acreage both above and below the bluff where they pastured several cows to supply milk, cream, and cheese for the hotel. I was always fascinated watching them use the cream separator and butter churn to process the fresh milk. They made their own cottage cheese, known then as "dutch" cheese.

Grandfather was a well driller by trade, and he also used some of his equipment to move buildings. In those days, gasoline-powered machinery wasn't extensively used, and horses provided the power for heavy jobs.

✛ ✛ ✛

The Barringers also operated a hotel. It was located in the building which is now the C and C Club, and was more of a stopover hotel than a tourist residence. It was used primarily by men who were to be in town for a few days for business reasons and needed a nice place to stay which served hearty, wholesome meals. In the late 1920s and early 1930s, high school students from Baileys Harbor and Egg Harbor stayed at the hotel during the winter months when travel between the towns became difficult. Gibraltar was the only high school in this part of Door County, and it accepted students from several neighboring villages. High school districts weren't well defined in those days, and it wasn't until many years later that state law mandated that all townships must belong to a high school district.

The Barringers also owned and operated the Maple Tree Cafe, which is now the Summertime Restaurant. It was a popular and attractive meeting place for summer visitors who wished to stop for a lemonade, a sundae, or a soda and sandwiches. The Barringers had a barn behind the cafe in which they kept several cows to supply milk for their hotel. I well remember the old bachelor gentleman Staner Olson, who cared for Barringer's cows and walked the herd down Main street to pasture every morning and returned with them every evening.

After Meta and Cora Barringer retired, they sold the hotel to a German gentleman named Joe Schwab and the Maple Tree Cafe to Mrs. Roy (Virginia) Kinsey. Virginia turned part of the cafe into an attractive gift shop and added an outdoor garden patio to the other part of the building where she continued to serve ice cream sundaes, sodas, and sandwiches. Everyone was pleased that Virginia continued the traditions of the Maple Tree Cafe, then renamed the Summertime Gift and Coffee Shop, and it became a popular gathering place for young and old.

✛ ✛ ✛

The Myron Stevens family owned and operated still another rooming house on Main street in the building that is now Cole's Tole and Country. The Stevenses were a large family, and the children were all assigned chores connected with the rooming house. Mrs. Stevens did all the cooking for the hotel's clientele in a large kitchen in the rear of the building. Myron worked out, operating a horse-drawn grader which maintained the township streets, and consequently kept several horses in a barn behind the hotel. In those days there were no hard-surfaced roads, and it was a constant chore to grade and smooth the crushed stone and gravel of the road surfaces so they didn't develop deep ruts from the horse-drawn traffic. It was the job of his two boys, Mynie and Freddie, to care for the horses by keeping them fed and cleaning the stalls.

There were times when Myron and his wife had differences of opinion, often resulting in Myron fleeing out the back door amid a small shower of pots and pans. But their quarrels were always patched up, and harmony would prevail until the next time. The Stevenses later bought one of the old school buildings which were sold when the new grade-school building was constructed. They moved it near to their hotel and operated a tavern in it. It has had several owners since then, and is now the Bayside Tavern.

✛ ✛ ✛

Many patrons of the Thorp Hotel bought property on Cottage Row from George Clark, a stove manufacturer from Chicago who had had the foresight to acquire part of a two-mile strip of shoreline and bluff property from Asa Thorp when it was available years earlier. He retained two fine building sites, one on each end, and sold lots down the shoreline to those who were willing to build homes of good quality and value.

As soon as the lots became available, many people from Chicago and St. Louis, including bankers, manufacturing executives, doctors and other professional people, bought them and built their summer homes. Many of those homes have been passed on to the younger generation and still retain the family names.

The Crundens were one of the early families. Mr. Crunden was associated with the Crunden-Martin Manufacturing Company of St. Louis, and Mrs. Crunden, a rather large lady with a "grande dame" personality, was very active in the social life of Cottage Row and of the community at large. She was always interested in community affairs and made an effort to keep many of the local men busy at community projects during the depression. She had a great fondness for stone terraces, and she employed several local men to bring in soil and rock and build the many terraced walls about her estate. If you seek out the house now owned by the Sidney Harris family on Cottage Row, you will be pleasantly impressed with the lovely stone terraces. Mrs. Crunden was also responsible for securing a grant and engineering the building of the large stone terrace at Sunset Park. That structure has been a source of pleasure for many years to vacationers wishing to view the colorful sunsets and islands over the waters of Green Bay. Mechanically powered machines were not much in use in those times, and one must appreciate the many man-hours that went into hauling and laying the stone and filling behind the wall that forms this beautiful terrace.

✠ ✠ ✠

The Clarks were another family that was always interested in the development of the village and also played an important part in the community. George M. Clark was instrumental in rebuilding the large pier and adding a warehouse on the site now occupied by the municipal pier. His pier made it possible for fairly large boats to dock at Fish Creek, which was a decided aid to the development of Fish Creek's fledgling industries. The land that is now Clark Park was a gift of the Clarks to the village. It affords pleasure to vacationers and villagers alike, besides being the site for many community activities and special events during the summer season.

The pier built by Mr. Clark was later replaced by the present one, which is built to stand the heavy pressures of shoving ice and strong gales. The new pier is also outfitted with electric and water service to accommodate the many yachts and sailing vessels which visit Fish Creek each summer.

✛ ✛ ✛

When the Lundbergs, who were another of the early families of Fish Creek, became interested in establishing a Baptist church in the village, they offered the land adjacent to their home as a site for a church. Mr. Clark, apparently sensing this to be an asset to the village, engaged an architect to draw plans and had them donated. The charming building now known as the Community Church still stands, and its classic design is very pleasing to the eye. Before the church was built, Mrs. Lundberg, who was very interested in children's Christian education, held Sunday School in the Town Hall, which at that time stood adjacent to the Thorp Hotel, where the Helgeson house now stands.

The Episcopal Church located across the corner from the Community Church was built in 1878. It was originally an unfinished dwelling of a fisherman named Charles Gessler, and is the oldest church in the village. It is a tiny building laid out in the shape of a cross, and it has retained its spartan furnishings, including straight-backed wooden pews, a plain altar, and an old pump organ. It is a delightful place to visit, but services are held there only in the summer months.

The Seventh Day Adventist Church is located a block south of Main street and is served by a pastor who also has the Sturgeon

Bay Church. The church in Fish Creek has now been enlarged and holds services year around. My great-grandfather Steven Norton, whose picture hangs in the foyer of the church, was one of its Elders when it was first established. Asa Thorp donated the land, and the church was erected in 1892.

The Community building in Fish Creek originally was built to replace two older school buildings, one for grades 1-4 and the other for grades 5-8. One of those structures became a tavern, and the other became the Catholic church. The Catholic congregation in Fish Creek met in a private home until they acquired the grade-school building in 1922 and moved it to its present site, just east of what is now the Community building. The Catholic congregation used that building for many years before they built the attractive new church located across from the Fish Creek entrance to Peninsula State Park.

✛ ✛ ✛

In the early 1900s, there were scarcely any autos, and the horse and buggy was the principal means of transportation. Hitching posts dotted Main street, and several stables were scattered about the village. Any day of the week it was common to see a row of wagons and buggies in front of the business places, usually people in from nearby farms doing their shopping or taking care of whatever other business they might have in town. I don't remember whether or how the streets were cleaned, but I am sure something must have been worked out. In the winter, horse-drawn cutters and bob sleds replaced the buggies and wagons as the means of transportation. We youngsters used to hitch rides by attaching our sleds to the horse-drawn sleighs. Needless to say, the owners didn't always approve.

In the early days it sometimes required great effort for the postal service to deliver the mail daily. Rail service brought the mail as far as Sturgeon Bay, but it had to be delivered to the villages north of there using horses. In summer, the mail came from Sturgeon Bay by wagon, but in winter it arrived in a large bob-sleigh fitted with a

Alex and Alice Lunderg in front of their store (now Alwes Food Market) ca. 1917. WW I posters can be seen in the store windows, and the Barringer Hotel (now the C & C Club) is across the street.

cab enclosure large enough to accommodate the driver and a small stove. The bags of mail were stacked in a box at the rear of the sleigh and were covered with a heavy tarp to protect them from the snow and ice. When the roads hadn't been cleared and the frothy, snow-covered horses pulled the sleigh into town, they were a sight worthy of a Christmas card.

✤ ✤ ✤

Winter always brought a spurt of activity to the town when ice formed in the harbor and Green Bay froze. Small tar-paper fishing shanties began to dot the harbor by the dozen as anglers waited for schools of herring to find the beaded hooks they dangled through holes in the ice beneath their shanties. A brightly colored bead was slipped over the hook to attract the unwary herring, and when a large school passed by, a skillful and lucky fisherman could catch his limit of fish in a few minutes. On the other hand he might spend an entire day on the ice and have to come home to his wife sheepish and empty-handed. Truly, fishermen's luck prevailed here.

Commercial fishermen set long gill nets underneath the ice in deeper waters, hoping to land a good catch of lake trout. This took a special technique involving long running poles and a series of holes in order to run the nets under the ice and secure them. A lifting shanty was hauled to the site, and the trout were removed from the nets and then cleaned and packed in the lifting shanty. Most fishermen had a Model-T Ford fitted with dual rear wheels and half-tracks, and with runners in place of the front wheels. A vehicle thus adapted could travel on ice in most any kind of weather. Travel from Fish Creek to Marinette or Menominee was accomplished with these vehicles, as well as with horse-drawn bob-sleds. Small evergreen boughs were set in the ice at intervals to stake out a "road" to follow. Since Marinette is only eighteen miles from Fish Creek by water and is the closest larger city, the road was usually well travelled in winter.

Downtown Fish Creek, about 1910, looking west down Main Street. Note nuggets of the road (right foreground) awaiting a street cleaner. Welcker's Casino (now the Whistling Swan) is the most distant building shown; the Barringer Hotel (now the C&C Club) is next, then the Lundberg (now Alwes Market) and Hill (now Norz) stores.

✤ ✤ ✤

Ice harvesting to fill the ice houses in the village was an activity that lasted about three weeks each February and employed many of the town's menfolk. There was no electrical refrigeration in those days, and the need for ice in summer was great. Most of the teams and bob-sleds in town were kept busy transporting heavy cakes of ice to the many ice-houses in the village. The cakes were cut almost through with a large motorized circular saw and then separated with an ice chisel. Once cut, they were guided to a narrow channel where they were lifted out of the water by an endless chain fitted with lugs and deposited on a large loading platform. The blocks were then loaded onto waiting bob-sleighs and transported to the ice-houses. Full appreciation of this great effort was only felt in summer when the ice was used to cool food or to enhance the enjoyment of a nice cool soda.

✤ ✤ ✤

On the lighter side, winter activities like skating, ice-boating and sail-sleighing provided recreation for the sports minded. Snow was cleared off a large patch of ice to make a community skating rink, and there was usually a bonfire built in its center, while many skaters spent happy evenings cutting figure 8's and trying to impress the opposite sex with their skating skills. It was clean, enjoyable fun.

My brother and I bought an old sail-sleigh from Gus Baxter, a retired fisherman who had used it when he did commercial fishing years before. It proved to be a good investment. We used it for many years, sailing as far as Chamber's Island and sharing rides with our friends. On a clear day and with ice conditions just right, we could reach speeds of 35 miles an hour. Several boys owned ice-boats and challenged us to race. Winning or losing wasn't important. The fun of the ride was the prize.

One day, a friend and I took the sail-sleigh for a ride to Strawberry Island in the very early spring. The ice near the island

A sail-sleigh (ca. 1912); wind-powered sleds like this one were used as all-purpose vehicles for transporting fish, lumber, and general supplies across the ice during the winter months.

had begun to weaken. Before we knew it, we had sailed onto this weak ice, and the sleigh went through the ice. Luckily the boom of the sail straddled the opening, and with a bit of careful maneuvering and balancing we walked along the boom onto safe ice. Then, with great effort we managed to pull the sleigh safely back onto good ice and sail it home. Needless to say it was our last sail-sleigh ride of the season.

✠ ✠ ✠

The extensive use of horses supported several blacksmith shops in town. The one I remember best was owned by George Schuyler. It stood next to the street on the site where the front cottage of Wesa's Edgewater Cottages now stands. We boys experienced the true feeling of "The Village Blacksmith" watching Mr. Schuyler crank the hand-driven forge, then pull a white-hot horseshoe from the glowing coals, and beat it into the desired shape amid a spray of sparks, before plunging it into cool water and fitting it against the waiting horse's hoof. The smell of horses, of hot coals, of the blacksmith's perspiration, and of the onlookers' pipe smoke all mingled together is still a vivid memory.

✠ ✠ ✠

During my early years in Fish Creek, electric, plumbing and phone facilities were quite limited or non-existent, though larger cities had electric power. Vacationers visiting Door County had to get used to the lack of these amenities. The power companies had not yet run electric lines to northern Door County, and kerosene lamps, Aladdin mantle lamps, and Coleman mantle lamps were the standard lighting fixtures in homes, businesses and hotels. What few autos there were used cresolene fuel for their headlights, and a tank of it was carried on the running board. There were several street lamps located on corners in the village which had to be cleaned and refueled regularly and which also had to be lit and extinguished each evening and morning. Several men in town took turns doing this chore. The Roy Kinseys still have one of the original lamps in front of their home on Main street.

My grandfather installed an early electrical system in the Nook Hotel. It consisted of a Delco light plant which ran on gasoline and charged up a small room full of batteries which in turn supplied electricity for the hotel and its many rooms. My dad later installed a Kohler light system which supplied electricity to our home and store and later, to the Town Hall, which stands kitty-corner to our original home.

When the Town Hall stood next to the Thorp Hotel, movies were shown there about once a week by Mr. Art Brungraber of Jacksonport. You may wonder how he could show movies without electricity to operate his projector. He solved this by having a large gasoline-powered generator mounted on his truck which he parked in front of the Town Hall when movies were to be shown. The cables ran in through a window and thus we saw Hoot Gibson, *The Phantom of the Opera*, *Frankenstein*, and many other exciting movies of the day. We boys often tried to see the movies by standing on each other's shoulders to peek in the windows, but, as a rule, Mr. Brungraber made periodic rounds outside and we had to scatter.

Indoor plumbing was rare in those days, and the hotels furnished large ceramic washbowls and pitchers of water in each cottage for their guests. The main building usually had one toilet on each floor, and water was supplied to them by being pumped from the bay to a large tank on a wooden platform on the hotel grounds. Water pressure was by gravity, and the water couldn't be used for drinking. Drinking water came from a well.

The streets in town were unpaved until some time in the early 1930s. The loose gravel and crushed stone streets required constant maintenance. Even the main highway from Green Bay had to be maintained by a grader in this fashion.

❖ ❖ ❖

The Albert Friedmanns of the Schuster stores in Milwaukee once owned the entire point where Hidden Harbor Condominiums and Sunset Park are now located. As the plotting of the village was laid out, some of the streets ran directly through the Friedmann property, dividing it into several pieces. Mr. Friedmann proposed that if the town was willing to close those streets and turn the property over to him, he would donate the strip of land now known as Sunset Park to the town. The deal was consummated and that is how Sunset Park came into being. The Friedmanns later had a circular lagoon dug at the north end of their property so that they could moor their boats in sheltered waters.

✛ ✛ ✛

Our town hall originally was a rectangular one-room building with concrete steps leading up to the entrance in front. Several years after it was moved to its present site, plans were made to enlarge it and provide added facilities because it was used for various meetings. Mr. Erwin Fuhr, a local electrician, was interested in producing one-act and three-act plays there, as was the local Women's Club and the grade school. When the hall was enlarged, Mr. Fuhr took charge of planning the stage, complete with footlights and overhead banks of lights, a raised curtain, two dressing rooms, and an assortment of scenery panels suitable for a variety of dramas. Mr. John Knuppel, a local painter of talent, agreed to paint the scenery. The stage isn't much used for drama today because the schools have their own facilities, but the scenery and stage stand ready if needed. A projection booth was added later, and a large stage screen can be lowered to show movies. At the time the hall was enlarged, restrooms and a complete kitchen were added, along with a good-sized basement room beneath the stage. When the town acquired its first fire-fighting equipment, a two-stall fire station was added to the rear of the hall.

✛ ✛ ✛

The peaceful little village of Fish Creek hadn't experienced a major fire in many years when, in mid-July of 1928, residents were awakened very early one morning to the smell of smoke and the eerie glow of impending danger – a FIRE. My parents awakened us to warn that a garage on the other side of our street was afire. It was threatening the Lester Anderson home, which was just across the street from us, and possibly ours as well. About a dozen men quickly gathered pails and organized a bucket brigade to pour water onto the threatened houses in an effort to save them. But, fanned by a brisk southwest breeze, the flames sent sparks and shards of burning wood onto the Seaquist house, a two-story structure that stood on the corner. The fire ignited the roof and the house was quickly engulfed in flames, and all attempts to save it proved futile. The Sturgeon Bay Fire Department had been called and duly arrived, but both the house and the garage burned to the ground.

Dad was president of the Fish Creek Men's Club at that time, and shortly after the big fire, the club made it a project to press the town into providing fire protection for the village. The recent fire was fresh in the minds of the town officials, and that made it quite easy to convince the townspeople of the need for their own fire department. The town ordered a new fire truck, and it was a festive day when the gleaming new red "Knotts Victor" arrived, mounted on a Chevrolet chassis with about 500 feet of hose and a sturdy pumper. The men then organized the Fish Creek Volunteer Fire Department, and Dad was made chief. From then on, the fire department was called quite often. Several major fires occurred, including some in nearby towns which didn't have fire departments of their own yet. Dad ruined many clothes in his duties as fire chief, but he served faithfully for many years until health forced him to resign. Our family nicknamed him "Chief," and though he is gone, we still speak of him by that name.

✜ ✜ ✜

In 1960, the townspeople became interested in establishing a library and the town-hall basement room was fitted out with bookshelves. Lois Schreiber was asked to serve as librarian, and the library operated from that location for several years until the town purchased a building on Main street from the Josh Bells and moved the library into it. Over the years, the old town hall has hosted movies, plays, minstrel shows, scout meetings, square dances, grade-school Christmas programs, town meetings and caucuses, and suppers and meetings by various civic groups, among many other activities. A few years ago, some felt that the hall had outlived its usefulness, but fortunately, under the able leadership of Virginia Kinsey and Ann Thorp, the Gibraltar Historical Association found public opinion to be very much in favor of making the repairs necessary to make the building a viable facility again. Its proximity to Clark Park and the harbor are much in its favor. To date, the foundations have been rebuilt, the roof has been repaired, and a new heating system has been installed, all part of an ongoing program by the GHA to put the building into first class condition.

Mr. Edgar Thorp, the hotel owner, once owned the property on which the town hall now stands. As the site of the original hall adjoined his hotel property on main street, Mr. Thorp proposed to give the site of the present town hall to the town in exchange for the property near his hotel. Apparently the proposition sounded fair to the town fathers; the exchange was made, and Mr. Thorp moved the hall to its present site.

✛ ✛ ✛

My grandfather owned the property below the bluff on which the Bonnie Brook Motel now stands, as well as about twenty acres above the bluff. When he had no more use for it as pasture land, he sold it to the Welckers. The two sons, Fritz and Victor Welcker, still retain ownership of it. In about 1935 Caroline Fisher, a recent college graduate, and her brother and sister became interested in forming a summer stock company in Fish Creek. They rented a piece of property from the Welckers behind the Bonnie Brook Motel and near the creek to produce their first dramas. From that small beginning, the Peninsula Players came into being. Today the Peninsula Players is a successful institution producing plays and musicals for the enjoyment of thousands of summer visitors each season.

✠ ✠ ✠

My great-grandparents Steven and Rachel Norton operated a farm in the Maple Grove area just east of Fish Creek for many years. When Steven passed away his widow bought a home in town on property where a gift shop called The Dove's Nest now stands. She lived alone there for many years until she became unable to care for herself and had to move into her daughter's home. Her home was then sold and eventually was moved to the corner lot across from the Adventist Church where it still stands today. It is one of the oldest buildings in Fish Creek.

✠ ✠ ✠

Another older home which deserves mention is the old Thorp House. It was built by Freeman Thorp, one of the early Thorp brothers who lost his life in the tragic Hackley sinking. The Thorp House has been tastefully restored and is now operated as the Thorp House Inn, a bed-and-breakfast inn featuring original recipes of its owner Chris Falck-Pedersen and her husband Sverre. It demonstrates that some of the very old buildings can be transformed into charming, unique inns which capture the attention of modern travelers, for such has been the case with the Thorp House Inn.

✠ ✠ ✠

The stately old Noble home still stands in the center of the village, a monument to one of the oldest families in Fish Creek. Alex Noble was responsible for platting the town eastward from about where the Community building stands.   His was one of two early town plats, the other being by Asa Thorp.   Mr. Noble operated a blacksmith shop in town located kitty-corner from the town hall.

There were several other businesses in the village, including three stores.  The store owned by the Vorouses was in a building that later housed the post office and also had a garage located at the rear of the building operated by two local men, Carl Seiler and Henry Stenzel.  That building now contains a shop called Hide Side Casuals.  Previously, the post office was in the Al (now Roy) Kinsey home across the street, with Mrs. Al (May) Kinsey as postmistress.

Another store, originally built and operated by Alexander Lundberg and his wife, was on the corner, and is now the Alwes store.  The Lundbergs were one of the early families and were quite active in community affairs.  The third store was in a building next to the Lundbergs and is now the Norz Fish Creek General Store.  It was originally built by Wallace Hill and run by the Hills, and it was then sold to the McLeods, relatives of the old Thorp family.   The McLeods later sold it to people named Poirer who ran it for several years before my father, Lester Schreiber bought it.  It stayed in our family for fifty-four years until we sold it to the Norzes in 1970.

The large upstairs of our store had served as a center for social activity for many years before my parents bought the store, and it had been the site of many dances and basketball games.  I'm told that the lively games and dances often shook the floor so violently that posts had to be added in the store below to strengthen the structure and prevent the floor from collapsing.  When my parents first bought the building, it was unheated, and they placed a large upright stove surrounded by a box of sand for safety reasons in the center of the room.  That stove had to be stoked with wood day and night to keep the merchandise from freezing.  Naturally the warmth attracted many of the town's men who sat around the stove exchanging stories and town gossip during the day.  This custom did not please my mother, as the men often spit in the sand and tracked in dirty snow, causing ugly puddles around the stove, but that was one of the joys of running a store in those days.

The Fish Creek business district, ca. 1914, showing the Lundberg (then Vorous, then Krause, now Alwes) store and the Hill (then McLeod, then Poirer, then Schreiber, now Norz) store.

✠ ✠ ✠

Peninsula State Park was established in the early part of the century by some forward-looking people at the state level. The thirty-six-hundred-acre tract which now comprises the park was the site of many farms, so it was a problem to establish the park as public land without seriously dislocating the families who lived there. The state wisely negotiated to buy the farms with the understanding that the families could live out their lives on them, at which time the properties automatically reverted to the state. This arrangement was agreeable, and thus the beautiful point of land between Fish Creek and Ephraim which we know as Peninsula State Park was acquired.

The totem pole which now stands near the ninth fairway of the golf course is a replica of an original that was fashioned and carved by Mr. C.M. Lasaar. The Lasaars spent summers in a cottage next to the shore road near Weborg Point and were very interested in the lore of the peninsula. Hjalmar R. Holand, a historian interested in the Indian background and activities of the peninsula, made the original sketches for the pole, and Vida Weborg, an artist who had studied Indian art for many years, worked out the final details of the sketches. The bear carving which graces the top of the totem pole was done by a man named Robert Petscheider. The pole was erected and the monument dedicated in 1927, with Chief Kahquados and thirty-two other members of the Potowatomie tribe hosted by nearby local residents present to witness the ceremonies.

Upon the death in 1930 of Chief Kahquados, the last of the chiefs of the Potowatomies, a burial ceremony which I attended was held at the stone monument. Members of the local historical society and other dignitaries spoke honoring the chief. I understood later that the chief had passed on some time during the previous winter, and his remains were kept frozen until they could be interred in the spring. The Potowatomies were a gentle and peace-loving people. The original totem pole deteriorated over the years, and it has been replaced by a new one carved by an artist named Adlai Hardin and erected in 1969.

The Peninsula Golf Course was established in 1921. It was designed by Mr. W.R. Lovekin as a 3500-yard nine-hole course, carved out of a scenic area in the park overlooking Eagle Harbor. It was ready for use by July 1 of that year under the auspices of the Door County Country Club, an organization charged with the course's operation. The course has since been revised and enlarged to an 18-hole course, and it remains one of the finest, most challenging courses in Wisconsin.

The old lighthouse standing in Peninsula Park near Tennison Bay is now a museum, but it guided many a ship through the waters of Green Bay in years past. Its light keeper was for many years an old-timer named Captain William Duclon, one of a family well versed in the operation of boats on Green Bay waters. As with most present lighthouses, it now has an automatic light.

Mention should be made of some of the interesting families and individuals who were among the last to relinquish their land to the park. The Kodanko family worked a farm on Middle road. They were Hungarian farmers who worked very hard to raise their family, having no machinery with which to clear and work their land or harvest their crops. Their children walked roughly four miles through deep woods to school in Fish Creek every day. During the winter months, the snow was often very deep, but despite their arduous trek, the three youngsters had one of the best attendance records in school. I'm sure their parents valued their children's education greatly to insist that they make that effort.

An old bachelor gentleman named Carl Anderson also lived on the Kodanko road and operated a greenhouse. At first glance, one might not be very impressed with him, since he usually appeared in rather scruffy clothing and was often in need of a shave. However, he was a well-educated man who apparently had studied horticulture and decided to come to Door County to open a greenhouse and nursery. His income must have been meager, because the nursery business is notably seasonal, though his customers included people on Cottage Row and other seasonal visitors. Many left their cherished plants with him for the winter and picked them up well cared for in the spring. He always had a friendly feud going with Miss Dyer, a retired school teacher who always addressed him as "Anderson" and was never quite satisfied with the health of her posies.

Anderson did have a flurry of business during the Christmas season when he allowed people to cut their own Christmas trees from his land. I remember him charging only fifty cents for a tree that we cut ourselves. My boys, who were only eight or ten years old at the time, looked forward to the experience of trudging through the snow with me to find just the right tree and dragging it out of the woods to take home and show their mom what a nice selection they had made. Carl always had a smile when he wished us a Merry Christmas as we left with our tree.

◆ ◆ ◆

Some may remember Camp Meenahga, a camp for teen-age and younger girls which was run for many years by Alice Clark and her daughter, both from St. Louis. They arrived every summer to open the camp which was attended by about thirty young ladies from the St. Louis area. The camp offered swimming, trail hiking, horseback riding, and other related activities under the supervision of qualified counselors. Thade Cornils had a riding stable near the edge of the park, so it was very easy to cut a bridle trail to Camp Meenahga and make riding horses available to the girls at camp.

Each autumn before the camp disbanded for the season, the girls and Mr. Cornil put on a gala horse show in an arena behind the camp, where they exhibited their riding skills and expertise in horsemanship that they had learned during the summer. There was a young Scotch boy who was a counselor and sailing instructor for the camp. He dressed in bright tartan-plaid kilt, scarf, and tam and played the bagpipes as the horses bearing young ladies high-stepped around the arena. The show attracted many visitors who applauded each act of the show with enthusiasm. Several times during the summer the girls would ride into town (either Fish Creek or Ephraim) dressed in their neat riding habits and would be a real traffic stopper. They often made their way to the Summertime for sodas and sundaes before returning to camp.

Two very interesting spinster sisters lived quite spartanly in an old house in the park, high upon an escarpment facing the waters of Green Bay. Their names were Ella and Vida Weborg. I used to deliver groceries to their home, sometimes having to climb up the icy hill with a fifty-pound sack of flour or a five-gallon can of coal oil (kerosene) for their lamps and oil stove.

The room where they did all of their living was small, dark, and cluttered with the activities of their life. Vida, the eldest sister was an artist who, incidentally, did the drawings for Hjalmar Holand's book *Old Peninsula Days*. Though she had very poor eyesight, she was talented and had an indomitable spirit. That spirit made itself felt in the community when she pushed hard for the adoption of the Townsend Plan, a forerunner of Social Security as we know it today. I'm sure that if she could have made her efforts felt at a higher level, Social Security would have been adopted earlier than it was.

The two old ladies had no means of transportation, and Ella, the younger sister, did all of the errands, walking a distance of about three miles into town to take care of shopping, mail, etc. In the dead of winter she could be seen trudging along the rutted sleigh tracks, shod only in a pair of canvas sneakers. She had many friends along the way where she visited, stopping for a hot cup of coffee, a little conversation, and a chance to warm up before continuing on the next leg of her journey. I'm sure, on looking back, that those two ladies' lives were quite drab and that they welcomed any available social contact.

Several other unmarried ladies lived in the park, some year around, others occasionally. Three sisters, Miss Gatter, who called her place the "Owl's Nest," Mrs. Bach, a widow who lived in a house on the shore, and Mrs. Eberline, who lived on an island near the park, were summer visitors to Door County.

Miss Agnes Keuchler lived in an old log home near the old Svens Tower, which has since been taken down. She was a spinster who had taught in a conservatory of music in Chicago and then decided to make her year-round home in the park after she retired. She was a fine pianist who gave music lessons and also sang and played at many local social events. She could often be seen driving her Model-T touring car with side curtains into town to shop and pick up her mail.

The old Dyer cottage, now removed, used to be a landmark near the Fish Creek entrance of the park. The Dyer sisters, Lilia and Lydia, were retired school teachers who came from St. Louis to spend summers in their log home. The home was sparsely but tastefully furnished and was kept immaculately clean. The two ladies loved to entertain, especially Lilia, who courted the friendship of many of the well-to-do people on Cottage Row. They had no transportation of their own, but could always rely on their Cottage Row friends to send their chauffeurs to pick them up for parties to which they were invited.

The last residents to leave their property to Peninsula State Park were Alfred and William Carlson, two brothers. Their home was also near Weborg's Point. I think they were commercial fishermen. The Carlsons had a housekeeper named Gertrude Lund who outlived them and stayed on in the home until her death.

Park history wouldn't be complete without mention of Alfred Doolittle one of the early superintendents of the park, if not the first. Al was a very strong-minded man, with definite ideas of how the park should be managed. He put many local men to work on projects of his own design making many improvements which were much needed in the development of the fledgling park. He carved out campsites, built a network of roads, cut hiking trails, and gave them names which still grace the signposts today. He was criticized for some of his projects, but the lookout terraces overlooking Green Bay and the large tower on Eagle Bluff that people like so well are all due to the drive and fertile imagination of Al Doolittle. People meeting him on the street would often ask "How are you today, Al?". As he chewed on his unlit cigar, his stock answer was always, "Never better".

While he was park superintendent Mr. Doolittle acquired and developed the piece of property on the left as one enters the park from highway 42. At that time the highway continued toward the park, turned to the right on Evergreen Street and came out on top of the hill above the Irish House. The state later rerouted it, cutting out the circuitous route. Mr. Doolittle built about twelve cottages, a miniature golf course, a coffee shop, and a filling station on his land. He rented out the coffee shop, the filling station, and the miniature golf course for several years, and he eventually sold the entire complex to the Lester Andersons. Lester ran the filling station and his wife ran the cottages. After various changes of ownership of different parts of the enterprise, the State of Wisconsin finally acquired the entire property, removed the last of the existing buildings, and annexed it as part of the park. It is now a pleasant area where people can wander down to the edge of the creek or sit on the benches and listen to the bird songs or just quietly enjoy nature.

At one time the Wiest Plumbing Company built a plumbing shop on the small triangle of land where the welcome sign for the park now stands. After serving as a plumbing shop for several years, it became a barber shop with living quarters above. Eventually that property too was acquired by the state, and it now serves to welcome visitors to the park.

During World War II, the large building about half way up Evergreen road on the right was used to house German prisoners of war. It had been a cherry camp, but it served as a dormitory for the prisoners, and the surrounding grounds served as a recreational area. During the cherry-picking season, the men were taken to nearby orchards and helped to harvest the cherry crop. Though they were under strict supervision, they seemed to enjoy the experience and could often be heard singing in the evening after the day's work.

As camping became more popular in the park, many people made camping there an annual event, and some arranged to spend the same vacation period there each year. Campers named Huber spent a good share of each summer at Weborg Point. The Hubers, were interested in theater and organized and built what they called the "Huber Theater" where they put on skits and plays using the current campers as actors. It became a going institution, and people looked forward to attending, acting in, and enjoying the entertainment and sing-alongs that they produced. Social life at Weborg's was anything but drab. Community sings led by Mrs. Byfield of Ephraim also took place at Nicolet Bay campground every Sunday night, but the Huber Theater was the most popular.

✛ ✛ ✛

I will not go into detail on the development and history of Chambers Island, the largest island adjacent to the Fish Creek Community, since an account of Chambers Island history is included elsewhere in this book. Suffice it to say that the Island has always held a special attraction, a sort of Bali-Hai charm, for mainlanders because of its secluded coves, protecting reefs, inland lakes and islands, and abundant woodlands. It has lured many fishermen, hunters, and just plain island adventurers over the years. A visit to Chambers Island will more than likely be a rewarding experience to the curious.

Adventure island is the largest of the Strawberry island group. For many years, Charles Kinney (nicknamed "Skipper") from Winnetka, Illinois, maintained a camp for young boys on the island. He was a small, amiable man who walked with a slight limp because of a stiff knee. His counselors and boys were all recruited from the Chicago area, and, while attending camp, they were taught skills in boating, sailing, swimming, lifesaving, woodworking, and safety and survival techniques. It was much like a scouting program, and the boys loved it, especially the remoteness of the island locale. Camp was in session for about ten weeks each summer, and some of the boys returned for several summers and then later became counselors to younger recruits.

The camp had a large boat built in the Viking style. Powered by a team of about twenty oarsmen and bearing the likeness of a Viking chieftain on the bowsprit, it was a striking sight entering Fish Creek harbor. As it is about three miles from Adventure Island to Fish Creek, the lads needed a great deal of stamina to make the round trip, especially in rough seas. Occasionally they made the trip in another craft, a large scow-like boat with a huge colorful sail which the lads called the Walloping Window Blind. It always created a sensation when it sailed into the harbor. Mr. Kinney was a kind and very likeable man, and he commanded great respect from his boys and counselors. I was sorry when he retired and gave up his camp, as it was an important part of Fish Creek life.

The other islands in the Strawberry group were of lesser importance. The middle one is owned by a private party. The smallest, called Jack Island, was uninhabited except for thousands of sea gulls and is not safe to visit without a sturdy umbrella and well-weathered leather boots. I would call it the Whitewash Capital of Green Bay.

✠ ✠ ✠

Around 1928, the highway department decided to widen the road on the hill coming into town from the south. Until that time the highway was little more than an unpaved country road leading into town. Large cuts were made in the bluff rock face which required heavy blasting and removal of many cubic yards of solid rock. I was in the eighth grade in the Fish Creek school at the time, and I remember a recess one afternoon when I was in the play yard with the rest of the kids. Suddenly, following a loud boom on the excavation site, a boulder about the size of a football came crashing through the roof of the school and landed on the floor of the classroom which we had just left. Luckily the room was unoccupied. As the school was a quarter of a mile from the blasting site, it surely must have been a heavy charge of dynamite. The blasters were made aware of the incident and were warned to be more careful in the future. All of the rock they excavated was transported to what is now Clark Park and left there for about two years, an eyesore on the town shoreline. But, one day a crusher was moved in and the crushed stone was taken away to be used to surface roads.

❖ ❖ ❖

Until about 1937, Gibraltar High School consisted of a large building divided into four classrooms. A separate building stood nearby which was used as a shop and agriculture classroom. Every year the student body let the school board and the surrounding community know that they badly needed a gymnasium. There was no place in the winter that young people could use to hold activities needed to round out their curriculum. Some of the other area schools had gyms. They maintained basketball teams and could hold dances, proms, exercise classes and dramas in their gymnasiums. Naturally our student body felt a bit disadvantaged. Apparently the message finally got through, because a large new gym was finally voted in and constructed, much to the joy of the students. That original gym is still in use today, though it is now part of a much larger structure, since subsequent additions have been made to the school. It has been the performance site for the Peninsula Music Festival since its inception in 1953. As this is being written, a new 750-seat auditorium is being planned and should presently be built adjacent to the Gibraltar High School. Funds for the project are being raised by private donation. When completed, it will be a worthy addition to the northern Door County community, serving as a home for the Peninsula Music Festival and as a center for drama, dance, and other cultural events.

❖ ❖ ❖

Fish Creek had its share of characters, as does every small community. I would like to share with you one of the street scenes I witnessed as a youngster one summer day. Clyde Duclon, a young man in his late teens and Harry Churches, a man in his forties, were two good friends who both possessed a dry sense of humor. Harry was a common sight, driving his four-wheeled wagon pulled by two sturdy draft horses through the village. One day while Harry was making one of his frequent trips through town, he spotted Clyde on the sidewalk, apparently on an errand. He beckoned Clyde to his wagon. "Young man, I wonder if you would be kind enough to direct me to the Federal Building?" he said.

"Why yes, I would be glad to," replied Clyde. "Continue on Main Street to the second stop light, then make a left turn, proceed over the viaduct and across railroad tracks. Two blocks further, you make a right and you will see a large brick building on the far corner. That's the Federal Building."

"Thank you my good man", said Harry, and he whipped his horses with a gentle giddy-ap and drove on. Neither man had cracked a smile.

✤ ✤ ✤

In those days traveling evangelists made their way up and down the peninsula holding revival meetings and attempting to make converts of as many local residents as they could. On one such occasion, a young man named Percy Fairchild was sufficiently moved by the services that he proclaimed his faith by submitting to baptism. It was early spring, and the ice had barely left the harbor. The baptism was to take place in the bay off the shoreline in town. On the appointed morning, Percy dutifully showed up with the other converts and awaited his turn. When the moment finally came, he was led into the waist-deep water; as the rites were pronounced, he was fully immersed for a fleeting moment in the water. Upon catching his breath and recovering from the shock, his first and only comment rang out to the silent onlookers, "JEE-E-Z IT'S COLD". A muffled snicker went through the assembled congregation.

✤ ✤ ✤

Though Fish Creek is just a small resort village on the popular Door County peninsula, it is typical of the profound changes that have taken place in small communities over the last three-quarters of a century. Young people who have grown up since may find it hard to believe stories of the way life was carried on in those days because they have grown up with television, autos, indoor plumbing, phones, electricity, and many other amenities which they take for granted. I think it's enlightening to know that happiness was possible without these things. A knowledge of our historical past is an important part of our education.

Many artists and craftsmen have made Fish Creek their summer workshop over the years, partly because their crafts were appreciated by the many tourists who visit the area each season. Glassblowers, potters, painters, enamelists, and weavers are among those to be found as one drives around the area. In the late 1960s, Madeline Tourtelot started the Peninsula Art School in a building near the Gibraltar High School, and became its first director. It offers classes to aspiring artists and affords them an opportunity to meet other pursuers of the arts. Previous to that, in the mid-1950s, a young potter form Milwaukee named Abraham Cohn acquired a location near the high school and established the shop known as The Potters Wheel. Abe is one of the original practicing artists of the area and is responsible for helping and promoting the careers of several other aspiring potters. Today his studio is abundantly stocked with his and many other artists' creations. Abe's exquisite work and imaginative designs are well-known throughout and beyond the midwest. A visit to his shop cannot help but stimulate an appreciation for the beautiful objects on display and you will undoubtedly find Abe at his wheel creating new ones.

The Peninsula Music Festival has highlighted our summer seasons for several weeks each August since its inception in 1952. It was organized by the Peninsula Arts Association and individuals interested in making classical music concerts available to residents and visitors of Door County. Music director Thor Johnson was selected to organize a symphony orchestra and present a series of nine concerts each season in the high school gymnasium. Soloists of national reputation have appeared on many of the programs, and new works by composers have often premiered there. Dr. Johnson remained the festival's director until his death in 1975. Because of the increasing popularity of the concerts, the Festival and its many patrons look forward to performances in the new auditorium.

⚜ ⚜ ⚜

Today, Fish Creek is a bustling little resort town, one of the busiest on the Door County peninsula. The large hotels have ceased operation except for the White Gull Inn, which operates as a charming country inn for patrons who wish to have lodging and meals included in one package. Meals are also served to the general public. The White Gull Inn is owned and operated by Andy and Jan Coulson, who have given it a unique and pleasant atmosphere, and it has been written up in several national magazines. Many new motels and condominiums, as well as numerous gift shops and restaurants have been built in and around the village. Though life styles have changed a great deal since the years of steamboat transportation, the popularity and charm of the village attracts many repeat visitors. The Peninsula Music Festival, the Peninsula Players, the art school and pottery studios, the Heritage Ensemble, and the proximity of Peninsula State Park all serve as compelling reasons for tourists to return. Village residents are friendly and eager to make summer visitors feel welcome.

# A Talk At the Women's Club (1975)
by
*Harry Schuyler*

I was born in the town of Clay Banks on April 17, 1897. My father, Frank W. Schuyler was born in the county in 1868 and my mother Jenny A. Templeton was born in Door County in 1875. My grandfather, Albert A. Schuyler, came from New York to Door County as a young man to install the first circular saw in the county. The mill was on the shore in Clay Banks, right near the Tufts pier. Clay Banks at that time consisted of a post office, saloon and boarding house for the men that worked in the saw mill.

Clay Banks is just north of what is now known as Bronsdorf Beach. Maybe some of you people have gone on County Trunk U and you know where Bronsdorf Beach is. Clay Banks was just north of it; there is a little creek that runs into the lake just north of Bronsdorf Beach, and it was just this side of the creek. I remember it very well – I got mail in the post office in Clay Banks. That is, my folks did, I was probably too young; but I remember going there. Of course I couldn't go into the saloon. That was bad!

My grandfather bought eighty acres of timber land and built a home there. There's a sign on a barn yet today – Old Schuyler Homestead. My grandparents raised a family of eleven children – five boys and six girls – there, and in their later life adopted a girl who needed a home.

My grandfather loved animals, he developed by books and practice quite a skill in veterinary practice and was known as "the horse doctor." Now a horse doctor at that time was quite a dignified person, I'll have you understand. He wouldn't dirty his hands on a dog or anything of that kind. He didn't like to even work on a cow. A horse was a very valuable asset.

My grandfather quit the farm and moved into Sawyer which is west Sturgeon Bay. I can remember when Sawyer had a post office and when trains stopped in Sawyer and you could buy a ticket from Sawyer to Green Bay or any place the train went.

Fish Creek in 1906. There are fish sheds and a sawmill (with the smokestack) along the water. The dock is being repaired and extended. The charred hulk of the *SS Cecilia Hill,* which had burned earlier that year, is tied alongside.

We lived on the homestead for five or six years that my grandfather had after my dad and mother were married. At the end of that time my dad bought a sixty-acre farm at Warrens Corners. Warrens Corners was just north of Salona. The Salona school, the store, and the cheese factory was known as Cheeseville. If you look on some of the old maps of Door County you'll find Salona and you'll also find Cheeseville.

We lived there until I was ten years old. My only sister Francis, later Mrs. Ralph Nygaard, was born there. About this time my father learned through his sister, Mrs. C.A. Lundberg of Fish Creek, that a Mr. George M. Clark and family of Evanston, Illinois had purchased a large farm just south of the village of Fish Creek known as cliff farm and that he was in need of a practical farmer to operate it. My father applied for the job and was hired.

Mr. Clark was a stove manufacturer from Harvey, Illinois. I shall never forget how nervous my mother was when Mr. Clark and his son Robert drove up with their team of shiny bay horses and one of these buggies with the fringe around the top. They got to our place around 10:00 in the morning and began to look over the place and talk with my father. They had never met my father but they wanted to talk with him.

I recall my mother was sure my dad would ask them in for dinner at noon. You know farmers were always very cordial. No matter what they had they were always willing to share it. But this particular time my mother was a little bit nervous because she didn't have a bit of fresh meat in the house. I'm sure of that, and at 10:00 it was too late to kill a chicken and get it ready for dinner so she had to do the next best thing that was possible in those days and that was to have salt pork. Salt pork and white gravy. So she was forced to swallow her pride and serve her old reliable salt pork and milk gravy. Of course we had a garden and plenty of vegetables for salad and homemade bread and homemade butter.

I put the homemade butter in because I wonder if any of you really ever tasted homemade butter. Maybe some of you have, but if you haven't, you've missed something because the butter you get today isn't butter compared to what the old butter used to be. That butter was made from cream that was raised in a pan and then skimmed off. The fat wasn't all churned up and broken up. When you put it in a churn, it churned very easily. The butter you get today and the homogenized milk you get today is just churned all up, breaks the fat all into small particles. It's quite different now; if you remember back when you bought a quart of milk, you had the cream in the bottle of milk. You don't have that anymore. Maybe it's better, pasteurized and homogenized, but it really isn't any better than oleomargarine is because oleomargarine is broken up in the same manner. It doesn't have much more taste than oleomargarine has. In fact, I prefer oleomargarine.

At any rate that's what mother served. She had fresh strawberries and shortcake, and mother always made very good sour-cream cookies, with coffee and so forth. I'm telling you this because it wasn't easy on a farm five miles from a store where you could buy anything to whip up a meal in a hurry.

But the Clarks were very complimentary, and I remember they ate considerable salt pork and said they hadn't had any for years and years and years. They also enjoyed mother's sour-cream cookies, and she used to make some for them after we moved to Fish Creek and they were living in the cottage.

You might be interested in how we moved to Fish Creek from Salona. You have to bear in mind that there was no transportation of any kind. Mail was carried on a small wagon from Sturgeon Bay north, and the mail that came into Sturgeon Bay from the outside was brought on a train. But there wasn't any other transportation. No means of getting around.

But the Reynolds and Rickles Pea Canning Company had two factories, in Sturgeon Bay and Sawyer. My father had sold peas for several years, and it was their policy to cut and haul peas with their own crews. They'd rent the land and have the farmer plant them, but they wanted to cut them and truck them so they could bring them into the mill in an orderly manner and not have it flooded one day and not have any peas there the next day. They had their own big flat racks.

Dad hired two teams with drivers and wagons, and he loaded the two wagons with livestock, furniture, and trappings. Dad was to establish a dairy farm at cliff farm, so he brought his six cows and two heifer calves, also two or three pigs and about eighty chickens. All this was in crates and loaded onto the two wagons except for the cows. Three of the cows were tied behind each wagon and they had to walk, poor things, all the distance from Clay Banks (or Salona) to Fish Creek which is a matter of thirty or thirty-one miles.

My mother and my sister were able to come up in our buggy with our horse, and they were quite comfortable. We got as far as Sturgeon Bay or Sawyer (west Sturgeon Bay) and had our noon lunch there. We left our old farm about 11:00 and had our noon lunch there along about 1:00. We left again as soon as we had lunch to get started up this way. Our biggest problem was when we hit the bridge.

You don't remember but there used to be a plank bridge that came all the way over from Sawyer to Sturgeon Bay. When those cows put their feet on the plank bridge, it was something entirely new to them and they weren't going to go another step. It took a lot of persuasion and a lot of pulling. If we hadn't had good strong ropes on them I guess they wouldn't have been able to come over. They finally did. We also had a collie dog who encouraged them to move along a little bit. After they got across the bridge, they weren't entirely out of the woods yet because they had to go down Cedar Street and there were a lot of noises there to get used to.

At any rate, we came on up this way. By the time we got about two-and-a-half miles south of Egg Harbor, we had got as far as the Grant Haskell farm and my father knew Grant Haskell. We stopped with the cows and put them in the barn there and came on up home to Fish Creek. We got to the Schutz's farm about 10 PM in the evening and it was about 2:00 AM before we got the beds unloaded so we could go to sleep.

Now I'm going to take a little different turn for a minute. I'm going to tell you what I found in Fish Creek on October 1, 1907.

Downtown Fish Creek showing Lundberg's store (now Alwes Food Market) and the Barringer Hotel (now the C & C Club) in about 1915. The wires carried by the pole in the picture are telegraph wires.

There were three stores: the C.A. Lundberg store, which is now Alwes; the McLeod store, which is the store the Schreibers had that Mr. Norz has now; and then over where the ice cream/gallery was this summer, and where the Fish Creek garage is in the back, was the Levi Vorous store. All competing within a block of each other. There were two blacksmith shops, of which George Schuyler had one. That was located where the Wesas are now, and then Mr. Noble (that was Gertrude Howe's grandfather) had a blacksmith shop just a little bit west of the house about where Gertrude has her garage now.

The Post Office was in the building that is now our library building and was taken care of by Mabel Vorous, whose husband died when the *Hackley* sunk coming from Marinette-Menominee. The Barringers had a hotel, and that is where the C&C Club is now. They had a barn and a place to take care of horses, and anyone traveling back and forth could stop there and put their horses in and feed them. They also had some cows and furnished their own milk for their hotel.

The Thorp Hotel was up where Founders Square is now. It wasn't as large as it is now. They built several cottages and they built an addition onto the hotel after the time when I came. Mr. Thorp also had a livery stable up there and he rented horses, buggies, cutters, and so forth as the season might be. They went all over the county. Mr. Putnam in Sturgeon Bay used to have horses and when I went to high school in Sturgeon Bay, I used to come home with a livery horse every once in a while. Alma Lundberg came with me and Mildred Thorp. We'd come home Friday night and go back Sunday afternoon.

Dr. Welcker had the resort and it was quite a large resort. The Casino (Whistling Swan) was right across from the big building of the old Thorp Hotel. That used to be over in Menominee; it was the clubhouse from the Menominee River Brewing Company, and Dr. Welcker bought it, tore it down very carefully, moved it over, and reconstructed it in the same shape as it was over in Menominee. He brought a lot of furniture along with it. He also had the Henrietta cottage which is presently the White Gull Inn, and then he owned all the cottages across from our place and almost that whole block. All of those where the Maple Crest is now; he owned all those cottages. Then Meta LeClair had the Maple Tree Cafe. She was a Barringer girl, and her husband was drowned on the *Hackley*. The Maple Tree Cafe was about where the new dining room of the C&C Club is. The primary school was up on the same lot where the village school is now. There were two schools, the primary and the upper grades. The primary school was moved down after the new school was built. It was moved down to the Pelke's Tavern (the Bayside Tavern).

The upper grade school was the old Catholic Church building which just moved across the lot. The Adventist Church is in the same location. I have a little story I think I ought to tell you about the Adventist Church, not that I'm prejudiced to the Adventist Church or anything but it's a good story and I think it's worth hearing.

I remember that they were having a revivalist there in the winter time and he was a very loud-voiced person and very out-going and he made quite a few converts. The Adventists were quite a large congregation at that time. Anyway, they had quite a few converts from this series of meetings that he held for about a week or ten days. It is the practice of the Adventists (like the Baptists) that they immerse in water and you must go down into the water and come up out of the water.

Among some of the so-called converts was a young fellow by the name of Percy Fairchild. He was one of the toughest boys in town. He was always in fights, drinking, and doing the things that all tough boys do. At any rate, he was the one that was going to be baptized. It was in the later part of November and very cold. They didn't have a baptism place to baptize these people, so they went to the bay because they didn't want to miss the opportunity of having him part of the church. I remember we kids who were not Adventists knew what was going to happen and we sat on the ice banks and watched them. When the minister got out in the water he called out his flock one at a time. When Percy's time came, they took Percy out and tipped him over and he went down under the water. When he came up he said, "Jesus, that's cold!" So they put him down under again to wash that one off and the next time he was smart enough and didn't say a word.

The Episcopal Church was there and just the same as it is now. There's one exception, and they never laughed at it at that time, but on Halloween we youngsters climbed up in the belfry and took a piece of telephone wire over into a cedar tree where nobody could find it and we could ring the bell anytime we wanted to.

The Town Hall was up where Clyde Helgeson's house was. When the Thorp's bought the corner lot where Bunda's Hutch is and added it to their properties, they wanted to get that building out of there, so they moved it down to a lot they had with the town's consent. It was a good deal for both the town and the Thorps. That was used as a Sunday school and a Modern Woodman Lodge and of course for all town affairs.

Fishing was the big industry in Fish Creek. At that time herring were very plentiful in the waters of Green Bay. Very plentiful. There were fishermen scattered all along the shoreline. Each one would have a single net (once in a while there was one who would have two nets) and a small pond boat. The pond boats were equipped with sails.

About the time I came down here, some of them were just starting to put gasoline motors in the boats. They would sail out, empty their nets and bring them in. If the wind didn't blow, they had a long sweep oar that they put on the back and moved by what we called sculling. They'd scull the boat out, load it up with fish and scull it back again. If the wind blew they could sail, so they only sculled in calm weather.

Many thousands of tons of fish were taken in this area over a period of years. Though necessarily, it required some packaging to take care of these fish. You have probably noticed when you drive around in the park (though you don't notice it so much now as you did years ago) that there were a lot of fireplaces in the park. Those weren't for heating cottages in most cases. They were used by the

The Fish Creek Episcopal Church in about 1914. This is the church tower into which Fish Creek youngsters climbed one Halloween to rig a wire that allowed them to ring the bell from outside the church.

coopers who made the barrels the fish were packed in. It was necessary that they be able to heat those barrels, which they did.

It was quite an art to be able to make a barrel, because you have to remember that they didn't have access to gang saws like we have now where you can saw any shape, any angle, and any thickness you want to. These barrels were made out of pine, the most choice pine that they could find. They'd split them out in about the thickness they wanted the staves to be. But to make a barrel round, you have to taper it on both ends and it has to fit together and be tight because salt brine went in them and that couldn't leak out. So it was necessary that work was done very carefully.

Most of the coopers were not particularly well educated. How do you make the inside of a barrel to fit the head? It was quite a little trick. They had a wheel and after they got the frame of the barrel set up, they ran the wheel around and had a mark on it to see how many revolutions and then to what point on the wheel it went and then they made the head that size to fit. Very simple. But in order to get the barrel to set, they used the chimney. They put all of the shavings inside the barrel as they . . . . (EDITOR'S NOTE: there is a gap in the recorded narrative here.)

I might also tell you how they dressed the fish, maybe you'd be interested in that. When they brought them in from the nets, they had a table in the shed that was about as high as this table is. They put the fish on the table, then they built a little block, a piece of two-by-four with a "V" cut in it. That was for the fish entrails to go down, and they put a barrel underneath. So the man picked up a fish, if he was right-handed he picked it up with his left hand. He laid it on this block and the first thing he did with the knife was take the fish's head off. The second thing he did was to split it right down alongside the dorsal fin, right down the back, through all the bones. That was always strange to me but that's the way they did it. When the knife went back, the entrails went in the hole in the bottom of the barrel. That was all the dressing the fish got.

After that it was taken and put in a big wooden vat. They always had the fish shanty out on the bay where they had plenty of

A nice catch of herring from a pond net, about 1909. Staner Olson is on the far left; Roy Thorp is third from left (looking into the camera); the boy sitting on the far side of the boat behind Roy Thorp may be Warren Baxter.

water, and they'd dip water out of the bay and pour it into this vat.
Then they'd take a scoop, wash the fish out pretty well, until the guts
all ran out of them. Then they put them out on the drying table and
the salting would start. They would put a layer of salt in the bottom
of an empty keg. Then they had a salt rack in front of them. They'd
pick up a fish and wipe the meaty inside through the salt. Then they
would take another fish and wipe it in salt, until they got a thick
handful. Then they'd reach down and put it in the barrel around the
outside. Next they would pack salted fish inside that ring until they
filled the whole bottom of the barrel. Then they'd put in another
layer of salt and do the same thing over again.

People didn't get rich working at fish either, because usually
they paid about twenty-five or thirty cents for dressing the fish to fill
one of those kegs, which held about 150 pounds. They paid the
women and children a nickel for salting the fish that went into a keg.
But don't forget that they sold the fish sometimes for about $2.50 for
a barrel of 150 pounds of fish, so they didn't have a very big margin.
I don't know what they had to pay for the cooperage, but that had to
be something. So that was the main industry in Fish Creek.

Now you might be interested in knowing who those
fishermen were. They were the Rockendorf boys of Fish Creek, Carl
Olson, John Melvin, Roy Thorp, the Duclons, the Chambers, the
Grahams, the Hills, the Weborgs, John and Andrew Anderson, The
Evensons, Joseph Tennison, and the Carlson brothers. All those
people were fishermen; all had fish shanties.

The Grahams had another industry that worked for quite a
while. They had a vessel that was a floating store, and they would go
over to Marinette to Lauerman Brothers. They'd get clothing over
there and they'd go to Green Bay to Morley Murphy Hardware and
they'd get some hardware and things that would be considered
hardware nowadays anyway and they had them all in the boat.
Displays around the hull of the boat were made of shelving, just like
a store. They went into each town and conducted store for three or
four days until they had sold all that people wanted to buy; then they
moved to another town. That was one way of making a living.

Transport by water came very early. Some of the first transportation was furnished by the Hills, who were residents of Fish Creek. They owned the *Erie L. Hackley* and the *Cecelia Hill*. They operated between Marinette/Menominee and here, but that was about as far as they ever went. Then we had the Hart Transportation Company, who had the *Sailor Boy*, the *Bon Ami*, the *Thistle*, the *Fanny Hart*, and the *Eugene Hart*. They ran all around Green Bay; from Green Bay they went to Menominee, from Menominee to Escanaba, from Escanaba over to Washington Island and then down the shore of Door County and back to Green Bay. That's the way they made the circuit. They carried whatever freight there was from one port to the other.

I remember one time when Hugo Becker (some of the Beckers still live out east of Fish Creek) was going over to Marinette to buy some furniture for the house. Probably his father had trusted him because Hugo was a pretty good boy. He brought him down to Fish Creek to go on the *Thistle*. I heard him in conversation with his dad when he was ready to leave. He said, "How will I know when to come back and get you Hugo?" Hugo said, "When you hear the *Thistle* whistle, then you know I'm on the *Thistle*.

Green Bay waters also had other transportation. The Goodrich Transportation Company had two boats up here in the summer. Though that was only in the summer months, that is what started the resort business up in this area. The *Georgia* and the *Carolina* ran from Chicago to Mackinac Island. Each boat made a round trip each week. They took a whole week to make it because they weren't very fast boats. One of them arrived here about the middle of the week, and the other one came at the end of the week, and they went back in the same manner. The boats provided one way for young people to get around; we could buy a ticket from Fish Creek and come over to Ephraim. Ephraim had a lot of good-looking Scandinavian girls over there. We didn't have many Scandinavian girls in Fish Creek, so we'd ride over on the boat to see the girls and then we'd walk home. But then when the boat came from the north, the girls would come over and then we'd have to walk the girls home. So it was a losing proposition - we always had to walk back after we walked the girls home. We had two walks.

I'd like to tell you something about crossing on the ice. After navigation closed it was still necessary to have certain supplies and to get rid of certain produce that we had in the county here. We had many different people that went across the ice in the wintertime with teams and a covered sleigh. Usually the sleighs had a little stove in them to keep them warm and to keep the produce they were taking along from freezing. That was another way, if you wanted to go to Marinette; you could ride over in the sleigh and come back with it again. I remember Mrs. Schuyler went over the first year she was here, the winter just after we were married. She decided she'd like to go over to Marinette/Menominee and see her sister. Mr. Will Jarman was going over with a team, and she went along with him. When they got out on the ice by Green Island they came to a crack. She didn't pay much attention. Mr. Jarman got out with an ice chisel and tried the ice around the crack. Then he turned to her and said, "Mrs. Schuyler, we're moving across a crack now. If you're nervous about it you can walk over and I'll bring the sleigh across." She said, "What are you going to do, Mr. Jarman?" "Well," he said, "I'm going to ride in the sleigh." And she said, " Well, I'll ride in the sleigh too!"

We had an old Scandinavian from up in Ellison Bay, Charles Ruckert, who used to have a store up there. He used to bring a lot of his groceries and dry goods and things that he wanted from Marinette himself. He had a team, and the family took care of the store while he was gone. Charlie was a fellow who liked to talk about what he did. He was telling me about one of his trips over. He said:

> We got off to that Chambers Island crack that goes to Green Island. When I look up the crack this way, I could see open water for a long way and then I look down the other way and I can see water down there for a long way. Finally I took the horses up pretty close to the crack and I took my whip out and snapped it in the water so they could see there was a crack there. Then I backed them off about a hundred yards and I put the whip to 'em. Then I thought, when they jump, they can make it in one jump and then they take two jumps!

Pulling a sleigh across a crack in the ice by hand during the winter of 1905-1906. This sleigh apparently had a stove inside it. Notice the evergreen tree standing behind the horses; such trees were placed on the ice to mark the route.

Sometimes the men who worked in the woods, the lumberjacks, would ride over with people who were crossing the ice. In one particular case there were a couple of young Scandinavian boys from up in Sister Bay that went over and took over some apples that they had to sell. On their way back a Mr. Sherm Kinsey came along with them. Sherm Kinsey was an uncle of Roy Kinsey. If any of you know Roy, you know he's very wide and not too high. His uncle Sherm was even more so. Anyway, he came back with these two boys, and, when they got into Fish Creek, they went to the Barringer Hotel and put their horses in the barn there. It was the middle of the afternoon, and they couldn't get any food, so they went over to the store and got some crackers and cheese and were having a lunch. Sherm had come in with them, and some of the natives were talking to Sherm. Sherm had on a new pair of these heavy wool pants that the lumberjacks always wear, and he had them rolled up because he was very short and he was so big in the waist. I suppose they had to be long somewhere, since they were for an ordinary man, but they didn't fit him. So one of the natives said, "Sherm, when you bought those very expensive pants, why didn't you buy a pair that fit you?" Sherm looked at him, sober as a judge, and said, "You know, when I bought them they fit me perfectly. But, out in the woods a tree fell on a fella up there. I lifted just as hard as I could and I just shoved myself together." These guys from Sister Bay didn't know Sherm as well as we did; we knew Sherm wasn't telling the truth.

I'd like to tell you a little about the settlements in and near Fish Creek. We have segregationists now, and we have groups of people who don't like to associate with each other. I think we had the same thing then to a certain extent. Not violently so, but it was that way anyhow. We had three different settlements right near Fish Creek. We had the German settlement, which was out near Maple Grove. Most of those people out there were Germans, including these families:   the Reinhards, the Stenzels, the Jarmans, the Zachows, the Rays, the Seilers, the Eckerts, the Polsters, the Ohnesorges, the Krauses, the Hermans, the Frankes, the Gaugers and the Kalms. All of German descent. Most of them went to school at Maple Grove; now the American Legion owns that building. Then there was the Scandinavian settlement at Juddville. In that settlement we had Olaf Weborg, Charles Witalison, Thor Hanson, John Broodie, Ole Christjohnson, Peter Peterson, Theodore Peterson, Nels Olson, Gus Berquist, Dick Runquist, Willie Olson, and Ole Carlson. If you go and visit the Lutheran Memorial Building you'll see pictures of all of the people up on the wall there.

And there was a Polish settlement (we had a school out on County F near that settlement, but it's not used anymore either). The Polish people included Martin Bureski, Leo Stanley Raiza, Joseph Zak, John Grey, Andrew Kazmarek, Ignatz Charnetski, Stanley Burnesky, Roman Kita, Roman Mazur, and Martin Zak. All stayed in a regular community there.

Of course, Ephraim was mostly Moravians, mostly Scandinavian. They were a part of the town of Gibraltar. I might tell you that the town of Gibraltar at that time had a population of between 1,400 and 1,500 people, including the village of Ephraim. It's quite different now.

Some of the firsts in Door County was a five-acre cherry orchard on cliff farm in 1911. That was one of the first beginnings of the cherry industry in Door County. Also the coming of the mechanical machines, like a tractor. That farm had a 1020 Titan tractor in 1917. The first rubber-tired tractor came in 1928. The first cooperative cheese factory in Gibraltar and in the whole northern end of the county was where Eva's store is now in Juddville (the Door County Farm Market). That building, the original building, was built by a cooperative that was formed there.

Max Wilson, a brother of Jim Wilson who had a store in Egg Harbor, was the cheese maker. He afterward lived over in Baileys Harbor township. I have a little story to tell you about that cooperative. Max, as the cheese maker, had a report to make at the end of the first year. Max kept pretty good records to give us. He thought he'd be good to the patrons of the cheese factory, so he got a pony of beer and some crackers and of course he had cheese there and he invited all the patrons to come in and hear the report and sit around in the cheese factory. Well, a pony of beer for about thirty-five men isn't an awful lot. I guess a pony is four gallons. Anyway the beer ran out in a short time. Herman Woldt who married an Olson girl, and is Dick Weisgerber's father-in-law, was living with the Olsons up there at that time helping Mr. Olson with the farming. So he came to the meeting and he was kind of full of the dickens anyhow, so when the beer ran out, he took the same pitcher that they had been putting beer in and he went out to the whey tank and he filled it up and he came in. He started pouring glasses of it. Frank Robertoy was the first one to try it. He never batted an eye, he just drank it.

It was always necessary to take your milk up every day to the factory. Seven days a week you had to haul milk to the factory. Of course, you brought back the whey, that you naturally would feed to the pigs when you came home. We had an old uncle living with us on the farm. He wasn't able to do a lot of heavy work, but that was one job he could do very well. We had one horse on a light wagon, and he'd load the milk cans on in the morning and take them up to the factory. They'd all have to sit around and wait their turn. One of the people that was there was this Ole Christjohnson that I mentioned a while ago. He would always be there, so this old uncle of mine got acquainted with Ole, and the two old fellows would visit with each other. One day old uncle said to Ole, "I'm getting in some new dentures, I wonder how they're gonna fit?" Couple of days after he had them. He went up and said to Ole, "Well, I got my new dentures in, they fit pretty good." Ole said, "What did you do with the old ones?" He said, "I have them at home." Ole said, "Would you bring them down tomorrow so I can see if they would fit me?"

Ole got me into more trouble than that. We had a man working for us on the farm, Ben Shields, who was an Irishman, not too intelligent, but a very good worker. He liked to pick stones. We used to let Ben pick stones whenever we didn't have anything else for him to do. There were a lot of things he couldn't do, but that he could do and do very well. But he loved tobacco, and he very often ran out. He just never could seem to remember to bring enough tobacco along to keep himself supplied. At any rate, one day Ole Christjohnson came along with his team, going down to the Lundberg Store to exchange his eggs and butter. You see, all the women made butter and sold it at that time. It was a cash crop for them. Ole was going down to exchange for tobacco, coffee, and sugar and a few little items they would use, because most all of those products were self-maintaining. As he came along, Ben saw him coming. He went out and he stopped him and said, "Ole, have you got any tobacco on you?" "Oh ya," he said, "I always got tobacco." And so he pulled out his pouch and he handed it to Ben. Ben took a big handful of it and put it in his mouth. He started chewing on it and talking to Ole. Finally he said, "Ole, this tobacco isn't very strong." "Ya," he said, "maybe on the ride I chewed it once." I have to explain that Ole was a very conservative fellow and after he chewed tobacco, he put it back in the pouch and dried it out and then smoked it.

All and all, I've had a most interesting life, an active life, these past seventy-five years. It was my privilege to serve on our Graded School Board, the Gibraltar High School Board as chairman, chairman of the Town of Gibraltar, chairman of the Door County Board of Supervisors, chairman of the Door County Hospital Board, director of the Fruit Growers Cooperative, chairman of the Wisconsin Soil Conservation Committee, a member of the Governor's Resource Committee, a director of the National Cherry Growers Association and Chairman of the Door County Republican Party. (Whether that's a credit or a debit I'll leave to the listener.) I'd like to say this, I can say without hesitation, that all of these privileges, activities, pleasures would not have been possible without the love, patience, faith and cooperation of a certain young lady who on October 18, 1919 was willing to step to the alter and change her name from Helen Mason to Helen Schuyler.

In my lifespan many changes have taken place in Door County. From simple, humble, quiet, orderly homes of sturdy people to a highly advertised and promoted resort area. What will the next fifty years bring to Door County? I shudder to think.

# COTTAGE ROW – FACT OR FICTION?
by
*Archibald G. Douglass, Jr.*

Asa Thorp's plat of Fish Creek names the road Resort Street, but later, when connected to Ula Street, it became Cottage Road. Where Cottage *Row* came from is anybody's guess. Perhaps a sign painter?

In the late nineteenth century, the cities of the central states were prosperous and growing. The huge German and Irish immigrations of the mid-century were being digested, and the demand for goods, services, and transportation was on the increase. New Orleans had its Exposition in 1886, the Columbian Exposition in Chicago was held in 1893, and the Louisiana Purchase Exposition took place in St. Louis in 1904.

This post-Civil-War growth and prosperity was the result of hard work and imaginative entrepreneurs. It had led to a stable and secure class of people who were in a position to begin enjoying the fruits of their labors. Demand began to grow for ways of relaxing and getting a change of pace.

This same period saw a decline in the old basic economy of the Fish Creek area. The lumber had been stripped from the land, and shipment by water was reduced as railroads speeded transport to Sturgeon Bay, Marinette/Menominee, etc. Fishing was on the decline, ship building not needed, and the lumber supply was depleted. The idea of running resorts had been in many people's minds, and Asa Thorp and (later) Dr. Welcker carried out their ideas with two commodious establishments. There was also The Nook and a smaller businessmen's hotel, the Fish Creek Hotel.

The timing was absolutely right for the attraction of people from the large cities of the midwest to Fish Creek. There was no air conditioning, and the stifling heat of great cities was something from which to escape during the summer. There were, of course, the old established resorts of the eastern seaboard and of the mountains of New York State and of New England, and there were also some

George M. Clark on a leisurely drive down the lane in about 1905.

older and fairly formal resorts in Michigan and Wisconsin. But, many people were looking for something simple and affordable. They were also looking for beauty, quiet, and relief from the crowded clatter of the cities.

George Clark and Frank P. Crunden were the first to build summer houses in Fish Creek. In 1895, Mr. Clark built a house for his family which later burned under the ownership of Curly Lambeau. In 1898, Mr. and Mrs. Crunden built a cottage which still stands, though in a greatly altered state. All of the additions and changes were made during Mrs. Crunden's life. She loved to build and also built the houses now owned by the Cadwalladers and the Hambletons.

Of course, the waterfront land was worthless to year-round residents. The trees had begun to be replaced with second growth, but there was no soil for gardens and no protection from the howling storms which came across the bay. Thus, the land was cheap and very suitable for families with children who wanted to swim, play outdoors and live for a while in clear and healthy air.

The Crundens were from St. Louis, the Clarks from Chicago. The first Milwaukee person to build a house was Howard Eldred. They called the house Ridgeway and it is a copy of a Russian dacha.

In the meantime, more and more people were coming to Thorp's and Welcker's, and the community was becoming an active resort. Almost everyone who eventually built on Cottage Row had stayed first at one or the other of those resorts. Welcker's catered to German-speaking people who had come to the U.S. due to the political unrest following the unification of the German states. These were not the tired, hungry, and poor of Statue of Liberty fame. They were doctors, professors, musicians – people of intellectual stature. Thorp's attracted businessmen, doctors, attorneys, etc. who did not have the Germanic origins of the other side of the street.

By the middle 1920s, Cottage Row was established pretty much as it is today. The Friedmanns, the Blakes and the Gilbert Smiths were among the last to build before the Depression; Friedmanns in 1923 and the others in 1926.

Growing up in this community was a lucky privilege. In the 1920s there was a group of twenty to thirty children who were all within a few years of each other in age. Travel time from the various home cities was as much as two days. Therefore there was no commuting. Entire households would move in for the summer. The fathers might come and go as they could and as their employment would allow.

These early days were a transition period between horse-drawn and motor vehicles. Women had never driven carriages in the cities, and many did not drive automobiles. A chauffeur was often necessary to give the family mobility when the husband was absent.

From the first, the families planned for their children's welfare. Many group activities made for a cohesive bunch of friends which exists to this day. When I was of kindergarten age, a teacher was brought up from Community School in St. Louis. Each morning, classes and activities suitable for ages five to ten were held in our side yard. There were many picnics on the undeveloped sand beaches on the Lake Michigan side, and there were tennis and swimming lessons, golf, and hikes to Wilson's for an ice cream soda. Later, the Fish Creek Yacht Club came with its fleet of sailing prams. Twice a week races were held, open to anyone. It was great training in boat handling and water safety.

Household chores were tremendous. There was no electricity and no telephone. We could all have running water because the cottages were used only in warm weather and a windmill or a noisy gasoline pump on the beach would fill a storage tank from the bay. We had no worries about freezing the pipes from the tank to the house, but there was sometimes a crisis when the gravity tank ran dry at the wrong time.

Ice boxes had to be kept filled with cakes from the ice houses. That was my first job to earn my fifty-cent-per-week allowance. I had to dig out the ice, wash off its insulating sawdust, haul it down to the house and lift it into the two ice boxes. For a twelve-year-old, it was a lot of work! The countryside was scoured for fresh produce (including homemade wine), fruit, and chickens.

The local stores did their best, but delays of shipments on the Goodrich steamers sometimes interfered with supplies. As time went on, a few people bought Delco electric systems, but most of us had the chore of washing lamp chimneys and trimming many candles each day. I remember going to one "Delco" house to watch some home movies. It was necessary to turn off every light in the house to get enough wattage to operate the projector.

There were no radios or television sets. Everyone read books. One of the subjects of daily socializing was what book was being read at the moment. Books were read to the very young at nap time, and they were read by young and old and discussed on many levels. One summer almost everyone was reading "Gone With The Wind" at the same time. You didn't dare discuss the book because you might give something away to someone who had not read as far. It was a wonderful thing to have had implanted at any early age. All the knowledge of the world is in books and most of the entertainment. Life can never be dull with books at hand.

One of my vivid memories is the jolting and discomfort when hopping a ride down unpaved Cottage Road on the rear of Harry Churches' wagon. No springs! Another was when I was age eleven Mother asked if I wanted to ride to the post office with her. I said yes, and when we reached the Model T, I asked if I could drive. She asked if I knew how and I assured her that Frank Churches (in whom she had great confidence) had taught me. Being somewhat naive, she reluctantly gave her permission. We climbed in, I started the engine and pushed the pedal, and we were off. She commented when we went right through the stop-sign at highway 42. She was surprised when we sailed right past the post office. And she leaned over and turned off the ignition when we came opposite the public bathing beach. All she said was "You can drive with Frank, but not with me." The difficulty was that Frank had been letting me sit on his lap and steer and push the pedal. but he hand not taught me how to stop. In those days there wasn't much to run into so no damage was done.

✛ ✛ ✛

One of the Goodrich Transportation Company steamships that served Door County in the early 20th century at the Fish Creek pier in about 1912. This is after the reconstruction of the dock shown in the photo on page 43.

I vividly recall being awakened at night to watch the sparkling lights of the *Carolina* or the *Georgia* sail past – a sight never seen on our street in St. Louis!

In 1923, there was a forest fire in Peninsula Park. Everyone with an automobile went out, and, for a couple of days, they drove back and forth from the waterfront to the fire with buckets and barrels of water on the running boards. My father's stories of his experiences gave me nightmares of being surrounded by fire.

In the 1920s, there was a smallpox scare. At that time there were five doctors on Cottage Row; it was a perfect vacation place for them because there were no telephones. Dr. Welcker, Dr. Lippmann (a St. Louis doctor who stayed regularly at Welcker's), and Dr. Egeland in Sturgeon Bay had vaccine and offered vaccinations free to anyone who would come. Dr. Blair used his house as a clinic, and the work was shared by Drs. Cole, Baumgarten, Blair and Fischel. Vaccination for smallpox is performed by scratching the skin and applying the vaccine to the wound. Stringently sterile conditions were necessary and the Blair's house was extremely sanitary for a few days.

As we grew older, there were parties, treasure hunts and other group events designed to keep us out of trouble and at the same time to teach us a bit about socializing with our peers and the groups to which we belonged in the winter.

In the period after 1930 many changes came about. The Great Depression affected almost everyone. I can remember how grateful we were to have the cottage. The cost of going to a resort hotel would have been out of the question. Most of the houses retained their original form of a single layer of clapboards on studs with no insulation. They have one advantage in that they cool off rapidly after a hot day.

National rural electrification came to Door County. My brother wired our cottage, and constant visits from Art Baraboo made sure it was all up to code. Housekeeping became much easier, which was a boon, as household help began to disappear. Telephones (with many parties on the line) became available through the Baileys Harbor phone system.

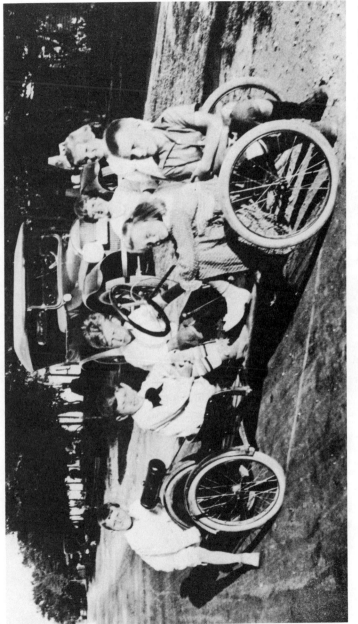

Some of the summer youngsters on the Main Street of Fish Creek with their "wheels" in about 1918. Rocky Wilms is driving, and Martha Hochmeister Cherry and Paul Guenzel are seated on the front.

In the 1940s, our group was finishing school and beginning to venture out into independence. Then World War II was upon us, and we all went off to Army, Navy or Air Corps duty. The women joined the Red Cross and other volunteer groups, and many served overseas. Things never returned to what they were before the war, but it has proven hard to pull up roots. One cottage is now being enjoyed by the fifth generation of the same family; and many others have third or second generations. Families with children often can no longer spend the entire summer, but they come back as regularly as the seasons. Even though we may not see each other for months at a time, we old-timers get together with a sort of trust and relaxation which is a great refreshment to us all. We are fond of our new neighbors, but a lifetime of memories together makes for a warm bond.

The great growth of short-term tourism and the slow suburbanizing of our once rural charm have made it impossible for many to even imagine what life was like only a few years ago. Can we be blamed for missing the slow pace, the courtesy of casual everyday greeting, the quiet evenings with no traffic sounds, the occasional hiss of a passing steam yacht instead of raucous roars from cigarette boats? About a year before he died, Bob Schreiber said one day to me how much he missed the shoppers who came quietly and pleasantly and combined a courteous visit with the business at hand.

These are my memories and others will have different ones. Some may even say "No, that is not the way it was." Well, that is the way it was to me, and it still is as of this September of 1989.

# First Impressions
by
*Lois Schreiber*

"Letter from a boyfriend?" Professor Lynn asked as he strode past my chair to his desk. "No," I answered, "from my father." The letter I was so eagerly reading was post-marked Fish Creek, Wisconsin, and was filled with almost ecstatic descriptions of the little village and its environs. Here I sat in a classroom in my last year of college in Southern California in that spring of 1934, longing to be finished with it all and to be on my way to the Eden my father described so vividly.

At last I was being met at the train station in Milwaukee. It was a long drive to the Door County peninsula, and the farther north we went, the more it seemed to me that we were on our way to the last outpost. But, as we rounded the curve and turned down the hill into Fish Creek, a sudden change overtook my mood, and I knew then that I would like this little spot, tucked cozily under a wooded bluff and overlooking the pure blue waters of the bay. It took no time at all for me to become entranced by the village, Peninsula Park, the countryside, and the people.

Helen Schreiber had fallen off the bluff just a week before I arrived in Fish Creek. Her life was still at risk, and I shall never forget how the whole village was so shocked by her mishap that they could think of nothing else, rallying around to help and comfort the family as best they could. Everyone in the village was relieved and happy when Helen returned home, to recover fully. I had never seen a town so "at one" in its concern.

I soon learned to enjoy the beauties of Peninsula State Park, and sometimes bush-whacked through its woods and meadows with my father, looking for blackberries or mushrooms.

Some of the women in the village went out of their way that first summer to make me feel at home. I think of Edna Thorp, Helen Schuyler, Henriette Volquartz, Alta Fuhr, and "Bennie"

Greene. There were many other women in and around the village who later became friends too.

Walt and Min Rousseff lived farther down our road, and I sometimes visited them. They were both artists, and Walt often told me teasingly that he would like to paint me. When I told my father, a minister, he said, "Well, I'm not so sure I want him to do that." "Oh, Dad", I said, "You can be sure I would keep all my clothes on." He needn't have worried; the picture was never painted, but the Rousseffs continued to be kind friends.

The days sped along, and summer passed through brilliant autumn into winter. I reveled in the snowstorms, sometimes choosing the stormiest day to walk down into town from our hill-top home (now the Potter's Wheel) just for the fun of walking in the snow, though perhaps also to buy a spool of thread or some other trivial item from that handsome blond who worked in his father's store.

It was a new experience for me to see white-tailed deer in their own habitat. We usually saw one or two at a time; but one cold winter morning, I could hardly believe my eyes when an entire herd of the beautiful creatures jumped the fence and loped through our yard to the apple orchard in back of the house. It was an awesome sight for me.

There were three older ladies in town whose names were all Annie: Annie Roy (Thorp), Annie Carl (Olson), and Annie Pat (Chambers). Annie Roy lived in a pretty little house on the corner across from the Episcopal and Community Churches. That home is no longer there, and the Main Street Motel now stands on that corner. Annie Carl lived with her husband and son, next door to the Community Church. Her son, Foster, eventually removed the house and built a new one in its place. Annie Carl was known for her beautiful hooked rugs. Annie Pat lived in a large house between the old Schreiber home with the stone fence (now a gift shop) and the Barringer Hotel (now the C and C Club). Annie Pat and her sister Edith (Mrs. Charles) Duclon had come here from Germany as young girls, and they entered school here with no knowledge of English.

The bluff entrance to Fish Creek in about 1912.

When I knew Annie Pat, she was a widow, and took teachers in to room and board. I stayed with her my last year of teaching here, after my family moved to Eau Claire. Also staying there that winter were Marian Chase, another teacher, and Alta Fuhr, whose husband's work took him away for a few months. Marian and I had all our meals there, and as I remember it, one of Mrs. Chambers' favorite and frequent meals was boiled ring-bologna, boiled potatoes, boiled cabbage or sauerkraut, and, for dessert, brownstone front cake. I enjoyed it all. Sometimes we would gather in the large living/dining room in the evening to grade papers or listen to the radio. I vividly remember King Edward VIII announcing the shattering news that he had renounced his throne for the woman he loved, and we often heard Kate Smith singing "When the Moon Comes Over the Mountain," and "God Bless America," one of Mrs. Chambers' favorites. Incidentally, the Chambers home mysteriously caught fire years later, and burned to the ground.

One evening that winter, Alta, Marian and I were invited up to Martha Fahr's home. She was managing the Welcker Resort after the death of her uncle, Dr. Welcker, and she lived behind and below what is now the Irish House. The evening was enjoyable, with food, conversation, and apple wine. Evidently, the wine had a more potent effect on us than we had anticipated, for, as though on wings, the three of us sang and danced all the way home.

After a year or two, I married the handsome blond and stayed in Fish Creek, never regretting for a moment my decision.

In spite of the changes in the village, and the present heavy tourist traffic, Fish Creek has never lost its charm for me. It remains, for me, a special place of bliss.

✣ ✣ ✣

# My Years With The
# Fish Creek Post Office
by
*Anita Schulz*

Just a year after we moved to Fish Creek in 1940, I started working in the Fish Creek Post Office as a clerk. Little did I know that someday I would retire as Postmaster from that same office. In those early years, the wages were low and the rewards seemed nil. I often asked myself whether this was to be my lifelong career. Now, in my retirement years, I often think about those years, and, if someone asked me whether I would do it again, I know that I would truthfully answer "Yes, I would!" I never got rich money-wise, but the memories I took with me mean far more than material wealth.

I started working in the old post office, which later was an ice-cream parlor and is now a clothing shop, across the street from the present post office (though the post office is about to move to the Community Center). It was a building owned by Carl Seiler, then postmaster, and Henry Stenzel, who owned the Fish Creek Garage. The post office proper was one room in the front of the building, with the garage occupying the larger part in the rear. Divided by a partition, half was the lobby; it housed a small antique table, two chairs, and a writing desk that was originally a Clark's Spool Case, sitting on a stand. The other half was the work area, with only one small window for ventilation. I worked in the building for twenty-two years, and it holds the most poignant memories.

I well remember my first "bad" experience – bad then, humorous now. I had worked only a few days when Mr. Seiler asked me if I would mind staying alone while he walked across the street to the Schreiber grocery store. I was very confident and told him I could handle any situation. He had been gone only a short time when I looked out the window and saw a truck stop. A man stepped out and walked toward the post office. He was dressed in bib overalls, and he had a beard that almost covered his face. Being a young girl from the city, all I could think of was that here was a man coming to rob the post office. I quickly and efficiently locked the door and hid behind the lock boxes. When he came to the door and found it locked, he mumbled something and walked away. Soon I saw him returning with Mr. Seiler, who introduced me to Claude Kihl, a well-known resident of Juddville. His gruff demeanor and appearance certainly was enough to ignite a young girl's vivid imagination and cause fear and trembling!

Although many people come to mind as I think back over the years, I will never forget Lilia Dyer and Ella Weborg.

Miss Dyer was a well-educated lady from Missouri who spent her summers in a log cabin near the entrance to Peninsula State Park. She always carried an umbrella (which she told me quite definitely was a "parasol") to shade her face from the sun as she walked the mile and a half to town. She came into the post office every day during the summer and asked me if I would please show her how to open her box. She knew how to open it, but it was her way of getting personalized attention – attention that she wanted NOW! If I was busy with other customers and told her to wait her turn, she would stand and pout. After I finally helped her, she would say, "You weren't very nice to me today." After twenty summers, this became an established custom; I became very fond of her.

Miss Weborg was a woman of limited means but with a wealth of knowledge. She always had interesting stories to tell when she came into the post office. Whatever the weather, hot or cold, you could recognize her dressed in an old cloth coat. When you saw her, you would think she had stepped out of an old photograph. Elliott Hodgins, the postmaster at the time, was a good photographer. He once asked her to sit in one of the lobby chairs to be photographed; I have often wondered what happened to that photo.

Miss Weborg loved making flowers from toadstools and fungus that grew on trees. She was constantly giving me these gifts she had made, not knowing that I was allergic to mold. I was grateful for her thoughtfulness and took them home, but, because of my allergy, I placed them on the window ledge in my father's toolroom.

The Fish Creek post office in about 1905. This building was later destroyed by fire. Left to right, the people are: unknown woman; Jess Thorp; unknown child (inside the door); Mr. and Mrs. Roy Thorp; unknown boy; Carrie McLeod (later Haddack); Edna McLeod (later Thorp); Keith McLeod; and Leon Mcleod. The McLeods are all members of the Duncan McLeod family.

Camp Meenahga, a girl's camp, was located in the state park. It seemed never to fail that on the hottest day of the beginning of the summer season we were deluged with duffel bags belonging to girls going to camp. Then, on the hottest day at the end of summer, we were again confronted by those same bags being sent home again. There was also a boy's camp on Adventure Island, and this was run by Charles Kinney, also known as "the skipper." The boys would come to town in an old boat that looked like a Viking vessel. Weather permitting, they would pick up their mail daily. It usually consisted of packages of various shapes and sizes containing goodies sent from home. They were never allowed to open them until they were back at camp, where each boy was made to share what he received.

In 1947, when Mr. Seiler transferred from postmaster to rural carrier, I became the acting postmaster until Elliott Hodgins was appointed postmaster. It was during the time he was postmaster that it was decided that a new post office was needed. A new building was erected across the street in 1960. Some people protested that the old building was in keeping with the quaintness of the town and should remain as it was, but the new post office certainly was a pleasure for those of us who worked in it. It was large and airy, with windows on three walls. We now had a washroom, a utility room with a furnace, and all new furnishings, including two new lobby desks.

When Mr. Hodgins moved to California in 1949, I became the officer-in-charge and then advanced to postmaster. I was the first person in Door County to be appointed postmaster under the then-newly-created U.S. Postal Service; previously, it had always been the U.S. Post Office Department. When I retired in 1973, William Wedepohl of Ephraim became acting postmaster until James Gogats became postmaster.

As I said, those years were rich in memories; many of them were happy, but some were sad. The saddest was the day an officer from Green Bay transferred all of my records to Mr. Wedepohl, and I lowered the flag for my last time at 4:30 PM.

# Growing Up In Fish Creek

# Fish Creek Memories
by
*Allen Schreiber*

My recollections of Fish Creek and Door County begin in the mid-1920s, but I will also include here stories that I heard from my parents and grandparents of much earlier times.

My life began in an old frame house that had been built in Marinette, Wisconsin and moved across the ice of Green Bay to the spot on which it still stands, the first house west of the present White Gull Inn. It is on the street leading to Sunset Beach, so named because people used to congregate there in the evening to watch the beautiful colors displayed in the sky as the sun slowly sank below the horizon. The view over the water was unobstructed, and the bay reflected the colors of the sky. This was also a vantage point from which my mother would look out over the bay to see if my father was headed safely home with his fishing tug, the *Amelia D.* At that time Dad was a commercial fisherman out of Fish Creek, setting and lifting gill nets about every three days.

As I remember, there were three so-called fish houses located on the shore across from the present Town Hall. My father occupied one of them, and our neighbor used another. His name was Don Chambers, and he fished with his son Ray. Their boat was the *Morning Star.* I don't recall who occupied the third building.

Trout and whitefish were the main catch, depending on where the nets were set. Gill nets were strung out in a long line with a marker buoy anchored at each end. This enabled the fishermen not only to find the nets but also to identify their own. There were wooden floats attached to the top side of the nets and lead weights fastened to the bottom edge so the net would stay extended during the set. The fine mesh was almost invisible in the water. Once the fish put its head through the mesh it was trapped. Extracting the fish sometimes caused tears, so, when the lift was over and the catch safely cleaned and packed in ice for shipping, the nets were wound on huge reels to dry. When the nets were taken off the reels, the men would mend the tears by hand with a shuttle full of twine before they were folded into a fish box for the next set.

The fish box was of a standard size with sloping ends and sides, with a hand hole in each end of the box. The nets had to be placed carefully in the boxes, because when the set was made, the nets were played out of the box at the stern end of the boat while moving forward. A snag on the box would cause tangling of the net. The work made the men thirsty, and they always kept a tin dipper handy in the boat to dip a cool drink out of the lake.

Gill nets were set under the ice along the shore during the winter. The mesh size was very small in order to catch the smaller herring which cruised the shoreline. This was a different operation than fishing from a boat. First they chopped a hole in the ice large enough to allow a three-quarter-inch board about four inches wide and sixteen to eighteen feet long to enter and float up flat against the bottom of the ice. After the board was pushed to its full length into the hole, a man at the other end would determine about where the end of the board was, then chop another hole in the ice, catch the end of the board and pull it through with a line attached to the trailing edge of the board. This process contined until they had covered the entire distance for the length of the nets to be set. Once the rope had been pulled to the desired distance under the ice the floats and leads kept the net extended.

When I was small, the waters of Green Bay were known as government water. That is, there were no restrictions on fishing outside the bays and inlets. My father and his old fishing partners Tim McCummings and Vet Judd had fishing shanties out along the southeast bar of Chambers Island. The water over the bar was only maybe twelve to fifteen feet deep, them dropping off abruptly to thirty-five to forty feet. There was a current of water along this bar, and the direction of the flow would change every so often. When this change occurred was when we were most likely to spear a nice big lake trout. Our record was a thirty-five-pounder. The shanty consisted of a light wood frame attached to a floor, which was built

Fish nets drying on racks at fish sheds in about 1920, near what is now the Retreat Dock. The shed on the left belonged to Ray and Don Chambers.

on wooden runners. The bottoms of the runners were covered by pieces of strap iron the width of the runners, and the iron protected the runner from wearing away when it was being towed over the snow and ice. The wood frames of the shanties usually were covered with tar paper, which, being black, absorbed heat if the sun was shining. Otherwise we had a little stove made from sheet metal in which we could burn coal or wood. A 4-inch pipe went through the roof to let out the smoke. The inside was quite comfortable, even when the outside temperature was below zero.

✛ ✛ ✛

When I was five years old my father sold the *Amelia D.* and abandoned the fishing business. We moved to a place that people knew as Green's farm, about a mile from Fish Creek on highway 42 south of town. Actually the farm was a cherry and apple orchard. There was a barn on the farm, but we didn't keep cattle or horses. The farm belonged to a man named Green from Chicago who also owned a house right on the corner of the big hill coming into town. He and his family stayed there during the summer months.

I remember the windmill that pumped water into a large wooden tank so that Dad could fill the spray rig and douse the pests that invaded the orchard during the growing season. The wind sometimes proved unreliable, so Dad hooked a one-cylinder gasoline motor with a very heavy flywheel to the pump. The engine would fire four or five times, and then it would coast while the heavy flywheel kept the pump in motion. As it slowed, a governor would kick in the magneto, and the motor would fire again. We called it the putt-ning as it would go putt-putt-putt-putt then ning-ning-ning as it would coast.

We always kept chickens, and they would run loose around the barn and other buildings. Occasionally a large hawk would swoop down and get one of the smaller chickens. Dad remedied that by getting some guinea hens. The hawks wouldn't attacked when the guinea hens were around.

✤ ✤ ✤

I started to school in the fall after my sixth birthday. Of course I didn't want to go, but our neighbor Harry Schuyler and his son Bob stopped and picked me up. I was hustled into the car and away we went to the village and the schoolhouse. Bob got out of the car but I refused. Mr. Schuyler was going to pick me up and put me out, but that didn't work very well, as I bit his hand, so he gave up and took me home. I was thoroughly reprimanded, and Dad took me back to school. I was a little late, but I was well-received by the teacher, Miss Timble. She became a good friend through my first four grades, so the trauma of the first day at school faded away. Mr. Ray Slaby was the principal, and he taught grades five through eight in what we called the "big room."

Baseball was one of Mr. Slaby's enthusiasms, and we played a lot of softball. Every recess sides were chosen, and we were always able to wrangle a few extra minutes of play at the end. In the fall, when the World Series was to be played, we chose sides, named our teams after the big league teams, and played a best-of-seven series. We also got in some football and basketball, as well as some snowball fights in the winter.

One of the really fun things was the merry-go-round. About four kids would get on the push-bars in the center, and the half dozen swings would start to go around. After it got going fast, one rider would put his feet down on the ground and hold the swing back; when the forward pressure got too great, his feet came off the ground and the swing would go far up and out, giving us a thrilling ride.

What did we do for fun? Here are a few things I remember well. When the sun started to warm things up in the spring, I used to go across the street from our house in the village and climb onto the roof of a shed that housed maintainance material for Welckers Resort. The shed had a gable roof, but one side extended down to within four feet of the ground. It was easy to get onto the roof, and I would just lie there, soak up the warmth, and watch the clouds and seagulls soar. Next to the shed was a wooden water tower, and when

I got a little braver, I climbed to the top and enjoyed the view until my mother saw me and almost fainted. Dad was informed and a stop was put to that.

All the kids had sleds, and we spent a great deal of time sliding on the alley hill. There were few cars, so it was a nice place for fun. As we grew older, we would post a guard at the bottom of the big hill on the highway leading into the village. When the guard called "all clear," we left the top of the hill on our sleds. What a ride we had! Picking up speed at the big turn we could coast almost down to the water's edge (ice at that time of year). When a car showed up during our trip down, the guard called "car-car," and we had to drag our feet and turn off the shoulder of the road. Probably dangerous, but a heck of a lot of fun.

Sometimes a few boys would get together on a nice Saturday morning, someone would bring a rope, and we were off for the woods. There was an especially good spot behind the State Park office where there were many tall trees two to three inches in diameter. One of the group would climb high into a tree and attach the rope to the tree trunk. Then, we would all pull on the rope to bend the tree down as far as possible, and when the kid in the tree had a good hold, we would release the tree and allow it to spring back to its upright position. What a ride that kid would have! Then on to the next tree. We could only get one ride per tree because the first one took a lot of the spring out of the tree.

Sometimes, we made masts and sails for our coaster sleds to ride the wind. Of course we could only ride in one direction – the direction of the wind – but we sometimes attained very high speeds and had to hang on for dear life. Occasionally one of us would hit a bump and the sleigh would turn over, resulting in quite a tumble and a few scraped knees, hands, and faces. Another version of this sport involved a triangle sail on a light wood frame with a hand hold that we used on skates if we had a large area of glare ice. Ice skating parties at night were always popular. We gathered wood and built large bonfires to warm up by. We played tag or just skated for the sheer joy of it. On nights when it was cold and still, we liked to call

The "big hill" down the bluff on the southern approach to Fish Creek. This is where the "big kids" used to coast on their sleds from the top of the hill clear down to water's edge. The photo was taken in about 1912.

out three or four words and then wait for the echo off the high bluff behind the village.

Like lots of kids, I started skating with clamp skates, and many a heel or sole of shoes were torn loose with those monsters. When we got our first shoe skates, it was nice not to be retightening skates and loosening and tightening clamps after every few strides. As we grew older we took up ice-boating on rigs that sometimes attained speeds of sixty miles per hour and more. We also liked cross-country skiing, and we occasionally took along food to cook over a bonfire and made a day of it.

❖ ❖ ❖

I remember going hunting for rabbits and squirrels with my dad and uncles. A friend of ours had a nice beagle hound called Cubby that we always took along. Cubby was good at finding rabbit trails and flushing rabbits out of brush piles, and once Cubby started to bay, we would go to our left, away from the baying, since rabbits always circle to the left when chased. We would pick a spot that the dog and rabbit would pass, listening for the dog to let us know they were getting closer. Then suddenly the rabbit would cross the open spot where we had chosen to stand. Dad's 12-gauge would roar, and the rabbit would do a cartwheel and lay still.

A good dog chases a rabbit by scent and so is always some distance behind the rabbit, which he hasn't actually seen. Once the gun is fired he senses the kill and comes up quickly to grab the kill and shake it. We had to take the rabbit away before the dog chewed it up, and then he would stand and look at us with tail wagging. Then, a few pats on the ribs and the words "good dog" and he was off searching for a new track and another chase.

If our bag limit was filled and we were close to hardwood trees, we might spend the rest of the day bagging grey squirrels. Cubby of course was put in the car, and we would saunter along watching the trees ahead. Once a squirrel was spotted we watched his movements as we came closer. Sometimes it would dart into a hole in a hollow tree and we couldn't scare it out. Then we tried the tactic of rubbing a stick against the tree trunk, and sometimes it would lose its nerve and dart out of the hole to perch on a limb. Now was the time for me and my 22-caliber rifle – a shot in the head and down it came. When we got home all the animals were skinned and cleaned, cut up in pieces, and put in salt water to soak overnight. The next day my mother would make a rabbit or squirrel pie with meat and carrots and onions mixed with a little flour and water inside a crust. How we did enjoy those meals.

A fellow by the name of Eugene Ohman hunted with us one time. When we didn't have a dog along, we never missed a chance to surround a brush pile and then have one man tramp on top. Well, this day, when one of the guys began jumping on the brush, a rabbit ran out and went right between Eugene's legs. He turned around and put the gun on the rabbit going away, but the surprise so stunned him that instead of pulling the trigger on the gun, he bit down on his pipe, and the stem broke and the pipe fell to the ground. Everyone had a good laugh over that.

✦ ✦ ✦

Life was simple, but we always had a lot of fun. One treat was to go to the bay in the winter and get a gunny sack full of ice. A gunny sack is another name for a burlap bag. The bag of ice was brought home and the opening tied shut, then laid on the ground and beaten with a flat shovel. This of course broke the chunks into small pieces. During the time it took to get the ice, Mother had prepared a custard made with eggs from our chickens and thick cream skimmed from the tops of milk bottles and saved until there was a substantial amount.

After this custard went into the freezer can, the paddles were put in place and the cover was fitted on top. The can went inside a wooden pail and fit over a pin on its bottom which allowed the can to turn easily. Next, a gear box was set over the shaft that turned the paddles and fastened to two clips on the edges of the wooden pail.

A handle turned the gears which turned the paddles inside the can. Next, we placed a layer of ice in the bottom of the pail, then some salt, then more ice, and so on until the bucket was full. A hole in the side of the bucket at the bottom allowed water to run out as the ice melted and cooled the custard. As the paddles turned inside the can, the custard got heavier and heavier until one could hardly turn the crank. That was the sign that the ice-cream was done. The wooden bucket had to be unpacked carefully so as not to get salt into the ice-cream when the cover was removed from the can. The lucky one was the person that got to lick the paddles, although they were scraped pretty clean before they were handed over.

On the day of a fresh snowfall, my grandmother would sometimes invite the grandkids over in the evening for a treat of snow candy. She would boil brown sugar and water until it started to thicken. A broom straw was plucked from the broom and a loop was tied on the end that came from the top of the broom. This loop was put in the sugar water, and when one could blow the start of a bubble, it was done. Then the hot solution was spooned over new snow gathered in a couple of big pans. Wow! Was that stuff good! Grandmother also had a popcorn party once each winter. I never could figure out why it always tasted so much better at her house.

✛ ✛ ✛

When I was about eight years old, I was awakened by my mother in the middle of the night. · She said, "Son, I don't want you to be afraid, but we have to leave our house. There is a big fire next door, and our house may be in danger." So we left and went across the street to my uncle's house to watch.

The fire had started in the garage next door and then caught in an old barn that was directly behind. That old dry wood really burned fast and sparks were flying all over. The house we lived in was tall, with a hip roof covered with wooden shingles. The men from town tried their best to save the house with buckets of water, but the heat was too intense for them to remain on the ladders. The portable pumper and hose from the state park was brought in and it helped some, but the fire was just too big. The Sturgeon Bay fire department had been called, but it took them at least forty-five minutes to get to Fish Creek. They doused water on the Town Hall as its roof was catching fire, then they pumped water onto our house to calm the flames. What a terrible night that was; it was a wonder that more buildings weren't destroyed. My dad had been out of town on business for the state park and he got quite a shock when he got home that day, but luckily no one was hurt.

✠ ✠ ✠

While we were still living on Green's farm, my mother's father became very ill. He lived in the village of Ephraim where his folks had been among the first settlers, and my grandfather's brother Barnt Oneson was the first child of European descent born in Ephraim. They had come first to Green Bay to settle and work in some kind of agreement with Otto Tank, but the group broke with Tank and eventually homesteaded in Ephraim. So, when my grandfather became ill, my mother was notified by Harry Schuyler, who was one of the few to have a telephone, to come to Ephraim.

Well, this was in February and we had just experienced a three-day blizzard; no cars were able to travel, so Mr. Schuyler hitched up the horses to a covered sleigh and took us to Ephraim. The sleigh had seats along the side and a stove which was bolted to the floor, with a pipe through the roof. It was warm and comfortable inside, but the poor horses really worked hard to pull us through the drifts. The ride was sort of rough, especially along the shore at Ephraim where the wind had piled up really big drifts.

✠ ✠ ✠

There was once a resort on Chambers Island. Several buildings had been erected and an airstrip cleared, but the project was abandoned when the depression hit. Earnest Steinseipher, a stepson of the Don Chambers whom I mentioned earlier, worked for a man by the name of Drake, who I think was connected with the resort and had a nice summer home on the island. Ernie came to town once a week for supplies with a boat called the *Islander*. One afternoon he had loaded the boat, including some heavy oil drums in the cargo, and then stayed in town overnight. When he came to leave in the morning, the boat was sitting on the bottom in about four feet of water. It seems the heavy cargo had forced the exhaust pipe from the motor under water and it flooded the boat during the night.

The town fire truck was brought down, and they pumped the water out of the inside of the boat. Then, after cleaning the motor inside, the cargo was rearranged and everything was back to normal.

There is one other story connected to the *Islander*. One fall day Kenneth Thorp and Roy Doughty, two local youths, talked Ernie into taking them to Strawberry Island where they were going to hunt ducks. Ernie was going to be out at Chambers Island for only a couple of days closing up the Drake home for the winter, and he was to let off the two boys with their rowboat and live duck decoys at Strawberry Island and then pick them up again the following day. During the night a violent storm erupted with high winds, and the next day Ernie got no response when he stopped to pick up the boys. A trip around the island revealed the smashed rowboat washed up on the beach. A tragedy had occurred. Apparently, the boys had left the live decoys anchored out overnight; when the storm broke, they must have gone out to retrieve them and overturned in the rough seas. Their bodies were recovered the next spring, one on Chambers Island, one near Tennison Bay in the Peninsula State Park.

Another drowning victim was a young man by the name of Warren Baxter, whom I remember as a youngster. I also remember the time when Roy, Pat, and Mart Kinsey were out on the ice retrieveing some nets in late March. Pat and Roy were young, but their father, Mart, was getting up in years. The ice was not the best, but they were being very cautious, and they had an open truck. One of the boys would get off the truck and test the ice with a chisel for some distance. If it was safe, the truck with the other two men would drive ahead to where the last test was made. Then the man with the chisel would walk ahead again some distance. The truck would them proceed again up to the last test. But something went wrong; the last test seemed OK, but when the truck stopped, the ice gave way and all three men found themselves in the water and the truck went to the bottom. No one panicked. Roy and Pat knew how to get back onto the ice, and they pulled their father to safety. It was pretty cold but the two-mile walk back to town wasn't too bad, they said, as their clothes froze, so the wind didn't get through and the heat of their bodies kept them fairly warm. Everyone came through the ordeal all right, though a bit shaken.

The next spring the trio went out in their boat and determined that the truck had landed on its wheels so they got some grappling hooks on the truck and some stout lines and towed the truck along the bottom all the way to shore. Quite a crowd gathered to watch as they pulled the water-soaked truck up on land. The motor was taken apart and cleaned, and that truck served the boys for quite a few years.

As I recall, my cousin Earl Bonville and my friend Joe Hogan also once went through the ice into the water, but they got out without gettin hurt. But, the two Jensen brothers, Emery and Alfon, were not so lucky. They had lived in Ephraim and fished on Green Bay all of their lives. They went through the ice near Eagle Bluff, but they never got out.

Door County also once had a plane crash. A dentist from Milwaukee had a small summer place on the hill next to the ski slide, right behind the old Frank Burr place. The dentist would fly up from the city on weekends and return on Monday morning. On this one particular Sunday night there was a very heavy rain storm, though on Monday morning the sky was clear. According to witnesses, the dentist got into the plane, started it up, and gunned down the runway without a warmup. The plane got above the trees just behind the Gustafson home before it sputtered and nose-dived into the woods. The plane caught fire and it burned beyond recognition before the fire department could get there.

✤ ✤ ✤

I shouldn't forget to tell a little tale on my cousin Edward Schreiber. He and his brother Bob built what we years ago called a water sled. Actually, it was a box with a rounded front designed to skim over the water. With a fin under the boat for stability and a 7½-horsepower Evinrude motor, the boat was complete. It provided a thrilling ride and could attain a good speed. At times, when the bay was calm in the early morning, Ed would ride down along Cottage Row and back before going to work in the store. But, on this particular morning he must not have tightened the clamps which hold the motor onto the boat. On the return trip, the clamps vibrated loose, and the motor started to sashay wildly; before he could get it under control, it threw him out of the boat. The motor sank, but Ed got himself and the boat safely to shore. They retrieved the motor later. That didn't stop them from boating, though, and Ed and Bob later built a nice racing hull and had many fun rides.

✤ ✤ ✤

I caught many a big yellow-bellied perch, sometimes two at a time, and spearing perch always stirred my blood. Minnows for bait were always plentiful. In fact they were sometimes so thick around the docks that one could dip them with a kitchen strainer.

✤ ✤ ✤

Putting up ice every February was great to watch after school or on Saturday. We always liked to catch a ride on the sleigh with Harry Churches since he was always jovial and fun to be with. We would ride up from the bay to town and then catch a sleigh going back for another load.

Making ice was quite an operation. First a large level spot was picked and a saw rigged on a sled would cut a perimeter line. The circular saw was set so that it did not quite cut all the way through the ice. There was a runner on one side of the saw which was placed in the previous saw cut, and in this way the ice cakes were all cut to a uniform width. After cuts were made in one direction all across the section that had been laid out, the saw went at right angles to the first cuts, making squares. Next, a channel wider than the ice cakes was cut leading to the loading dock and cleared of ice. Then, the first row of ice cakes was sawed completely through by hand, and the blocks were floated down the channnel. The next rows were broken free by jamming a chisel into the saw cuts. Men with long poles herded the ice cakes to the channel and over to the loading dock, which had an endless belt with flat metal pieces sticking up. When an ice cake was floated up to it, one of the flat pieces would get behind the ice cake and push it up onto the loading dock, where men would slide the cakes to the sleighs waiting to load.

When the cakes had been hauled to the ice house, they were unloaded onto a bed of sawdust, with sawdust packed between cakes and spread over their tops; this in turn was covered with other layers of ice packed in sawdust, until the house was full. The ice house had double walls and the space between them was also filled with sawdust. These ice cakes lasted all through the summer, and they were delivered to private homes to fill and cool old-fashioned ice boxes.

✤ ✤ ✤

I remember our first radio. It was a box about three feet long, with a big horn for a speaker. There were no end of dials on the front to tune in the programs. The power came from batteries. Most of the programs came from Chicago, and we usually listened to the WLS Barn Dance on Saturday night. There had to be a long aerial outside the house – usually a long wire stretched between the house and a high pole, with a wire leading in through the window.

Dad would get everything ready and turn on the switch, and the speaker would emit a series of yowls and growls, but finally, after turning dial after dial, we heard music. Dad would sit down to enjoy, and the sound would fade; he'd turn the dials some more and the music would return. He would sit down again, and it would start to yowl again. Once in a while, we might enjoy ten minutes or so without interruption. However, radios improved rapidly, and within a few years one could enjoy an entire program without much interference. Bradly Kinkaid and "Heine and the Grenadiers" were a couple of early favorites. Then a little later, "Jack Armstrong," "Little Orphan Annie," and the "Secret Three" are some I remember, along with Fred Allen, Jack Benny, and George Burns and Gracie Allen. "The Lone Ranger" was one of my favorites.

✤ ✤ ✤

Cars were always of great interest to my father. Some of the early models I remember were the Saxon, Graham Paige, Model T Ford, Hupmobile, Star, Willies Overland, Franklin air cooled, Auburn, Essex, Studebaker, Hudson, Terraplane, and Cheverolet.

✤ ✤ ✤

There was a man named George Jerasick who came to town and got a job at the state park. He decided to live close to his work, I guess, so he built a house boat for himself and his wife Gretna. They anchored it in the bay just south of Weborg Point campground. One night there was a severe storm. My father said a huge wave came into the bay, and it carried the houseboat over about thirty feet of beach and deposited it in the trees alongside the main road in the park. George passed away shortly after that. In time his wife Gretna married a fellow by the name of Merton Grimmer. The houseboat was repaired and was set up almost where it had landed on the beach, but a few years later it was moved to a spot just below the crest of the hill near the high school. It still stands there today although it has been added to and remodeled; it is now The Irish House.

❖ ❖ ❖

One summer afternoon I was down at the store, and some of the kids were talking about an airplane that had landed in the hayfield on the Clark farm, just above the hill from the village. We decided it was worth the half-mile trek up the hill to see such a sight. It was a biplane with an open cockpit. Quite a crowd had gathered to see such an unusual sight, not to mention the thrill we had when we were allowed to sit in one of the cockpits. I never heard why the plane landed there, but it was a great happening anyway.

❖ ❖ ❖

During the summer we used to watch for posters announcing the arrival of the circus in Sturgeon Bay. They were colorful and exciting pictures, especially those of the lion tamer and the trapeze artists. Sometimes we actually got to go and see the show, but mostly it was just wishing we could go, and a lot of imaginative talk went around among the kids.

❖ ❖ ❖

Swimmming was a fun part of summer. After picking cherries all day or caddying at the golf course, one would get very warm. A nice cool dip in the lake was very welcome. We were all good swimmers, learning how at an early age.

❖ ❖ ❖

Electricity was a luxury in Fish Creek, but I don't know in what year it was first possible to get it. I do know that we used kerosene lamps up until I was nine years old, and I think Ed and Lottie Schreiber, my grandparents on my father's side, were among the first people in town to have electric lights and indoor plumbing.

# The Seasons In Fish Creek
by
*Helen Schreiber Allen*

Thinking of Fish Creek in the 1920s and 1930s brings back memories of many places, things and people long gone but also of many that are still here and unchanged. How different Fish Creek and our lives were then. Perhaps the best way to organize these memories will be to take you through the seasons.

## Fall

As a child it did not matter what the calendar said, fall started the day after Labor Day. On that day the world turned around for everyone who lived in Fish Creek. Suddenly the village belonged to us after a summer in which all actions and thoughts were geared to tourists. Children had to be back in school and only a rare person thought of taking a vacation in the fall.

That sudden silence after the last hurrah of the Labor Day weekend was to be savored. Neighbors and friends had time to stand in the sun and catch up with the news beyond the snatched greetings of summer. On the streets, in the post office and stores, no matter where; it was just good to see familiar faces and have time to visit.

School opened the day after Labor Day, and, since Fish Creek's population did not always provide companions, I often walked alone. However, I remember admonitions to hurry up or be late, and I suspect I was a laggard. I can remember sitting on the top step outside Mr. Slaby's door waiting five minutes before being allowed in the room – the allotted punishment for being late.

School was the rear portion (soon to be destroyed) of what is now the community building. How tall that front facade looked to me as a child! In truth, the two flights of stairs inside the doors (one entrance for boys and one for girls) leading to the classrooms were very steep.

One of the Goodrich Transportation Company steamers being met at the Fish Creek dock by most of the people who happened to be in town when it arrived. This photograph was taken in about 1906.

The sun shone brightly in the morning through the windows of Miss Timble's room (grades one through four) as we did our morning exercises. When I hear now the music that accompanied them, it brings back a vision of rows of us students standing in the aisles at our desks, arms and legs flying in and out, up and down. On Fridays we dutifully took the iodine pill supplied by the state to counteract the lack of that element in our Great Lakes area.

The room was typical of one-room and two-room schools of the day. A little circle of chairs next to the teacher's desk faced the blackboards. Behind them were rows of desks, and at the back wall was a small collection of extra reading books. Books read and reported on merited a gold seal for the reader. This was affixed to a certificate provided by the state with the title written in the appropriate spot. At the end of the year pupils proudly took them home, although some may not have made it that far.

As to all generations, recess was a joy. The boys and a few brave girls played baseball where the fire station and the tennis courts now stand. October brought the World Series, and, as a great baseball fan, Mr. Slaby sometimes prolonged recess to catch another Cardinal hit or a Yankee homer. Sometimes we played Aunty, Aunty I Over at the shed at the back of the lot. Back of the school a spot in the fence, probably tramped down by years of students, gave us easy access to Mr. Hotz' woods. On its paths the boys played War, and Cops and Robbers. Disdaining such wild behavior, the girls played house and admired the wild flowers and mosses. It was a beautiful woods and we probably shouldn't have been there, but we went wherever curiosity and fun took us. I wonder if Mr. Hotz knew what he contributed to our childhood.

One night in 1928, my mother awakened us and told us to get dressed. There was a fire across the street in Lester Anderson's garage. The closest fire equipment was in Sturgeon Bay and it took almost an hour to arrive. Fire was a dreaded word in Fish Creek with no equipment.

My father had discovered the fire and was already outside organizing resistance. Dressed, we huddled on the front steps shivering in the fall night, or was it from fright? Aunt Ella (Schreiber) came over carrying Charles and leading Allen by the hand; Uncle Hollis was helping the men. They lived in the big old ramshackle three-story house on the corner across the street. As the fire spread to the sheds ringing the back lawns, furniture began to appear on our lower lawn. Soon a veritable store of sofas, tables, dressers and beds from three households packed our lawn, although our house, too, might have been consumed if the wind had been right.

What an eerie scene it was. Everyone in town was there, and there was a great confusion of helpless people milling around. The fire fighters shouted directions to each other. The huge blaze by that time had enveloped the house on the corner and was threatening the Town Hall. Aunt Ella was crying, and the incongruity of furniture on our lawn had all of us scared, especially when a sudden gust of wind blew sparks toward our house.

Through all this commotion, ears strained for the sound of the Sturgeon Bay fire truck arriving. It got there only after the fire was under control, but how reassuring it was to have them there, since the fire continued to burn through the night.

Out of the ashes of this fire came the Fish Creek Volunteer Fire Department – the first one north of Sturgeon Bay. The fire engine was purchased, and my father was made chief in recognition of his efforts during the fire. He served faithfully until the mid-1940s.

Gradually the green trees of summer left us. We took the seasons for granted, so autumn's miracle was lost on us. But not so the adults. Autumn's colors were a reminder that winter was coming. Hotels and cottages were closed and windows were boarded up for winter. The smell of burning leaves permeated the air, and storm windows replaced screens. The dock, which rarely had more than four of five boats even in the summer, looked deserted as fishermen brought their boats in for winter. Morning mists rising from the bay reminded us that the days were getting cooler.

The year they rebuilt the road into town, they brought the excess rocks and boulders that had been blasted out into the park next to the main dock. This created an eyesore that shut off our view of the bay for several years. But, living across the street, it provided a challenge we couldn't resist. We climbed and played on it, oblivious to danger. Fortunately, no one was hurt and it eventually was removed.

Then the sounds of summer were gone. The frogs croaking in the creek were silent and only the winter birds remained. Time to get apples for winter. One fall day my mother and Aunt Ethel Bonville piled the children in the car for our annual trip to our great-grandparents Stephan and Rachael Norton's farm on Highway F. The old house and orchard were deserted and both were falling down, but the Hyslop and Whitney crabapples (the best kind for apple pickles) and the Russet and Snow apples made the trip a success.

Now walking to school, we felt the crisp air of late fall. Fred Schuyler's blacksmith shop (where Wesa's Cottages now stand) was a wondrous and warming sight on our way. The old forge was roaring and the sound of clanging came from the dark innards of the shop.

The trees were bare by Halloween. We did not trick or treat, and costumes were unheard of, but the silent deserted streets and the moon floating in and out of clouds gave the night an eerie air that a whole street of young witches and ghosts today cannot conjure. Knocking on windows was the norm for young children. Once, with cousins Ora and Mila Bonville, we rang the dinner bell at Thorp's Hotel. This daring feat sent our legs running, sure that old Asa's ghost would emerge from the deserted hotel and chase us. We were too innocent to know that older boys were overturning privies and putting wagons on top of sheds.

One Saturday in November always brought a bit of excitement. For many years, Pelke's Tavern (next to our store) held a turkey shoot one Saturday before Thanksgiving. Shooting from the back of the tavern toward the bay put the target just east of our back yard. Our garage would deflect a poor shot, but it was still a little dangerous with adults, children and dogs milling around. I had strict orders not to leave our back step, where I sat to witness the excitement. Eventually the best marksman was determined and went home in triumph with his turkey. I suspect many people were relieved when the shoots were discontinued.

Thanksgiving was the gate between fall and winter. There occasionally was snow – usually just a skiff – but often the ground was bare. Many extended families still lived fairly close together in the 1920s and 1930s, and ours was no exception. We gathered at Auntie and Grandpa (Edward and Lottie) Schreiber's home across the street from Thorp's Hotel and Welcker's Resort. That home is still standing, surrounded by a stone wall. We walked that wall to display our balance, and parental admonitions to stay off the east porch of Welcker's made it even more enticing. We crept onto the large open porch, pretending the great deserted building was haunted. Through its tall windows we could see the reception room with everything covered with sheets. Back in the house we played innocent games like Button, Button, Up The Stairs which kept us out of the dining room/kitchen traffic.

There were no buffets for dinner then. Tables were set with the best one had, however humble it might be. As children, we were banished to the kitchen where we could do less damage. This turned out to be a grave mistake one year when someone (not I, of course) got carried away and began tossing turkey bones across the table. The ensuing melee brought the stern admonitions from parents and Auntie who did not seem to approve of this activity. We do not, however, tell our children about this gross behavior.

Eventually the big day came to an end. The next day it was more like winter than fall.

## Winter

The first snowfall announced the arrival of winter much more vividly than the calendar. Today's children probably greet it with the same joy we did, but in much lighter clothing. With winter came the much-hated long underwear, long stockings (sometimes of wool), sweaters over blouses or dresses, snow pants, heavy wool jackets or coats, knit caps and mittens, mufflers over noses on really frosty days, and, of course, four-buckle overshoes.

We built snowmen, made snowballs, and used up whole afternoons making forts for five-minute battles. Great blizzards brought huge drifts which could be dug out like caves. But our greatest joy was sliding on Alley Hill. I don't know how many hours of fun this provided for us children, but someone was always there after school and on Saturdays. The Alley Hill was an unused town road between Greene's house and Mr. Hotz' woods. We would plod up that hill again and again for the few thrilling moments of flying down past the Seventh Day Adventist Church and ending up in the ditch at the southeast part of Noble's yard. Older boys, competing for the longest run, posted someone on the main street to watch for the occasional car and slid across that street into Kinsey's yard. My brother Bob, the proud owner of a Flexible Flyer, was undoubtedly one of them. When dusk began to fall we headed home, noses and fingers nipped, cheeks ruddy, mittens soggy, and toes icy, but what fun it was.

We shed our buckle overshoes at the door and carried them inside, and how hard it was to open those buckles with frosty fingers. Then we got out of our wet clothes over the big heat register in the hall where warm air from the gravity furnace brought feeling back to our fingers and toes and also dried the clothes we laid out on its grill.

Once warmed, we turned on the Clarion, Jr. radio and listened to Jack Armstrong, The All-American Boy, or to Buck Rogers In The 21st Century, which we thought must be at least a million years away. If we could only get our mother to buy Wheaties so we could get the secret decoder instead of always having oatmeal or that awful Farina or Cream of Wheat for breakfast.

Teenagers went sliding at night on the "big hill" (the main road coming into town). Here, except for the rare car, they had a clear run to the bay, if they could reach it. This sport ceased as the number of cars increased. Cars on the crossroad (Bluff Road) also stopped the fun on Alley Hill. Today it is grassed over and forgotten.

The students of Fish Creek grade school in about 1910. Perhaps you can recognize an old friend; the blonde girl in the middle of the picture directly in line with the teacher in the back row center is Mildred Thorp.

Before we had a radio I remember a portable victrola which my brothers used to crank up before pushing a lever increasing the speed to send *Valencia* racing. Here I first heard *My Blue Heaven, Tiptoe Through the Tulips, Painting the Clouds With Sunshine*, and other musical hits of the day.

My brothers Ed and Bob had a small steam engine. I can still see them playing with it in the hall the night they set the rug on fire. My mother quickly doused the conflagration before it got out of hand.

Christmas was coming, but not until the first week in December did signs of it appear. For the most part, we gave presents only within our immediate family, and each person got only one major item each. There was little Christmas buying this early in the month and Christmas cards also came later. Plenty of time to do that before the big day.

One of the more pressing things was the making of costumes, for Mr. Slaby had announced plans for the annual Christmas play at school. What was it about? Even more important, what part would each of us play? One year I was a candle, and one year I was a Japanese girl; the rest of my roles are lost to memory. Learning our lines occupied most of our evenings.

At our Community Church, the Christmas pageant was being planned. Alice Lundberg (the driving force in founding the church), Edna Thorp, and Hubert Woerfel were in charge. Mrs. Stock, who had an exotic collection of costumes, and Henriette Valquarts, who played the violin, helped with the program.

One day a tall evergreen made its appearance at the main intersection where the road turns to Ephraim. That night and every night until the first of the year, the tree with its Christmas lights reminded us of the holiday season. Fish Creek looked almost like a European village with its snow and quiet Christmas tree.

Mothers began baking and cleaning the house for the holidays, even though fall cleaning was not that far in the past. Everything must be done so that the week between Christmas and New Year's could be devoted to visiting friends and neighbors.

No long epistles adorned Christmas cards; a simple signature told friends and relatives you thought of them. If the flaps of envelopes were tucked in instead of sealed, it took only a 1½¢ stamp rather than 3¢ for a sealed envelope.

Santa Claus was a much more exciting figure then because he was so remote. He was at the North Pole making toys, not standing about on every street corner and in every store. One year, however, I do remember being taken to Sturgeon Bay to see Santa arrive on the train, and one Christmas Eve Santa peeked in our windows. What a lark for my mother, who admitted that it was she when we became a little more knowledgeable. It wasn't until the third grade that such innocence faced reality, such was our sheltered life then.

For children, shopping was easy. We were given twenty-five cents to buy gifts for our parents and siblings. Sometimes we made gifts, but a nickel bought a big candy bar and once I went to Lundberg's corner store to buy a five-cent White Owl cigar for my father, his favorite.

Then came time for Christmas vacation! That meant days of sledding. But first, the school Christmas play. Because transportation and roads weren't as reliable in those years, social events in the village were well attended. What suspense! What excitement! The town hall was packed with young and old, for Mr. Slaby's plays had an excellent reputation. In costume backstage, we desperately tried to remember our lines, nervously fidgeting and giggling as we peeked around the curtain, trying to find our parents. Fortunately my lines were simple. I did not inherit my mother's talent for acting. (She organized a series of Women's Club plays and was usually the star.) Backstage, confusion reigned, especially in the small dressing rooms where things were lost and found with regularity. Finally the curtain went up and the play was on!

If only camcorders had been invented so that we could have a record of those wonderful plays. Would they still seem wonderful today? They were simple pleasures, but what memories they provided for all who had a part in them, including the audience.

Then it was over, and we stood on stage beaming at all the clapping. But wait! Suddenly Santa appeared, coming down the aisle with his big pack of candy. Every child in the Town Hall received a box of Christmas candy from Santa. This was usually the only sight of him for the season and most of the younger children were so in awe that they were mute. Then the big night was over.

The Sunday night before Christmas we all trooped to Church for the pageant. The girls all hoped to be Mary, but my round face didn't fit the part. The boys opted for the Magi since Mrs. Stock's gold and silver costumes made them feel like much more splendid creatures than the shepherds in their faded bathrobes. Afterwards, we walked with our parents to the village Christmas tree and sang Christmas carols in the quiet night.

Christmas came in the night. When we went to bed after setting out Santa's lunch on the kitchen table, there was no sign of decorations, tree or presents. Only empty, everyday stockings hung at the fireplace. In the morning the decorated tree was there with presents underneath. Sometime in the night Santa had come, put up and decorated the tree, filled the stockings and eaten the lunch. What magic! We received one present each from our parents (a sled, skates, a game, or perhaps a bike, as we got older), one from each sibling, and one from Aunt Lena, my godmother. For my father there was always a box of chocolate-covered cherries, his favorite. Stockings held candy, an apple, and a huge orange, a real treat since oranges were not as available then as today.

One Christmas morning Auntie Lottie (Schreiber) brought over a cold English pork pie for my father's breakfast. I can still see the layer of lard under the crust. For dinner the families gathered at Uncle Bill and Aunt Ethel Bonville's house. New Year's was also my mother's birthday and was at our house. We always had homemade ice cream for dessert, which my father churned in the basement. That was no chore for him, since he loved ice cream. We children always managed to make our appearance after the dasher came out.

Once the holidays were over, we settled down to the long winter. Measles, chicken pox, whooping cough, mumps and other children's diseases popped up and spread rapidly as school resumed. By law, they had to be reported to the health officer, so Dr. Sneeberger came from Ephraim to tack a quarantine sign on the door. There was no going out until it was removed.

Colds with a cough were also not to be sneezed at (but they were), and out came the mixture of goose grease and turpentine which was rubbed on our chest until the cough loosened. Between our chests and our long underwear we wore an old wool sweater whose sleeves and bottom had been cut off. This was supposed to keep the fumes in to penetrate and loosen but it never completely did. What an indignity to wear these when we were in the upper grades, sometimes for two or three weeks. I now realize that in the absence of antibiotics, mothers were very much on their own when illness came. Vanity was put aside for whatever worked because the threat of pneumonia was always present.

Card parties blossomed (Five Hundred was the game of choice) and ladies spent many afternoons quilting or tying quilts at various homes. I remember an afternoon at Annie Chamber's with five or six ladies; they surrounded the quilt, gossiping and exchanging news and ideas, fingers carefully taking minute stitches. Woe unto the sewer whose stitches were too large. Aunt Ethel's strong point was hooked rugs; she always had one set up in the dining room in winter. Annie Olson also made beautiful rugs.

One day the powers that be decided that the ice was thick enough to cut. Ice boxes were still in wide-spread use in the 1920s, and ours was in the basement stairway because it was cooler there. My first view of a refrigerator was in the pantry at Auntie's and Grandpa's house, a marvelous thing with a motor on top looking like a stack of trays.

Such excitement! I could watch from our back steps as team after team came by. Each pulled a heavy sled with runners, no sides, and only an occasional brace. Sometimes there would be four or five lined up waiting to be loaded with great chunks of clear bluish ice. The cordoned-off hole got larger every day as men cut the chunks and floated them over to where a conveyor belt with cleats caught the blocks and carried them up to be loaded. Then the teams of horses pulled the creaking sleds to ice houses in town and on farms. The ice house next to the northeast corner of our lot was filled, and sawdust was packed between the blocks to keep them from melting.

Then it was over, and the water in the large open square froze so smooth that all the skaters came. Sometimes at night they built a huge bonfire of old tires to keep warm.

Alma Lundberg Waldo, who belonged to my father's generation, recalled skating as a young girl with friends from the village to the lighthouse in the park for a get-together with the Duclon family. The Duclons were a musical family and full of fun; skating over there evidnetly was a lark.

My brothers skated well, but I was never much of a skater. We did play on the ice sometimes and I remember one occasion when my brother Bob and cousins Earl, Ora, and Mila Bonville, and I took our sleds onto the ice. Earl and Bob had driven nails into the ends of short sticks so that with one in each hand we could push ourselves along the ice. Following the leader we decided to go under the big dock. It was very dark and damp as we maneuvered among the wooden pilings. As we came out I could see open water around the pilings, and ever since I have wondered how thick that ice was upon which we so blithely pushed ourselves?

A great deal of activity took place when the ice was thick enough to hold trucks and cars. Commercial fishermen set their nets and fish shanties were everywhere. Fresh herring from these ice cold waters was delicious. Sometimes in the summer my mother met the fish boats as they docked and bought a whitefish to bake. No restaurant fish can compare with those herring and whitefish.

My mother was born and raised in Peshtigo along with nine brothers and sisters, so the trip across the bay to Peshtigo and Marinette was a shortcut to visiting many relatives. This was especially important since time away from the store was limited to Sunday. We would get into our Studebaker touring car with its side curtains and isinglass windows, with heated bricks and car robes tucked around, and off we would go.

Sometimes cracks in the ice had to be spanned with planks to get across, and, by March other problems surfaced. My mother told of one return journey in late winter when some areas of the ice were black and rubbery and they drove through much water on the ice to arrive home. The next day the ice broke up and went out. "Never again," said my mother, and subsequent trips followed the 115-mile route that skirted the bay.

When a good old-fashioned blizzard roared through town, all school children rejoiced. School was closed and, even better, the whole town was closed in, as snow piled up on the roads. Snow removal machines then could not cope with really bad blizzards, and it might be several days before the road from Sturgeon Bay was plowed out. In that time we were shut off from the world –no mail, no deliveries, no cars –only teams of horses could make it in from the country. It was a quiet wonderland that drew the village together. Drifts across the streets and in the yards gave a whole new meaning to the word play. We made the most of these "stolen" vacation days.

March came with its hint of spring, but also with late blizzards that dampened our spirits. The snow became dirty and slushy, the old forts and snowmen slumped, and the rivers of water running to the bay spoke of spring.

## Spring

Spring came on soft southern winds that took away the snow and revealed bits of green grass. The ice looked black, and in high winds you could hear it cracking. Around the edges, open water appeared. Then one night the frogs at the creek began their croaking. Spring was officially here; the creek was running.

The ice began to break up and one day a strong wind from the right quarter would carry it out. It was always disappointing when the wind shifted and brought it all back. But its days were numbered. Now I could hear the waves lapping on the shore, and they lulled me to sleep. There was only a natural shoreline then.

Most important, we could shed our long underwear, long stockings, mittens, scarves, and boots. The boys in the village appeared in knickers and high top boots, top fashion for the day. Sleds disappeared; wagon, scooters, and hoops appeared. My brothers made stilts and walked on them. They played knife and marbles, while I found hopscotch, jacks, and jump rope much more interesting.

There was a new bustle in town as adults put aside the relaxed days of winter and began preparing for the "season". With the same fervor that they praised the end of the tourist season in the fall, they now looked forward to it.

House cleaning became the order of the day. Clotheslines sprouted rugs which were dutifully beaten with a wire rug beater. My mother started early, cleaning the store. Everything was taken off the shelves and washed (along with the shelves) and put neatly back. Next she scrubbed the floor on hands and knees and then varnished it. And then she came home to clean house.

Cleaners descended on hotels and cottages. Lawns were raked, gardens were plowed and planted, and boats were readied for the launch. At our house, the chicken coop back of the store also had to be cleaned; that was my brothers' job, thank goodness.

Until I could go on my own, it was my brother Bob's job to take me up to George LeMere's barber shop for haircuts. George's tiny shop was on Main Street across form Mart and Bertha Kinsey's house (now Osaki's shop), and he cut hair there for many years.

Brother Ed also had to take care of me at times. He was eight years older than me, and, with my mother in the store, it was his boring job to wheel me around in the buggy. One day he took the buggy up the big hill as far as Green's house and let it go to see how far it would coast. Fortunately for both of us it did not tip over. I've never held that episode against him, though.

Sometime in the spring elections were held. The word didn't mean much to me then, but I knew it was important because there were so many cars parked around the Town Hall and in front of our house. No one ever parked in front of our house in spring and rarely

The "cross-roads" in Fish Creek, looking up what is now Hwy 42 toward the bluff entrance to town, in about 1912. The Maple Tree Cafe (now the Summertime Restaurant) is on the right; the Nook Hotel is the white building across the intersection on the right.

in summer so it had to be something special. Mother made sure she went over to vote, something women had not been able to do a few years before. The town meeting was held with the same response.

May Day came and we made May baskets at school. On the way home we picked May flowers to put in them. Then we slipped our little cone-shaped baskets onto the doors of relatives and friends, knocked, and then ran and hid to wait for the look of surprise as the door was opened and searching eyes sought the giver.

School was out about the middle of May and we were already looking forward to a whole summer of play. But first came the annual school picnic at Weborg Point. All eight grades arrived with an abundance of mothers; fathers occasionally showed up for lunch. It was too early for campers, so we roamed the point freely, falling into the water, getting into poison ivy, and having a wonderful time. The tables in the shelter held the "dishes" the mothers brought, and the line moved slowly with such a variety. Then the word went around. Pleck's Dairy had delivered the big yellow tubs of ice cream packed in ice that were donated by the two teachers. You could run as fast as you could, but it was never enough to put you first in line. Ice cream cones were a real treat which we did not often have.

The town was polished and ready. The cherry and apple trees had bloomed, bringing a few tourists. At the two campgrounds in the park, Nicolet and Weborg Point, an occasional tent appeared, placed by regulars who wanted to claim their usual spots for the summer. We visited the game farm on one of our many Sunday drives through the park. Everyone was poised for summer. For us spring ended with the end of school. Summer started the next day.


### Summer


June brought long days to play. Sometimes we walked the shore to Aunt Ethel's, overturning rocks to look for crabs, and we occasionally arrived with a bloodsucker attached to an ankle or a leg. Once it was removed, we were back at play. I think now about how carefree we were, and I wonder about today's structured children. Even as very small children, we roamed Fish Creek freely (and usually barefoot) with no fears. We absorbed the lessons of nature, and we learned about society and its values from the broad spectrum of people who came to our village.

Some days we went to the old barn back of Fred Schuyler's to play. It was near the water and deserted, but enough hay was left so that we could jump down from the haymow, and we devised all sorts of implausible plots and daring deeds. Some years, however, the barn was rented and filled with riding horses tended by young black men. We could still walk the path past the barn, but play there was out for the summer.

It was too cold to go swimming, so we went instead to the creek to play. You could follow the highway to Blanche Brunswick's house, take the lane that bordered the woods, and then go through the meadow to the old wooden bridge (no railings) that crossed the creek. No homes or mowed lawns spoiled the creek, no beer cans or garbage floated in its clear waters. Instead you could find newly hatched polliwogs, fish and frogs; blue bottle flies hovered overhead and turtles and snakes crawled the sandy banks. Black-eyed susans, and butter-and-eggs daisies were in abundance. We could play the whole afternoon and not get bored. Then we would walk the path along the shore to the bathing beach and home.

In May and early June, boys in the village were smitten with raft fever. The sight of one log on the shore sent them on a mission to find two or three more which they straddled and paddled home. Nailed together, they were launched and maneuvered around the bay with a long pole, sometimes all the way around the shore to Hen Island or the slough. One spring my brothers found an old propeller and fastened it on a long shaft with a hand crank on the other end. This was added to the raft, and they proudly took their invention for a spin around the bay, finally liberated from shallow water. Turning furiously, since it took an incredible amount of energy to push that heavy raft around the bay, they made the grand finale – a tour down the length of the old dock for all the fishermen to admire. Alas, the anglers were not astounded at the young geniuses passing by and told them in no uncertain terms to "get that @*!%$#! thing out of here, you're scaring the fish!"

Another summer, when I was probably three or four, an encampment of gypsies made their appearance between the general stores. Stories of gypsies snatching children and stealing were rife at that time so my mother was nervous. My dad was calm; things like that did not bother him. Nonetheless, one day Sulie Anderson (now Sulie Hansen) and I decided to take the path between the stores (no fences then) to the main street. Hand in hand we scurried past the tattered camp, glancing at the lounging figures who watched us pass. A few days later they were gone and we never saw them again.

In June 1934 I fell off the bluff back of Thorp's Hotel. I didn't realize when I went to retrieve my cousin's shoe, which was almost at the edge, that the rocks were fractured and would not hold even a twelve-year-old's weight. What did come out of it was a realization of how much a community can mean to us. Small towns have their minus sides, but when trouble comes, their concern and caring gives us the support we need and it was certainly so at this time. I should hate the bluff but I have a special caring for it.

Remembrance seems to come in fragments that appeal to our senses. Another scene imprinted on my mind from my very early years is of great clouds of steam rising as my mother lifted clothes with a thick stick from the copper boiler. The old iron range, complete with warming ovens and water heating compartments, had been relegated to the basement when the new stove appeared. Here, my mother boiled the white clothes before washing them – insurance against "tattletale gray." Mondays were always washdays, Tuesday was ironing day and Saturday was cleaning day, like it was in stone. Washdays the basement took on the appearance of a steam room. There the Maytag washer chugged and jerked while Mom (usually in rubber boots since the floor was often wet) fed clothes through the wringer into two rinse tubs next to it. Starch for shirt collars and dresser scarves stood at the back of the stove. What a production washday was. However, this arrangement was a great improvement

The Main Street of Fish Creek, looking east from in front of the Thorp Hotel (where Founder's Square is now) in about 1915. The taller building just to the left of the horse and buggy is Schreiber's store, and the building just to the left of it is Lundberg's store.

over earlier days when she had had only a washboard, and even rugs
were scrubbed by hand, section by section.

Dryers were yet to come, so all clothes were hung outdoors
on clotheslines. In winter, fingers and clothes froze almost
immediately. When dusk came and it was time to take them in, they
were often still frozen – sheets came off like boards. Everyone
owned a clothes rack where clothes were draped to finish drying.
After our hall register was removed, my mother strung lines in the
attic, and in winter or on rainy days she carried the clothes up three
flights of stairs and hung them there to dry.

The basement was also the scene of another activity —
making root beer. Like ice cream, soft drinks were a special treat
which we did not often have. But, once during the summer, Mom
would make root beer using the little square bottles of Hires extract.
I'm not sure of the process, but we had a manual capper that sealed
the bottles before they went up to the attic to develop their fizz.
Sometimes too much fizz developed and a bottle would blow up, and
some never made it because we felt impelled to test a bottle before
it was ready.

My brother Ed remembers summer Sundays (probably
around 1918-1919) when my mother and dad took soda from the
store to an area between Eagle Tower and Eagle Terrace and sold it
to vacationers and picnickers. He also remembers eluding the
watchful eye of parents and drinking up some of the profits.

Moving pictures were fairly new in the 1920s (at least in Fish
Creek) and were a great fascination. The fact that all this took place
across the street in the Town Hall made it even more exciting, not
that we were allowed to go very often. Mr. Brungraber would set up
his projector once or twice a week, and on hot summer nights the
door was left open for ventilation. Every kid in town had his own
method of trying to outwit poor Mr. Brungraber, but it was easy to
stand close to the open door so we could see the movie. Suddenly
discovered, we would be shooed away, only to drift back. Persistence
finally paid off by the third reel; Mr. Brungraber gave up as the
movie neared its end. So we usually saw the hero kiss the heroine.

The 4th of July was both glorious and awful with 5 AM firecrackers (no injuries) and great fears on the part of my mother and dad that a careless cigarette or match would set off the stock of fireworks in the store and burn the whole place down. Fortunately, that never happened. I think we were allowed fifty cents worth of firecrackers, and the decisions were terrible. Packages of firecrackers and snakes were only a nickel or a dime but there was still a lot of agonizing until the final decisions were made.

At night, my father gathered Roman candles, sky-rockets, sparklers, and a variety of other things available at that time, and we all went to the shore at Aunt Ethel and Uncle Bill Bonville's. We dashed around with sparklers, held Roman candles as they shot off, and ooohed and ahhhed at all the rest. Around the bay we could see other fireworks. I'm sure that my mother and many others slept better that night than the night before.

Some time (determined by mothers) in the later part of June, the water was warm enough to go swimming. From that day until the start of school, we spent hours every day at the beach. The beach at that time really consisted of three portions, separately fenced. We could take the lower path around Al Kinsey's barn, past Fred Schuyler's sometimes-deserted barn, through the tramped-down place in the fence to Aunt Ethel's. There we picked up cousins Mila and Ora, and, since their beach was stony, we followed the road (no sidewalk beyond Al and May Kinsey's) to Welcker's or Thorp's beach. Both contained big old bath houses that were used by hotel guests but not by us since we already had on our wool suits. Between Welcker's and Thorp's beaches was Friedmann's private beach (they owned the point where Hidden Harbor is located). That was not a barrier, however, since we could walk in the water around the fences, although we never played on their beach.

Sun bathing was as popular then as now, but more of the sunbathers swam. Men had tops to their suits, and ladies had been only slightly liberated from suits at the knees and elbows. There was, happily, no sea wall at Thorp's, only a wide arch of sand where we played for hours. We learned to swim ourselves, as there were no lessons then, and we finally opened our eyes underwater to look at the minnows, crabs, and sand patterns. You could also walk from sandbar to sandbar until it was deep enough to swim to the raft. The beach and swimming were probably the most important part of our summer.

In the early years, my father walked a two-wheeled cart which he made down Cottage Row to deliver groceries. Earlier in the day he walked the Row to get orders. In my childhood I remember a Model A Ford truck parked near the gas pump he had installed in front of the store. In perfect harmony next to it were several iron shafts with rings where horses were still tethered at times. Occasionally, he allowed me to go along when he was taking orders for delivery. At a couple of cottages I was allowed to go into the kitchen with him, and the cooks would give me a cookie. Such excitement for a three or four year-old.

In the 1930s, a few cottages were beginning to appear in back of private residences. In the 1920s, cottages were primarily at the hotels and on Cottage Row, though the "cottages" on Cottage Row were really large homes used in summer by families from St. Louis and Chicago. They would arrive in the later part of June with their entourages. Rolls Royces, Deusenbergs, and Packards appeared on the streets, often with chauffeurs in attendance. Natty yellow convertibles made our new black sedan look drab, and they gave me a lasting desire to have one.

The only telephone in town where one could make or receive a long distance call was at Thorp's Hotel. Fortunately or not, only a grave crisis required such a call. In the 1920s and 1930s, Thorp's was at its height of strength and popularity. Around the middle of July townspeople would pass the word to each other that Thorp's was full. This was a signal for rejoicing, since it meant a good season was at hand for all. The faithful had returned to their cottages and the main lodge was turning them away.

One cottage was reserved. It was Ted and Tilda Thorp's old home and was still occupied by them (preserved now by Founders Square). I remember Ted as stooped and moving slowly with a cane.

The baseball team out for a joy ride and stopped in front of the Maple Tree Cafe in about 1918. Blaine McSweeney is the man in the dark coat standing in the back of the car, Henry Blackfield is pouring water into the radiator.

Usually, he would be sitting in the sun in front of the cottage observing the activity. Tilda was still up and about, active enough to be in Ladies' Aid in winter.

Thorps owned quite a bit of land around Fish Creek, including the land on which our home was built. That land had previously held Alex Noble's blacksmith shop. Recently, while digging in a flower bed, I turned over bits of iron from the old shop. In 1922, however, it was barren and overgrown; my mother was pregnant with me and was hoeing in the large garden back of the store when she was approached by Ted. "You shouldn't be climbing all those stairs with your family and another one coming," he said. "You talk to Lester and get him to buy that corner lot below the store and build a house." The stairs he referred to were a long, open stairway on the east side of the store which led to the living quarters above it. My dad agreed to that suggestion, and so our home came to be.

After he retired from his lighthouse duties, Captain William Duclon, lived in the house across the street. He was a jovial fellow, full of fun and he teased my mother when our house was being built, claiming that it would shut off his view of the bathing beauties on the beach.

Besides working in the store in summer and caring for a large vegetable garden, my mother had flowers. My dad helped her plant them, but from then on they were primarily her care. When I was about three, my brother Bob and I took bouquets she had cut to Thorp's cottages to sell. One sure sale was the Del Banco sisters who lived in the Bide-A-Wee Cottage (now the Confectionery). Five to fifteen cents bought a bouquet. That money went into our steel banks from the Bank of Sturgeon Bay, except for a nickel apiece which we exchanged for an ice cream cone at Meta LeClair's Maple Tree Cafe (now the Summertime), the only shop in town at that time.

Toward the end of July, the cherries were ripe. From about four years of age on, children from the area picked cherries. We were outfitted in old clothes, given a rope with a snap and a lunch, and walked up the big hill to the orchard. For some years Uncle Bill managed Greene's farm (where the clock shop is now located), and we picked there. The going rate was three or four cents a pail, and we thought it was a lot of money. The only trouble was that on hot days (and it always seemed to be hot), perspiration began to roll and we were soon covered with sweat and sticky cherry juice which attracted flies and began to make us think about swimming. By noon when we ate our lunch, such thoughts overwhelmed us and we invariably walked home and went for a swim.

One day of cherry picking stands out in my mind. We were picking at Schuyler's (later Clark's and now Lautenbach's) orchard. It was hot, sultry and sticky. Visions of that cooling swim were tempting me, but I knew I should stay. Suddenly a beautiful, clear tenor voice began singing "When It's Springtime In The Rockies" from far off in the orchard. It revived us all. I stayed.

At night we played Hide-and-Seek and Red-Rover on our north lawn. August nights were special. We could sit or lie on the grass and look for the big and little dippers. Some nights a star would fall or the northern lights would move mysteriously across the skies; fireflies would sometimes be out. No cars lined the streets; no one disturbed the quiet – that is, until sometime in the 1930s when the word went around that our north lawn was full of nightcrawlers, an overweight form of angleworm. Sometimes in the middle of the night we would wake up to the flashlights of fishermen matching their speed with that of the nightcrawlers. Fortunately, that era passed with the onset of a drought.

My first brush with death came when Grandma Norton died; at least, that is the first death I remember. Grandma Norton was really Great-Grandmother Rachel Norton, and she was a Jarman before she married Stephan. Both the Nortons and the Jarmans were pioneer families in Door County and had come from England. My dad remembered her saying to her son Homer: "'Omer, go out into the woods and get an 'ammer 'andle." That may be a clue to her origins, but I am still researching all this. I understand that she made an elixir which she sold around town. I always try to conjure up an image of her as a young girl who caught the eye of one of Asa

Thorp's champion wood splitters – or were they already married in the 1860s when they came to Fish Creek?

I knew her only as an elderly lady, very heavy, blind, and always dressed in dark clothes. My mother would remind us that the hours were long for her and that we should stop and see her. In summer she could often be found sitting in the sun on her back porch; other times she was in her little room, crammed in with her belongings and her bed. She often produced a peppermint from her apron pocket for each of us, but my brother and I never ate them. She was a quiet, kindly soul, but I suspect that when she was young she had an indomitable spirit.

She was ninety-three when she died. I was about six or seven years old. The funeral was at the Seventh Day Adventist Church, and, true to the custom of the day, the casket was open throughout the service. It was my first sight of a dead person, and, with all the weeping, it produced an awesome impression on me. With it came the realization that this too would be my fate. In true Scarlet O'Hara fashion, I decided I wouldn't worry about that yet. It would be a long time before I was that old.

The store was central to our existence. My parents bought it in 1916 and immediately set to work scrubbing the entire interior until the cat smell was gone. It took three scrubbings. Apparently, cats had been allowed to laze away in the cracker barrels and such. My dad took jobs outside the store to help them get on their feet, and my mother worked in the store. In the evening dad was in the store while mom worked in our living quarters above, doing all the chores that normally would have been done during the day. Those were hard years; no water or electricity, no varnish on floors that were scrubbed on hands and knees – not until they could afford it.

Many discouraging things happened. One of the worst was when the last boat of the fall sank before it reached Fish Creek loaded with the store's supplies for the winter. There was no insurance; everything had to be reordered.

Sometime in the 1930s, I began to be more conscious of the store. At fifteen, I changed places with my mother. I worked in the store with my dad and two brothers, and she stayed at home renting rooms for $12 to $14 a week. Until World War II, the store was open at 7 AM in the summer and 8 AM in the winter; closing time was 9 PM, but the cleaning up in summer lasted until 11 PM or later. It was an arduous routine. Each spring we looked forward to the season; each fall we were glad it was over. There was no self-service then; a clerk got each item for the customer, and it was a time-consuming job. Cookies came in bulk in big square boxes; the coffee grinder was often in use; nails came in barrels and had to be weighed. Even in the early 1940s, quarts of milk came in large iced tubs.

When my brother Ed was old enough, he took over getting the orders from Cottage Row. Then he struggled to fill them while we waited on customers. As business increased in the 1930s and 1940s, it was often 3 PM before he could get all the orders delivered. Then he came home for lunch. Dinner was at 9 PM.

The war changed everything. Orders for delivery were no longer taken, and checkout counters appeared, to the relief of the clerks. I fondly remember those days when the whole family worked together. There was a sharing and closeness that even hard work could not destroy.

The end of cherry season heralded quieter times. One big weekend remained – Labor Day. Once again came the crush of people and cars and long hours in the store, but by Monday noon the cars loaded with people headed up the hill. School would start the next day. Suddenly, it was all over and the next day it was fall again.

# The *Hackley* Tragedy
by
*Richard J. Boyd* and *Michael J. Boyd*

Perhaps the most notable disaster in the maritime history of Green Bay was the violent sinking of the steamer *Erie L. Hackley* on October 3, 1903. Although it did not involve an immense loss of life or fortune, the tragedy nevertheless produced a classic set of personal and community hardships such as often followed a Great Lakes shipwreck.

The *Hackley*'s story began in Muskegon, Michigan, when Captain Seth Lee decided to expand his ferryboat business on Lake Michigan. Lee had been established as a Great Lakes shipmaster since the age of nineteen, and he launched a new vessel on August 11, 1882, at the Boon Company Dock. The ship was built by the J.P. Arnold Company and was christened the *Erie L. Hackley* in honor of the daughter of C.H. Hackley, Muskegon's leading citizen, tycoon, and philanthropist. Captain Lee was a neighbor and close personal friend of the Hackley family. Enrollment certificates show that C.H. Hackley owned a half-interest in the vessel until the end of September of 1882.

The *Hackley* (official register number 135615) was not a large or particularly impressive vessel. She was 78 feet long by 17.4 feet wide, with a 5.2 foot draft; her gross weight was 91 tons, net 57 tons. Power was supplied by a 200-horsepower steam engine built by Wilson & Hendrie of Montague, Michigan. Steam was supplied to the 14 x 18 inch cylinder from a 7-ton boiler constructed by Turnbull Boiler Works, also of Montague. The approximate value of the ship was $3000.

For the sake of historical clarity, it should be mentioned that C.H. Hackley also had a ship named after him. This was a 124-foot,

* The Authors wish to thank Professor Walter Hirthe for research assistance, and Sue Boyd and Jeanette Burda for technical help in the preparation of this article.

three-masted schooner called the *C.H. Hackley* and was a sister ship to the renowned *Rouse Simmons*. The longevity of the *C.H. Hackley* was almost legendary; it was built in 1868 and finally sank in 1933. Captain Lee already owned several small boats including the *Mary M. Mentor* and the *Centennial*. With the addition of the *Hackley* his North Muskegon Ferry Line became a thriving operation. The area surrounding Lake Muskegon was experiencing a boom in the logging business. Besides timber interests, the towns adjacent to the lake were developing a considerable tourist trade, a fact upon which Seth Lee hoped to capitalize. For the small sum of twenty-five cents, a passenger could obtain transit aboard the *Hackley* to the various resorts. Another option allowed passengers to ride all day for only fifteen cents, but they could not disembark at the various ports of call. Accommodations aboard were described as elegant and cozy, and the vessel was generally said to be a model of neatness and beauty. The *Hackley* spent fourteen uneventful years in the passenger and freight service around Muskegon. In 1888, the ship apparently was outfitted with new boilers and generally rebuilt. Then, in 1893, ownership passed to Captain Peter D. Campbell and associates when Seth Lee sold out.

Campbell placed the *Hackley* on the Muskegon to Whitehall run until 1898, when he moved to Charlevoix. The vessel then spent the next few years delivering mail and passengers to Beaver Island. In 1902, Peter Campbell sold the *Hackley* to Benjamin and Franklin Newhall of Chicago, but he stayed on as captain. The steamer ran the Manitou Island Route for the season of 1902. During the ten-year period from 1893 to 1902, various structural changes were made on the hull of the *Hackley* to enhance her seaworthiness for Great Lakes transits; the most notable were the addition of high bulwarks on the bow and addition of a raised pilothouse.

In April of 1903, four men from Door County, Wisconsin, formed a transportation service to serve the ports along the Green Bay shoreline. Levi Vorous and his son Joseph, E.T. Thorp, and Henry Robertoy organized the Fish Creek Transportation Company and obtained the *Hackley* from the Newhalls for several thousand dollars and another vessel, the tug *Lily Chambers*. The latter vessel was taken to Beaver Island, where it became one of the first steam tugs to be utilized in that island's thriving fish trade. Eventually the engine and the boilers of the *Chambers* were recycled into a new tug, the *Shamrock*, but her hull still remains in St. James Harbor today.

The *Hackley* was promptly moved to Door County and scheduled to run several times weekly from Sturgeon Bay to Detroit Harbor on Washington Island. The route ran via Menominee, Michigan, and back to the Door Peninsula with stops at many of the villages along the bay shoreline. This shipping venture commenced in late spring of 1903 and enjoyed immediate success.

By August of that year, the vessel was doing a banner business in freight and passengers. Newspaper reports indicated that the freight cartage alone was almost more than the company could handle. The *Hackley* performed nobly during her first season, missing only a few trips due to a minor boiler problem on one occasion and a loose shaft coupling on another. She also suffered a routine stranding at Washington Island in September of that year.

Events proceeded smoothly for the *Hackley* until Friday, October 3, 1903. On this fateful day, the vessel departed Sturgeon Bay at about 11:00 AM with a full complement of cargo and passengers. Green Bay was quite rough due to a crisp southerly wind, but the steamer crossed to Menominee without incident. Although the weather was apparently deteriorating, captain and part-owner Joseph Vorous decided to press onward. The ship cleared the harbor about 5:45 PM en route to Egg Harbor some 14 miles away. The sea was steadily building, but the *Hackley* made consistent progress and eventually passed Green Island about 6:00 PM. With the halfway point behind him, Captain Vorous expected to make Door County in approximately an hour.

Suddenly the wind abruptly and violently shifted to the southwest as a fierce squall descended upon the bay. Almost instantly the *Hackley* was halted in her wake as the waves grew from large to monstrous. Captain Vorous attempted to bring the bow into the face of the gale, but the steamer, which had been cruising almost directly east, came around no further than southeast before she became entrapped in the troughs of the giant waves. The foaming combers crashed down on the stricken vessel, splintering off both the pilothouse and cabin and washing the stunned passengers into seething waters. The *Hackley* plummeted 115 feet to the bottom below within minutes of the squall's onslaught. Terror, confusion, and panic reigned among crew and passengers. Eye-witness accounts vary as to exactly what happened next, and the following account has been compiled from numerous newspaper stories and other reports.

Of the nineteen persons aboard, nine probably drowned immediately, including four men who apparently went down inside the hull. Two others perished within the next several hours, and eight eventually were rescued after severe ordeals. Passenger Nels Nelson, cook Carl Pelkey, and deckhand Hugh Miller probably never escaped the foundering hull; Nelson was probably asleep when the ship plunged. Captain Vorous probably had no chance to escape, and he was not able to swim; as the great waves boarded the ship, the pilothouse was torn from the hull with Vorous still inside, and the structure was spun about on the wave crests like a giant pinwheel, taking him to his doom. The pilothouse drifted ashore intact the next day, with the wheel, ship's papers, and the captain's clothes all unscathed and with the life preservers still hanging in place. The bell from its roof was retrieved and used for many years as a fire and dinner bell by a resort in Ephraim.

Purser Frank Blakefield was in the pilothouse with Captain Vorous when the storm struck. Both men struggled for several minutes to turn the wheel in a vain attempt to maneuver the ship out of the wave troughs. When it became apparent that this action was fruitless, Blakefield rushed aft to aid the panicky passengers and to lower the yawl. As he stepped to the deck the upper works exploded from the hull, but Blakefield leaped clear of the flying debris into the dark waters and managed to swim to the remnants of the ship's superstructure. Here he encountered Milton Hanson, the ship's fireman, and passengers John Haltug, Martin Olson and his son Milton. All had escaped the drowning hull and had taken asylum this large piece of flotsam, no small task in the darkness and the raging storm. Self-rescue was especially difficult for the Olsons since Martin was about sixty years of age and his young son had been convalescing in the Menominee hospital. Within minutes, these five were joined on their makeshift raft by passenger F. Mathieson and second fireman B. McSweeney.

When the storm hit, Mathieson was thrown across the rocking deck and landed in a small lifeboat which had broken free but which immediately capsized, sending Mathieson flailing into the water. As he thrashed about, he managed to grab a floating rope which luckily was attached to the separated upper works, and he soon was pulled aboard the raft with the other survivors.

McSweeney had realized very quickly that the ship was going down. He dragged seventeen-year-old Edna Barringer out of the disintegrating cabin with assistance from Lawrence Barringer, Edna's brother. As they entered the cold waters, McSweeney grasped the girl's hand, but the suction generated by the foundering hull pulled them down and apart. Edna and McSweeney popped back to the surface, but Lawrence was never seen again. McSweeney came up next to the ship's yawl which had broken free from the steamer, and he struggled into the boat and hastily paddled toward Edna Barringer who was frantically treading water nearby. As McSweeney reached out for her, the yawl suddenly swamped and pitched him back into the waves. When he resurfaced, she was gone. Unable to do more, McSweeney swam to the raft which supported the other survivors.

Both other women aboard the *Hackley* also perished. They were two sisters named Ethel and Edna Vincent, and they also were passengers. These young women were teachers on Michigan's Upper Peninsula and were intending to visit their mother in Egg Harbor. As the hull settled, the girls leaped hand-in-hand into the swirling seas. Several castaways reportedly attempted to pull them onto floating debris, but these efforts were in vain. The girls soon slipped beneath the waves and were never seen alive again.

Orin Rowin, the ship's engineer, climbed from his flooded engine room onto the side of the dying ship and pounced upon a floating plank. The crashing waves continually knocked him from this flotation and caused him considerable fatigue. In a flash of lightning, Rowin spotted a piece of rope attached to the end of the plank and used it to lash himself to the flotsam. Much later, after the storm had subsided slightly, Rowin managed to get aboard some remnants of the deck which had separated from the cabin and pilot-house, and he drifted slowly northward with them, suffering greatly from both exposure and his general state of ill-health. When finally rescued near Hanover Shoal off Chambers Island, eleven miles from where the *Hackley* sank, he was in serious condition from hypothermia.

Henry Robertoy, another part-owner of the *Hackley*, also succeeded in extricating himself from the ship and tried desperately to stay afloat. Survivor Orin Rowin reported that he heard Robertoy screaming for a life preserver, but the cries soon ceased and the storm claimed another victim. There apparently were plenty of life preservers aboard the *Hackley*, but there was no time to use them.

Freeman Thorp and George LeClair rapidly disembarked as the steamer took its death plunge, and each crawled onto a piece of the scattered wreckage. LeClair clung to the same debris which later also supported Orin Rowin. He drifted before the worsening storm, frequently being washed from his precarious raft and having to regain its sanctuary. Finally about midnight, George LeClair was swept to his doom. Thorp's legs and ankles were badly cut, and he was washed northward toward Hat Island where his lifeless body was discovered on Sunday, still entangled with floating debris.

Atop the remains of the upper works, the survivors huddled together as the gale intensified. Blakefield suspected that it would not continue to support seven persons, as their weight already had the raft partially submerged. He lashed several planks together and struck out on his own in hopes of relieving the strain on the raft.

The storm raged for many hours. Toward morning, the wind eventually switched to the west and began to diminish. Nonetheless, the seas remained large and violent. At dawn, Blakefield observed that five individuals were still aboard the large raft, and at least one other survivor was drifting nearby. Around 7:00 AM, the castaways received a lucky break. The steamer *Sheboygan*, with Captain Asa Johnston in command, was cruising south from Washington Island, running far behind schedule due to the overnight storm. Lookouts on the steamer were alerted to a possible mishap by a debris field floating near the Strawberry Islands and soon spotted the survivors. Although the seas remained high, Captain Johnston maneuvered the *Sheboygan* as close to the raft as possible while the first mate lowered a lifeboat, and five survivors were soon safe aboard the steamer. A mile further along, Frank Blakefield was plucked from the water, and three miles beyond that, a seventh survivor was rescued from the chilly lake. Finally, Orin Rowin was pulled to safety near Chambers Island. The castaways were fed, clothed, and then transferred to a passing fishing boat which took them to Fish Creek.

Once the survivors reached Fish Creek, word of the sinking spread quickly. Door County communities mobilized to search for other survivors and for the unpleasant task of recovering the bodies of the victims. A general state of confusion reigned because initial reports of the number and identity of those aboard were incorrect. So-called eyewitnesses had up to five women on board the vessel, including a baby and an elderly lady, and several men were incorrectly said to have been aboard. Survivors were unsure exactly where the *Hackley* had sunk, though everyone agreed that the size and abruptness of the squall was incredible. No one had had time to secure a life preserver or follow a calculated course of action.

Other reports confirmed the violent nature of the storm. Weather records for October 3 indicate that a tornadic wind cut a swath across Chambers Island. Captain Fred Johnson and the tug *Fischer* were three miles off the Sturgeon Bay Ship Canal near Sherwood Point when the gale struck. He estimated the wind velocity at 60 mph. Death and injury reports attributed to the storm came from Racine, Oshkosh, Waupaca, and Independence, Wisconsin. Wind damage throughout the upper Midwest was very widespread.

To recover the *Hackley* victims, the U.S. Lifesaving Service and the local fishermen joined forces. Much wreckage, cargo, and personal effects of the passengers were found by the recovery teams and beachcombers, but, of the eleven victims, only the body of Freeman Thorp had been found by October 10. By then muddled and exaggerated stories were circulating which suggested that certain bodies and the purser's desk held large amounts of money. Nels Nelson of Ellison Bay was said to have had at least $400 on his person, and Purser Blakefield supposedly had $1000 in his desk. The latter account was fallacious, but the former one proved to be true. In fact, part of the money held by Nelson belonged to his neighbor, and thus two families suffered hardship from the loss. There was talk of hiring a diver to recover Nelson's body, but no such action was ever taken, probably due to the water depth.

Roy Thorp, brother of victim Freeman Thorp, had had a strange dream on the evening prior to the sinking. In it, he envisioned the *Hackley* perishing exactly as she did. Thorp was terribly disturbed by the dream and considered phoning his brother to warn him, but he had not done so because he felt foolish and thought that no one would believe him anyway.

Serendipity saved the lives of several would-be *Hackley* passengers. Mr. V. Reimers and his family, formerly of Whitefish Bay, were moving to an Egg Harbor farm. They had loaded all their possessions aboard the steamer and then at the last moment decided to drive around to Door County instead of taking the steamer. They arrived safely, but their worldly goods never made it. Several other potential passengers fortuitously "missed the boat."

The sunken *Hackley* was finally located on October 15 by searchers pulling a long cable between two fish boats. The position was about two miles northeast of Green Island in over 100 feet of water. At that date, only one body had been retrieved, but a week later, the bodies of the Vincent sisters were recovered by grappling methods. The girls were located only twenty-five feet apart, lending credence to the report that they drowned almost simultaneously. Their bodies were transported first to Menominee and then on to Stephenson, Michigan, for burial.

The next day the searchers returned to the buoy marking the spot where the Vincents had been found; when the buoy line was pulled up, the body of Henry Robertoy floated up with it. Finally, on October 31, one week later, the remains of Captain Vorous were grappled to the surface. Lawrence and Edna Barringer, Carl Pelkey, Nels Nelson, Hugh Miller, and George LeClair were never found.

The demise of the *Hackley* produced considerable fallout in the communities adjacent to Green Bay. The mother of the Vincent girls suffered a series of severe mental disorders following the loss of her daughters and had to be institutionalized. Engineer Orin Rowin had been in poor health prior to the disaster; he never fully recovered from his ordeal and died a year later. George LeClair was married to the older sister of Edna and Lawrence Barringer, and that family thus suffered a triple loss, creating an anguish that persisted for years. Many of the victims left sizeable families behind, with only meager insurance or other resources to maintain them. To irritate matters, con-men in southern Wisconsin took up collections for the bereaved families and then promptly absconded with the funds. The *Hackley* and her cargo were totally uninsured, and so all was lost.

The funerals for the victims from Door County whose bodies were recovered were well-attended and extremely sad affairs at which hundreds of citizens paid their last respects. Henry Robertoy was buried at Juddville; Captain Vorous was interred in his family plot at Blossomberg Cemetery within the boundaries of present Peninsula State Park. Freeman Thorp was buried at the Clafflin-Thorp family cemetery within Peninsula Park. Vorous and Thorp have nearly identical headstones, but whether by design or chance is not known.

Considerable controversy arose regarding the seaworthiness of the *Hackley* and the seamanship of her captain. Several individuals suggested that the vessel was too old, small, and top-heavy to be safe; others went so far as to condemn all steamers of the *Hackley*'s class for use in passenger service on the Lakes. Some boatmen stated that Captain Vorous had made several serious errors in his handling of the *Hackley*. Captain Johnston of the *Sheboygan* pointed out that the storm was so severe that he had sought shelter overnight in the lee of Washington Island; he was amazed that Vorous had ventured out into such deteriorating conditions.

A poster commemorating the sinking of the *SS Erie L. Hackley*, which occurred at 6:05 PM on October 3, 1903. Eleven of the nineteen people aboard were killed in the disaster.

Other seamen also felt that Vorous was errant in turning the *Hackley* into the storm. A ship with a right-hand revolving propeller can turn more effectively to port (left) due to the development of greater screw suction current and associated stern thrust. During a starboard (right) turn, the vessel swings slower and with less power because of reduced propeller side thrust. At the onslaught of the storm, Captain Vorous instinctively turned to starboard toward the southwest because it was the shortest way to turn into the face of the storm. Although a turn to port would have required a swing of over 180 degrees, it would have generated a stronger screw suction current and enhanced turning power.

These allegations contributed to the convening of a Federal Marine Inquiry Board chaired by Inspector General George Uhler and Supervising Inspector Wescott of the Detroit District, and various *Hackley* crew members, owners, and shipyard workers testified at the hearing. Purser Frank Blakefield and other survivors gave considerable evidence, as did various ship outfitters and repairmen. The investigation lasted about a week during November, after which the inspectors retired to Detroit to contemplate the data and render a decision. The official verdict was weeks in coming, but it totally exonerated Captain Vorous and the condition of the *Hackley*. The consensus was that the steamer was hit by the same tornadic wind which sliced up the forests on Chambers Island and that this storm could have sunk any ship of the *Hackley* class. Thus, rumors of pilot error, owner neglect, and unseaworthiness were put to rest.

The *Hackley* was rediscovered by scuba divers from Mystery Ship Seaport, Menominee, Michigan in 1979. During the next two years, the ship was surveyed and photographed, and a comprehensive investigation took place. In 1981, two partial skeletons were removed from the wreckage and properly buried in Door County. In late 1981 there was an ill-fated salvage attempt, almost exactly a hundred years after the date the ship was launched in Muskegon. It resulted only in the recovery of a thirty-eight-foot section of the rail being brought to the surface. The remainder of the *Erie L. Hackley* remains on the bottom of Green Bay.

BIBLIOGRAPHY

*Algoma Record-Herald,* October 9, 1903.

Beaver Island Historical Committee, "Names and Places of Beaver Island," *Journal of Beaver Island History* 1(1976): 183.

*Door County Advocate,* April 2,9; October 10,13,17; November 7; December 29; 1903.

*Green Bay Advocate,* October 5, 1903.

Gregg, P., "Beaver Tales: The Mail Contract," *Journal of Beaver Island History* 1(1976): 136-137.

Interview with Molly Mayheu, daughter of past owners of Knudtson Lodge of Door County, May 10, 1981.

*Marinette Eagle Star,* October 9,10,27, 1903; June 3, 1980.

*Menominee Herald-Leader,* July 20, November 2, 1981.

*Milwaukee Sentinel,* October 4, 1903.

*Muskegon Daily Chronicle,* August 9,11, September 15, 1882.

Norberg, C.A., "Biography of the schooner *C.H. Hackley*: Lumber Hooker . . . Trader . . . Pirate Vessel," *Inland Seas* 37 (Winter 1981): 244-251.

Research Publications, Inc. *Portrait & Biographical Research of Muskegon and Ottawa Counties, Michigan* (Chicago: Biographic Publishing Co., 1893): 257-258.

U.S. Dept Treasury, *Records, Bureau of Marine Inspection & Navigation - Customhouse of Grand Haven, Michigan (1882),* National Archives Records Group 41.

U.S. Dept Treasury, *Records of the Bureau of Customs, Milwaukee, Wisconsin,* Wreck Report Series (1903), National Archives Records Group 36.

U.S. Dept Commerce, *List of Merchant Vessels of the United States,* (Washington, D.C., 1903): 227.

# Notes From A Conversation
# with Elsa Bartelda Carl
by
*Erna Carl Gilliam*

Elsa Carl first came to Fish Creek as a teenager in about 1912. The following is based on a series of conversations I had with her.

We wouldn't think of walking through town in bathing suits. We changed clothes in a bathhouse at the beach. Our bathing suits were like dresses with bloomers, skirts, sleeves and sailor collars. All the ladies wore big straw hats when they went swimming. From shore it looked like hats floating around. The bath house had little private booths with curtains. There were always corsets hanging on the hooks, wet ones that had been worn in the water, or dry ones. The aisle between the booths was very narrow.

One day when a friend and I were changing clothes, a man —maybe Staner Olson —was driving his cows down the street. One strayed and came clomping up the wooden walk and into the bath house. The ladies shrieked and giggled and the poor man couldn't turn the cow in the narrow aisle and had to lead it through, out on the beach, and back again.

I've been talking about Welcker's bathhouse, which was near our present public beach. We stayed at Welcker's. One had to be "recommended" to stay there. Our Aunt Louisa knew Hedwig Enger Welcker, and she had recommended us. We came to Fish Creek by boat —usually the *Carolina*, a Goodrich Line boat. When we arrived at the dock we were met by Dr. Welcker who had a horse-pulled dray, and our trunks were put on it and taken on. We were invited to follow the doctor on foot up the hill to Welcker's Resort, which was west of the Thorp Hotel (now Founders Square).

The resort was run like a camp. There was no running water or electricity in the cottages. Some of the help came in and filled our oil lamps and water pitchers. There was a bathhouse for bathing, and outdoor toilets. The ladies paid about twenty-five cents and someone

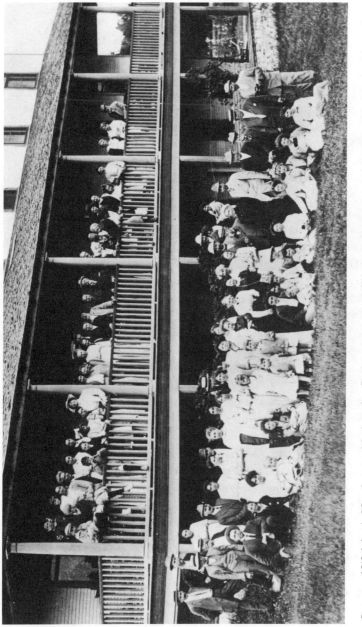

Guests of Welcker's Hotel assembled at the Casino (now the Whistling Swan) in about 1912. Obviously, ideas about proper vacation attire have changed since then. The man on the extreme right seems to be holding a camera.

lighted a fire to heat water and they bathed in the bathhouse. Children bathed in the lake.

What is now the Whistling Swan was then the Casino. We danced on the first floor to records put on the Victrola by Mrs. Welcker; there was also a room with desks and tables for writing letters and playing games. The basement had pool tables and a "Spinne" for beer and drinks where we helped ourselves and wrote on a piece of paper what we had taken and put it on a nail on a piece of wood. We were then charged on our bill. Dr. Welcker said he never lost a penny there.

Meals were delicious and were served at long tables with Dr. or Mrs. Welcker at the head. We had to be prompt. We were called to meals by *Erste Glocke* (first bell), *Zweite Glocke* (second bell) and *Dritte Glocke* (third bell). If we didn't appear by the *Dritte Glocke* we got no meal. When that happened we went to the Maple Tree (now the Summertime), where we could get hot chocolate and cake. Silent hours were observed from 1:00 to 3:00 PM, and lights out at 10:00 PM. If Dr. Welcker saw a light (candle or lamp) after 10:00, he threw pebbles at the window to remind us.

One day I was standing near the front gate with Dr. Welcker when a big car with a family, obviously rich, drove up. They wore veils and fancy clothes and one of them asked for accommodations. Dr. Welcker waved them on saying "the hotel for transients is next door." They had not been recommended.

Cottages had girls names: Tina, Matilde, Hedwig, Teckla, Helena, and Minna. What is now the White Gull was the Henrietta. The price for staying at Welcker's was twelve dollars a week, including room and board. There were many beautiful trails in the park, or what was later the park, and walking was a popular pastime. We stayed at Thorps too, in later years, and, at the end of each season in fall, Welcker's closed earlier. Thorps was run much the same, with dinner bells too. There were men at Thorps who took out fishing parties and the cooks would gladly clean and cook our fish and serve them to us.

THE HART
TRANSPORTATION COMPANY.

BON AMI

THE BON AMI
FISH CREEK, WIS.

7-11

The *Bon Ami* (ca. 1911), a steamer of the Hart Transportation Company that carried passengers and freight between Fish Creek and other Green Bay ports.

I remember when there was only one car in Fish Creek. It was a seven-passenger Studebaker with jump seats, and it belonged to Bill Vorous. Mr. Vorous took people for rides in the park. There was also one car in Ephraim. Its owner, Sam Rogers, also furnished taxi service. Since Ephraim was dry and Fish Creek wet, he did a flourishing business bringing folks to the tavern in Fish Creek and back.

There were three small boats that ran from Fish Creek to Ephraim, Sister Bay and Egg Harbor. They were the *Sailor Boy*, the *Bon Ami*, and the *Thistle*. We often walked to Ephraim and came back by boat.

Trails in the park were well marked. We often started at the park superintendent's office and went past Devil's Pulpit and Balsam Bench. At Balsam Bench we rested and enjoyed a view of Green Bay. The trees were not so tall then, and we could see over.

Cottages in the park were available to rent. My brother and his bride rented what was later Miss Dyer's log cabin and came down by canoe. In the 1930s, Mr. Doolittle, then park superintendent, allowed my nephew and a friend to camp on Hen Island. They came to Thorps daily by rowboat for dinner.

# Growing up in Fish Creek
by
*Duncan Thorp*

My father, Merle, was the only son of Roy Thorp. He had four sisters – May, Bertha, Grace, and Pearl. Each married a local man and launched another line of cousins, uncles and new branches. Then there were the other Thorp brothers who came from New York state, and they left branches all over the nation. Old Truman in Oswego had a lot of children, including Asa, who founded Fish Creek; Levi and Jacob, who founded Egg Harbor; Roland, who drowned at age 22; Byron, who froze to death on the ice; and Herbert and George. Grandpa had another brother, Truman, who perished in the sinking of the steamer *Erie L. Hackley* in October 1904. Every old family in Fish Creek lost someone in that disaster.

Our front yard originally was a pine grove, and Dad and Granddad cut the big pines and hauled them to Larson's Mill in Ephraim. From the lumber they built the farmhouse, barn, well house, chicken coop and had a pile of lumber to boot. They left a few of big pines standing in the yard, fifty feet to the first limbs, one at each corner of the house. Being the tallest objects for a long way around they attracted lightning bolts from the frequent thunder storms and were repeatedly ripped and seared by direct hits.

Lightning was a special hazard. Grandpa Roy was something of a psychic and his ESP often warned him of danger. He also worried a lot about the weather. If a thunderstorm raged in the night, he would rise, dress and walk through the pouring rain to our farm, enter the kitchen quietly and check both fires to make sure winds in the chimney had not started fires from scattered sparks of lightning bolts. He lost a lot of sleep and walked a lot of miles with wet feet to assure we didn't burn up, but the worst that happened in twenty years was a couple of close calls.

Once, while Mother was walking the floor and trying to sing my baby brother Kenneth to sleep, a lightning bolt hit one of those pines. The charge followed a barbed-wire fence stapled to the tree the length of the farm to a corner of the pasture fence, where Dad and Granddad were milking cows tied to the fence with wet ropes. One cow was knocked flat on top of Grandpa. Mother was knocked from her feet, the baby flew across the room and landed miraculously on a springy cot serving as a day bed. Except for mud on Grandpa's clothes and milk in his mustache no harm came to anyone.

Next morning, Grandpa began to cut those four great pines at the corners of the house. It took over eighty years to get rid of the stumps. You can see the roots in the yard to this day.

When the pioneers arrived, the land already knew what it took settlers a century to find out the hard way. The land of the peninsula is good for growing trees and nothing else! Now, after sixty-odd years, the pines are regenerating on the peninsula. Some trees were no more than husky juveniles left here and there when the big sticks were cut and milled, but with sixty years of growth added, they are now forest giants, their vast tops leaning against the sky. Nature is incredibly forgiving if you meet her half-way.

I have enjoyed watching the timber recover Chambers Island after the collapse of the Chambers Island Corporation, a Chicago developer's plan for a unique island resort that went bankrupt in the depression. In only a few years the forest and grass came back. The earth ate the stones. The regrowth drowned the foundations. The beams and lumber made compost and today you will have a hard time finding any evidence of the ambitious project which included a large air field, a watered golf course and two sturdy piers.

Tree culture has become popular with a generation of city retirees who have bought farmlands and planted their surplus acres to crops of conifers. They get double profit from this investment: first, tax savings under the forest crop law, and second, sale of Christmas trees while the young conifers are growing. Endless scores of pines are now flourishing all across Wisconsin for the same reason – a subsidy to reclaim the forests. It's educational to learn that restoration of resources is vastly encouraged by the same process that extinguished the resource in the first place - *money*. In any case, my blessing on every forest cropper. I hope you prosper long with

Love in bloom in June; a self-portrait of Merle Thorp and Edna McLeod (later Thorp) in about 1910. Notice the white "shadow" across Merle's leg of the string that was used to trip the camera shutter.

your orderly rows of pines and spruces, and I know my grandchildren will rejoice in the shade of your forests. This is one taxpayers' bounty that renewed a resource instead of burying it.

Our lives in the first half of the 20th century centered on fruit trees. Every frosty morning in June Dad would be out in the orchard, slicing cherry buds crosswise with his pocket knife. If the center was black the buds were frozen and would not produce fruit. It was a matter of percentages. If you cut ten buds and seven were black in the center, you had lost 70% of that year's crop.

Frost damage was capricious. Sometimes it would blast everything from ground level to three feet up, killing only the lower limbs. Other times it would strike just the tops of the trees, and there were freak levels that cut across midlines of the orchard. Because the yield was light the fruit was large and of high quality.

In the early years we slaved at the rows of small fruits planted between the trees. We packed sixteen-quart cases with currants and raspberries. Then, the farm wagon was driven up beside the veranda where we did the packing, and we loaded the heavy cases to be driven a mile down the dusty road to the Main Dock, as we called the old dock in the village. There a small package freighter from Marinette waited to haul our fruit to a commission house across Green Bay.

Everything moved by water. If we ordered clothing or hardware from a mail order house, we waited for it on the dock. Tourists and automobiles came off the Chicago boats.

During the cherry harvest, the orchards were hives of activity. Pickers were from local families, mostly farm people who had their fields seeded and sprouting while Pa, Ma and the kids picked cherries to earn a few extra bucks. They rose early, toting a generous lunch for all hands, and parked their buggies and horses all over our yard. When the pickers were at work the air was loud with hilarious yells, yodels, whoops, snatches of song, giggles, and general noises of exuberance. There was something inspiring about being up in a treetop on a picking ladder in the blue morning air. It was the Roaring Twenties and the young folks chanted the popular songs of the day: "Bye Bye Blackbird," "Barney Google," "Show Me the Way to Go Home," "Marie," "Long Long Trail," and "Pack Up Your Troubles".

The work was hard and dirty. Cherries were ideal throwing missiles, squashy and bullet-shaped. We hurled them at each other. Each had a thin coating of Bordeaux Mixture tree spray on its surface which combined with the juice and mud from our faces. It was a nice cool place on a hot summer day; an excuse for a break was always welcome. We also ate a lot of cherries, which had a definite laxative effect and provided additional "work breaks".

The hub of the activity was the packing shed, a partly-enclosed shell on skids which was dragged about the orchard by horses as the harvest moved along. The popularity of the back house (Chic Sales) was such that frequent relocations had to be done during picking time. Later, trucks and tractors replaced the horses, and Frank and Nell, the two old farm blacks, were retired.

When we got a spray rig and gas engines at the wells for pumping, the air was loud with the exhausts of our engines. We installed large gas tanks to fuel the engines. A 40-acre farm wouldn't support all that machinery, so we used our equipment and labor to till, spray and harvest another orchard next to ours, which about doubled the operation. Dad was the family mechanic. By some legerdemain he contrived to keep all those engines running well enough to get the orchard cultivated and the trees sprayed year after year. Our well was powered by an ancient one-cylinder Fairbanks-Morse gas engine; the neighbor's well had a Lawson engine. The sprayer was a Myers and also had a Fairbanks-Morse for power. The tractor was a Fordson. The truck was a 1917 Model T with a Ruxtel special transmission for low power.

For a few years Dad sold Fords for Moeller's Garage in Sturgeon Bay, and he often had bonanzas. The thrifty farmers would decide to go mechanized after years of saving, and more than once Dad sold a neighbor an auto, a tractor, a truck, and an orchard disc and drag all at the same time. The new owner would pull up a loose board in the floor of the barn, dig up a can full of big bills, and pay cash for the whole thing.

All the thousands of acres of orchards were intensively cultivated, but after all the disking and dragging was done every tree had a green square of quack grass around the trunk. Our hired man "Long Arch" appeared every spring in time to do much of the cultivating and to help with the spraying. Arch would take his heavy sharp-edged hoe and hack the tough mats of quack grass around the trunks. Arch was tireless. He would begin before the dew was dry, with his back bent over his hoe, and stay with it until sundown. A hired man was expected to work a ten-hour day back then.

I waited impatiently for the day I would be old enough to drive the tractor, because then I could earn money working at the neighbor's orchard. The price was $1.75 an hour for tractor and driver – 40 cents an hour for the driver, the rest for the machine. Dad's rule was that you could drive the tractor when you could spin the crank and start it. Starting that old Fordson was something. They burned kerosene or distillate, which was not sufficiently volatile to fire on a cold morning, so they had to be started and warmed up on gasoline, then switched to kerosene. Spinning the crank was a little dangerous; if the engine "kicked back" it could break the arm of the cranker. In spring months, you would often see farm boys with their cranking arms in slings, sort of a badge of maturity and a source of envy. I was eager to wear my sling like the big kids, but, although that old tractor backfired more than once, I always escaped the coveted stigma.

There were other perils. When the disk dug deep and developed an enormous weight behind the drawbar in the loose soil, it was possible to jerk the tractor over backwards and kill the driver. Also, our tractor had a tiny leak in the carburetor from which drops of kerosene continuously dripped down on the hot exhaust pipe and vaporized. The vapor blew up in the driver's face and was inhaled. The drone of the engine was monotonous, and long hours in the sun inclined the driver to sleep. One time while driving the tractor, I grew drowsy and careless. An apple limb combed me off my tractor seat and I was dumped onto the soft orchard earth between the tractor and the disc. Without thinking I swung my legs about and braced my feet on the scraper bar of the disc. The tractor kept on going, dragging me and the disc down the row. The belt of my trousers and the waistband acted as a scoop and collected a great mound of loose dirt and filled my pantlegs and seat until they were packed tight. Then the driverless tractor ran into a stout apple tree and the engine killed. I got up, scared witless, emptied my bulging pants of Door County loam, and resumed cultivating.

There were other hazards of the machine age. Granddad never got used to handling the clutch. He would try and try, but every time he drove the tractor he would let out the clutch carefully and slowly up to the last inch, then remove his left foot abruptly. The tractor and sprayer would take a leap.

Granddad had to drive so that Dad and Arch could handle two spray guns, one on each side, spraying two rows of trees each way and covering the orchard in half the time. Once, when the spraying rig with Grandpa driving took one of its accursed leaps, both men on the sprayer deck were dumped abruptly and each lost control of his spray gun with 30 pounds of pressure on the nozzle. The guns jumped around all over the place blasting Dad and Arch with Bordeaux Mixture, hard enough to sweep a man off his feet. We tried using horses, which Granddad could drive as well as any teamster born, but even then there were incidents in which a carelessly dropped spray gun blasted the horses in the rump. This made them skittish when hooked to the sprayer and provoked more dropped spray guns. But, somehow the trees got sprayed year after year.

Finally, the long summer would end and the crops would be stored: canned fruit, potatoes, squash, pumpkins, pork and sauer-kraut in the cellar; hay in the barn; silage in the silo; butchering all done and hams and bacon smoked; fish and cucumber pickles in big crocks; a barrel of cider vinegar stored; and a big pile of poles for winter wood in the yard. Then Dad would reckon up his accounts and find insufficient funds from the crops for next season's fuel, spray, seed, and fertilizer, so he would go out and get a winter job to make ends meet. At various times he sold Model T Fords, worked in construction on Chambers Island, stored ice, ran a trapline, helped at a sawmill, worked at a quarry, and helped to raise a barn.

Hotel Thorp

# Fish Creek
# Families and Personalities

# The Hill Family and Steamboat Line
by
*Harwood William Hill*

The Hill Steamboat Line was a family affair in the beginning in Fish Creek, where the Hill family is related in various ways to the Thorps, Kinseys, Fairchilds, Chambers, Stevens and other Fish Creek families. Will Rogers was part Indian and delighted in poking fun at people who take an inordinate pride in their ancestry by pointing out that his ancestors were at the dock to meet the Mayflower. Both figuratively and historically, his ancestors were also at the dock to meet the Hill family at Windsor, Simsbury, Sacketts Harbor, the Fox River, Beaver Island, Drummond Island and Wonewoc in its journey across America to Fish Creek. Some of his relatives were hostile, but most were friendly.

I have many nostalgic memories of summer vacations spent on a farm north of Ephraim in the 1930s. The area along Highway 42 between Ephraim and Sister Bay was mostly undeveloped at that time, and there was no speed limit on the highway. The twice-a-day adventure of bringing the cows from their pasture on the west side of the highway to the barn on the east side is especially memorable. The farm was auctioned off in parcels in 1950, and nothing recognizable remains of the old farm except the Red Barn and the cherry orchard where I picked cherries for five cents a pail.

It was not until 1954 that I became interested in living in Fish Creek, and I purchased property there at the south end of Pine Street from Ferdinand Hotz the following year. A few years later, an acquaintance retrieved a volume of Hjalmar R. Holand's *History of Door County* from the Fish Creek village dump where it had been discarded. It was from this book that I became interested in my Fish Creek heritage. In 1917, Holand wrote:

> Two other prominent citizens of the county, whose families have since moved away, also settled in Fish Creek at the close of the [Civil] war. These were L.P. Hill and L.M. Griswold. L.P. Hill came from Beaver Island, the famous

Mormon island kingdom in Lake Michigan in the 50s where he
won his wife from the household of King James Strang in a most
romantic manner. L.P. Hill's sons, in the 90s organized a
steamship company and for many years operated passenger
boats on Green Bay with headquarters in Fish Creek. They
later moved to Kenosha, where they are operating a line of
boats between Chicago and Racine.

In 1902, just before the headquarters of the Hill Steamboat
Line was moved to Kenosha, twenty-five Hills resided in Fish Creek.
The principal means of transportation north of Sturgeon Bay at that
time was by water, and the Hill boats, the *Cecelia Hill* and the
passenger and freight boat *City of Marquette* competed in the crowded
Green Bay transportation field. Soon after it became evident that the
navigation season was too short on Green Bay to support the growing
Hill family, plans were made to move the steamboat line to Kenosha,
where the big boats could operate all year long in the expanding
package freight business. However, the Hill Steamboat Line
continued to serve Fish Creek during the navigation season on Green
Bay for over two decades after its headquarters was moved.

## EARLY HISTORY OF THE HILL FAMILY

Over three hundred years ago on April 1, 1667, Luke Hill,
the progenitor of my branch of the Hill family in America, took
charge of the Rivulet ferry crossing the Connecticut River for 12
pounds per annum "besides what he gets from travellers and persons
by night." The event is recorded in the town acts of Windsor, CT.

Evidently ferrying was not lucrative at Windsor, for Luke Hill
left there for the new town of Massacue in 1669. Massacue was the
Indian name for Simsbury, CT, which was burned by hostile Indians
in 1676. Luke Hill's home and more than 40 other cabins plus other
buildings were destroyed. A large stone monument marks the site of
the first meeting house in Simsbury built in 1683 "near Luke Hill's
land," and Hills Ferry on the Farmington River west of Simsbury
appears on at least one map prior to the Revolutionary War.

It was not until 1807 that Luke Hill's descendent, Jedediah Hill, moved from Simsbury to the vicinity of Sacketts Harbor on the shore of Lake Ontario, where eventually he built a tavern with living quarters on the first floor and a ballroom with a spring floor upstairs. I suspect that this is where the idea for a dance hall above the Hill's store in Fish Creek originated. The historic red brick home is in the hamlet of Rural Hill, New York, where Jedediah was the first settler; it is described today as one of the most attractive of the old homes in Jefferson County.

The War of 1812 revived the danger from Indian tribes who sided with the British. The Hills joined with other settlers in constructing a log blockhouse for their protection at Sacketts Harbor. Jedediah's sons John, Ludlow and Ebben were soldiers in the New York Militia in the war. They received no compensation from the government for their war service except land warrants for 160 acres each. Thus, after the war, the family started to split up, drifting west looking for a place to redeem the warrants. L.P. Hill's father, Ludlow Hill, left with his family on a lake boat when L.P. was ten years old. They were several weeks traversing Lakes Ontario, Erie, Huron, and Michigan on their way to the Fox River, below Elgin, Illinois, where he had purchased the 480-acre Farnsworth and Hubbard claim on both sides of the river. The voyage over the waters of the Great Lakes in 1839 was a never-to-be-forgotten adventure for young L.P. Hill.

The Hill farm on the Fox River was the subject of a letter written in 1846 by a representative of James J. Strang:

> A gentleman by the name of Ludlow Hill owns some of the most beautiful locations on the Fox River or in the State of Ill. It affords one of the best of opportunities for flouring mills factories and other machinery in all this country.

The letter was written with the approval of Strang to solicit "capitalists" to develop the land for the Mormon Church, but the plan never materialized. Today the land is a memorial park and a statue of the Indian Chief Blackhawk dominates the landscape. The ruts left by General Scott's army where it crossed the Fox River in 1832 in pursuit of Chief Blackhawk are still visible.

## LUDLOW PRESLEY HILL (1829-1915)

Ironically, the boat carrying L.P. Hill toward his new home on the Fox River sailed near Beaver Island in northern Lake Michigan eight years before King James Strang discovered the island in 1847. Two years later, Strang established his famous Mormon Island Kingdom on Beaver Island, and the Hills were among the first colonists to arrive, investing their entire fortune on the island immediately after reaching there. L.P. had just reached his majority and secured the appointment as lighthouse keeper, but he kept the job just long enough to fall in love with Cecelia Seaman and marry her. Holand says that "he won his wife from the household of King James Strang in a most romantic manner."

According to Ludlow Presley Hill's recollections, the site on Beaver Island was a "splendid property," but the Hills were among the first disaffected families to leave the island kingdom of Strang, selling what they could and abandoning the rest. L.P. purchased the schooner *Emmilin* from his father and stayed behind to extinguish the light and close the station. In the intervening years, nature has obliterated all traces of the Hill family's occupation of the southern end of the island except the lighthouse a few miles to the west. Some of the same Indians who helped the Mormons survive their first winter on the island, probably local fishermen, drove the Mormons from Beaver Island in 1856.

As luck would have it, a man by the name of Delando Pratt was offering a choice of any two lots in the frontier town of Wonewoc, Wisconsin, to anyone who would erect a house there and cover it with a coat of paint. Winter was approaching, and he had few takers, but then, according to early records, the Hills came to Wonewoc. Deer were plentiful that winter, and a thousand pounds of venison was cured by smoking; with berries and other game they were well cared for. L.P. and Cecelia survived that winter on Drummond Island, arriving in Wonewoc with their little family the following year.

Drummond Island was the last outpost of the British Empire in the United States. There were a number of Indian families on Drummond Island, but American history began there in 1853 with the arrival of Daniel Murry Seaman from Beaver Island in a two masted boat, a schooner named the *Seaman,* aboard which were a family of twelve, a cow, a calf, and a pony. Cecelia had already married L.P. Hill on Beaver Island, and they stayed behind until the end of the 1853 navigation season. They arrived on Drummond Island just in time for the birth of Wallace on October 16, 1853. Their second son, Onnie, was born in Wonewoc in 1855. After engaging in lumbering and agriculture for a number of years, the Great Lakes called L.P. back to Drummond Island, where his three sons grew to manhood and became involved in the commerce of Door County long before moving there. All the Hill memorabilia in the Betsy Seaman Memorial Museum on Drummond Island dates from this period.

Fish Creek was conveniently located half-way between the Seaman family on Drummond Island and the Hill family in Wonewoc. After his sons settled in Fish Creek, L.P. made it his second home. A letter written at Wonewoc by one of the relatives in 1888 notes:

> Aunt Cecelia and Addie [L.P.'s wife and sister] are talking of going to Fish Creek where Uncle Lud and the Boys are. They are the greatest family to be always moving. They seem to make lots of money but spend it going from one place to the other.

The Hill steamship *Kenosha* was one of the last wooden ships built in Sturgeon Bay by the Universal Shipbuilding Company. Oldtimers may recall that in 1925 the *Kenosha* under the command of Captain Wallace E. Hill rammed the drawbridge in Sturgeon Bay and was badly damaged.

L.P. Hill was the directing head of the Hill Steamboat Line up to the time of his death in 1915, when he was eulogized as one of the most interesting men who had been influential in building the lake commerce. His early experiences and his family background were logical steps to the business in which he engaged.

## CECELIA SEAMAN (1835-1901)

The wife of L.P. Hill referred to by Holand was Cecelia Seaman, a descendent of Captain John Seaman who gained his captaincy in the Pequot Indian War in 1646. Seaman is a name familiar to Fish Creek genealogists. Cecelia's sister married Sam Chambers and their daughter married Roy Thorp. Another sister married Charles Fairchild. According to family legend, the Seaman family originally was Danish. In old Norse times, families banded together and sailed the seas in their beautiful ships, getting what they might and holding what they could. On one of their excursions they landed off the coast of England, whipped the natives and held the land. They remained in possession until subdued by the Norman conquerors in 1066. They passed under the name of Seamen, or men of the sea.

Both the Hill and Seaman families resided in America for several generations before the Revolutionary War, and a unique relationship existed between the antecedents of the two families long before the marriage of L.P. Hill and Cecelia Seaman.

Cecelia's antecedent, Caleb Seaman, enlisted in a loyalist regiment in the Revolutionary War. After years of intrigue and adventure involving two escapes from prison, Caleb went to Canada where he received a grant of land for his war-time service. L.P. Hill's antecedent, Jedediah Hill, enlisted in the American Army, and, after the war, left Connecticut with his family to settle near Sacketts Harbor on Lake Ontario, in time for the second war with the British.

The organizers of the steamboat line in Fish Creek identified by Holand only as the sons of L.P. Hill were Captain William Wallace Hill, Captain Ludlow Leonidas Hill, and William Seaman Hill, who was more interested in farming than he was in steamboating.

## WILLIAM SEAMAN HILL (1866-1928)

William Seaman Hill, known as Will or Willie, was the youngest son of L.P. Hill, and a story concerning him involves one of the saddest days of his life in Fish Creek. While watering his favorite team of horses at the bathing beach, the animals were spooked, became entangled in their harness, and drowned or had to be destroyed.

No history of transportation in Door County would be complete without mention of Myron H. Stevens and the principal means of transportation in the wintertime. Myron was the father-in-law of Willie Hill. According to Holand, it seems that one winter he was riding along behind a slow horse, blue with cold, and with his teeth visibly chattering. A passerby called to him, "Say Myron, why don't you get out and walk and get warm?"

"N-n-no" replied Stevens in frozen dignity, "I'd rather sit and freeze like a man than run behind like a dog."

The centennial issue of the *Door County Advocate* recalled that Myron Stevens was known for being witty and claimed to be well informed in the law. He acted as something of a lawyer in the town, and tried cases and really kept law and order in the community. His marriage in 1860 to Anna I. Graham produced six children, including Hattie Bell Stevens who married Willie Hill in Fish Creek in 1889. Hattie died shortly after my father, Floyd Stevens Hill, was born, and my grandfather then married Hulda Hofferman whose parents owned the Red Barn. Myron and Hulda Stevens lived for a time in the apartment above the store on the corner of Main and Pine streets in Fish Creek, where a son, Leonidas, was born in 1902.

Lonny, as Leonidas was called, was the purser on the *SS Marquette* in the early 1920s. Lonny had two things that he especially remembered about sailing on Green Bay. One was the box sliding around under his bunk that turned out to be dynamite caps put there for safekeeping by his brother. The volatile caps were destined to be used in blasting out what became Hidden Harbor. The other was the time the *Marquette* put into the harbor of refuge at Horseshoe

Island to wait out a storm. Lonny had an important date with a pretty school-teacher, so he shoved off in a row-boat and crossed to the mainland. He then walked about five miles through the woods to Fish Creek to see his future wife, Ruby Olson.

Ruby graduated from the teacher's college in Algoma and taught school in Door County before marrying Lonny and moving to Kenosha in 1923. While in Fish Creek, she lived across the street from the Welcker resort, and frequently helped her mother, Lany (Resler) Olson, with housekeeping chores in the cottage known as the Henrietta (now the White Gull Inn).

When Holand's *History of Door County* was published in 1917, Willie Hill was vice president and agent for the Hill Steamboat Line. That year, he disposed of his stock in the company and purchased a large stock farm which he named Hillsdale Farm. The farm became known as one of the leading Guernsey dairy farms in Kenosha County. Failing health forced him to retire from this several years later, and the youngest son of L.P. Hill was the first to die, on Christmas Day 1928.

### WILLIAM WALLACE HILL (1853-1949)

William Wallace Hill, known as Wallace, was the eldest son of L.P. Hill. He was born in 1853 on Drummond Island, about 150 miles northeast of the lonesome dwelling of Increase Clafflin in Fish Creek. Increase Clafflin, of course, was the first settler in Door County, and Wallace was said to have been the first child of European descent born on Drummond Island.

Many fishermen built their own boats on Drummond Island and according to tradition were entitled to be called "Captain," but, as master of the steamer *Islander*, Wallace held the distinction of being the youngest licensed captain on the Great Lakes. The *Islander* was often seen in Fish Creek, where Wallace had many relatives. In 1884, he married Christy McLeod on Drummond Island and soon afterwards moved to Fish Creek, where he joined his father and brothers in the Hill Steamboat Line.

A crew of men working to rebuild the Fish Creek town dock during the winter of 1905-1906. The *SS Cecilia Hill* of the Hill Steamboat Line waits for a thaw.

Wallace was the designer and shipbuilder in the family, and he brought his prize-winning sailboat *Rosina* to Fish Creek with him, where he gained a reputation for building some of the fastest sailboats on Green Bay. His prize-winning *Lena Delta* was built in Fish Creek in 1892. This was followed by his first steamer, a 60-ton boat named the *L.P. Hill* after his father, and, four years later, by a 100-ton steamboat named the *Cecelia Hill* after his mother.

In the 1890s, the road from Sturgeon Bay to Fish Creek was in poor condition and had natural obstacles at Plum Bottom, Egg Harbor, and Fish Creek. No doubt that is why Wallace was transporting a steam engine from the railhead at Sturgeon Bay to Fish Creek over the frozen waters of Green Bay when the engine broke through the ice and went to the bottom of Green Bay somewhere off Egg Harbor. The engine was destined to be used in one of the steamboats he was building, and it was salvaged with the aid of a diving bell. In later years, Wallace blamed his failing eyesight on excessive air pumped into the diving bell from the surface while he was recovering the engine.

In 1928, a generation later, Wallace had a vision of a vessel that would carry his name and built his last boat, the diesel-powered *W.W. Hill* of Kenosha. Though then seventy-four years old, he worked at the construction of the boat alone. However, he needed the help of his sons in sheeting the sides with steel plate. In an effort to conserve his failing eyesight, Wallace worked with his eyes closed whenever possible. Coming to work on the boat one day, he ran his hands over the steel sheeting applied by his sons with his eyes closed. He detected ripples in the sheeting and ordered it removed.

Among the structures that were built on the main street of Fish Creek before the turn of the century is the house built by Wallace Hill. Today that house is a gift shop owned by John Cole. Wallace's six children included Duncan and Roland Hill who became lake skippers and thus remained in contact with Fish Creek. In 1906, when Duncan was seven years old, he watched from his upstairs bedroom window in the sturdy old house as the *SS Cecelia Hill* burned while tied up at the dock. Sometime after this, if Duncan's

The charred remains of the *SS Cecilia Hill*, one of the steamers of the Hill Steamship Line, are tied to the Fish Creek town dock after the ship was destroyed by fire during in spring of 1906.

memory served him right, Wallace sold his water-front property to George Clark for $3200. The property adjoined the municipal pier in Fish Creek, and Clark's son Robert donated it to the town for a public park.

Wallace was described in *The Kenosha News* as "a tough old salt; a man of many and varied talents, capable of extracting his own teeth when necessary, and playing 'The Irish Washerwoman on his fiddle for enjoyment." He lived to be 95, dying in Kenosha in 1949. He is buried beside his wife and his son Roland in Blossomburg Cemetery in Peninsula State Park.

## LUDLOW LEONIDAS HILL (1855-1938)

Ludlow Leonidas Hill, always called Onnie, was the middle son of L.P. Hill. He was born in Wonewoc, Wisconsin, about 150 miles southwest of Fish Creek. Shortly after the Civil War, L.P. Hill moved his family from Wonewoc back to Drummond Island where Onnie began to devote his life to marine interests.

Onnie Hill first became identified with lake transportation in Door County about 1885, when he operated a sailing vessel that he sailed alone, freighting fish from Washington Island to Marinette and Menominee, Michigan. The following year, he purchased his first steamer, named it the *Eva M. Hill* after his sister, and moved with his boat and family to Fish Creek where he bought a house on Main street in 1887. The little house was home to Onnies' ten children, and since he was capable of pulling teeth, it also served as a dentist office. Although he was sympathetic towards the temperance movement in town, everyone knew about the bottle of whiskey reserved for his patients.

Onnie was town chairman in 1895, and his opponent in the election was a character known as "Doctor" Hale. According to Holand "there also existed between the two quite a business tangle. It is said that Hill and Hale had a hell of a time but Hill finally won out both in business and politics." Although he concentrated all his energy on his business interests, Onnie was not always successful. He almost went bankrupt after leading a futile strike by local fishermen, who withheld their fish from market too long. Overzealous creditors may have started Onnie thinking about long boat trips at about this time.

L.L. Hill had been to Kenosha a number of times, according to a newspaper article,

> but rarely under conditions as trying as on an occasion in the winter of 1904, when the wooden *City of Marquette* found itself locked in the ice off shore. Hill, the first mate, walked the mile to shore over the floes to report that the ship and its twelve-member crew was in no danger, having plenty of food and fuel on board.

In 1938, while salvaging a wrecked tanker and siphoning its gasoline cargo off Charlevoix, Michigan, Onnie, his fifty-year-old son Leon and three other crew members were killed in an explosion which destroyed the boat.

When Fish Creek was the home port of the steamboat line, the Hill Brothers pier was at the center of activities there. After receiving a postcard featuring a turn-of-the-century picture of the pier, Ruby Hill Wons, Onnie's daughter wrote:

> That might well have been Uncle Wallace supervising the dock repair. The *Cecelia Hill* was as I remember her – and the pile driver too, as I remember it. There was always one somewhere on the beach and we kids used to climb around and up it like monkeys – and the smell of tar comes back to me quite clearly.

Diversification was the key to survival in the early days of fishing and steamboating in Fish Creek, so the Hills also built and operated a general merchandise store on Main Street. It was eventually sold to Duncan McLeod, Wallace Hill's brother-in-law, and this same store has changed hands several times since. It is now owned and operated by Gary Norz and his wife. Recently, after viewing a postcard picture of the old store, Ruby wrote again:

> That picture sent me all the way back to Fish Creek
> and my childhood! The dance hall, the Duclon boys who played
> the music for the square dances in the hall above the store, the
> big trees in Uncle Wallace's yard, the Lundberg store, Alma
> Lundberg, my friend of about the same age, the occasional
> minstrel show selling Cardew's(?) Curative syrup and giving away
> gold watches. All those things, and especially the music and
> dancing schottische square dances, which I could only watch,
> seemed wonderful then. And the chocolate cigars for a penny
> apiece at the store.

Ruby Hill was born in Fish Creek ninety-six years ago. She was one of the Hill's mentioned as residing in Fish Creek in 1902 and is the last survivor. She worked for the boat line in its heyday, and, according to Ruby, any member of the family who wanted to work was given a job and everyone was paid the same. A clerk in a store at that time earned about $18 a month, but she was paid $150 as a clerk for the boat line. "If that was not enough to bankrupt any company, what was?" Ruby once remarked.

About this time, the company did come close to bankruptcy when the pride of the fleet, the *Flora M. Hill*, named after Onnie's wife, sank in 45 feet of water two miles off Chicago's harbor on March 11, 1912. The company eventually made good the uninsured loss, and in 1926 the Hill Steamboat Line merged with Westports, a competitor which was itself taken over in a reorganization of the Goodrich Company in 1929. The prolonged business depression and the expansion of truck competition finally ended all lake freight service in 1933.

## HOWARD CHAMBERS (1900-1974)

The *Door County Advocate* for a number of years published articles by a Charley Noble, and one of his favorite subjects was the Hill Steamboat Line. Also, in 1976, Vantage Press published his book entitled *Tales of the Sea*. Charley Noble identified himself to his readers for the first time when he wrote in this book: "The head of [my] family was the owner and captain of a 65-foot steam tug, the

*L.P. Hill."* The former Hill boat was purchased by the Chambers family and used as a fishing boat. My copy of Noble's book, given to me as a gift by Mrs. Kenneth Nash before she died, has an inscription that reads: "To Mrs. Nash with Best Wishes. A Lady who could keep a secret. From the Author Capt. Howard Chambers." One of Howard Chambers' antecedents once went from Drummond Island to Cecelia Hill's home near Fish Creek for a visit, where she met and married Sam Chambers. The Chambers' family history then closely parallels that of the Hill family in that they moved from Drummond Island to Fish Creek, and then to Kenosha where they continued commercial fishing for many years, sharing the same harbor as the Hill Steamboat Line.

✢ ✢ ✢

Articles in the *Door County Advocate* by Charley Noble carried such headlines as "Marine Bravado Came Easy For Guest Skipper At Helm," "Discarded Came Back To Haunt Captains," "Sleigh Becomes A Hot Rod," and "Potato Load Proved Bad Deal". The potato load story is worth retelling as Charley Noble wrote it.

## Potato Load Proved Bad Deal
### by
### *Charley Noble*

Late one fall, after the *City of Marquette* had made her last scheduled trip for the season, she was lying at the Booth dock on the west side of Washington Harbor, loading potatoes.
Captain Hill himself was in command. The weather looked bad, dark scudding clouds, spitting snow mixed with rain squalls, and a lowering barometer.
Potatoes were cheap that year, and wagon teams were lined up (there were no trucks in those days) each farmer unloading and selling for cash.
Captain Hill had to refuse the last few loads, for the *Marquette* was getting low in the water and the weather was getting more and more ominous. All summer long her loads

had been lighter and her upper seams had dried out so she started to leak rather badly.

As soon as she poked her nose around Boyer's Bluff into the sea coming from the northwest, she started to leak still more. When she squared away to go up the county, she started to roll and that made her leak still worse.

About abreast of Little Sister shoal, the chief came to the pilot house with the good news that his pumps would no longer hold her bilges clear of water.

Sister Bay harbor offered no protection, but soon he saw Horseshoe Island looming ahead out of the murk. Some romantics now call it Eagle Island but it was always Horseshoe Island to seamen. The open end of the horseshoe was toward the mainland, so it offered fine protection. It had to, for the fireman was in water up to his ankles.

The captain rounded up into the protection of the harbor, but his troubles were not over yet. In those days the law did not require that anchors be carried outside and ready for dropping. The *Marquette's* were not. So they got one up to the bow, but now they had to knock out a shutter that had not been disturbed in the memory of man.

They knocked it loose with a timber without figuring it was going to go overboard, but the wind was in the right direction so it drifted astern to the gangway, and they lowered a cargo hook on a heaving line and brought it aboard. They stretched out on deck what chain they thought they would need, shackled the bight of the tow post and prepared to let go. "Everybody get out of the way, and the Devil take the hindmost."

No one got caught in the chain and they could almost drop it on the beach, the land was so steep-to. Now let 'er snow, let her snow.

By morning the weather had cleared but there was still a dead swell and that chain and anchor had to be brought in with an old hand windlass. That shutter also had to be well caulked from the outside with oakum and a caulking iron. The mate was lowered on a bosun's chair for the purpose, while the captain held her low up against the beach, so the job was soon done. The chief had rigged another steam syphon so the leaks could be contained.

Layover in Sturgeon Bay for coaling, then on the next day. The west shore of Lake Michigan abounds with good harbors, Two Rivers, Kewaunee, Manitowoc, Sheboygan, etc., all the way to Kenosha where she was going to sell her cargo. By the time she reached Kenosha, wages and fuel had used up all but a small margin of profit, so that was not tried again.

## WALLACE E. HILL (1882-1959)

Captain Wallace E. Hill (Wally) was vice president of the Hill Steamboat Line when management decided to issue stock after World War I in order to purchase three new ships. These ships, the *Kenosha*, the *Sheboygan*, and the *Waukegan,* each had a carrying capacity equivalent to thirty box cars and were the strongest of their type ever launched on the Great Lakes, according to the prospectus. Wally was contemporary with his cousins Duncan and Roland, and in the 1920s they were in command of the *Kenosha*, the *Sheboygan*, and the *Waukegan*, all occasionally seen in Fish Creek where all three resided in 1902. Duncan was born at Fish Creek in 1899 and he was the last of the three to command a steamer. But I am not prepared to say that the family's love affair with Lake Michigan ended with his death in 1980.

✣ ✣ ✣

The Hill's invariably went "down to the sea in ships" in going from one place to the other, beginning with a perilous voyage across the Atlantic in the early 1600s and ending on Lake Michigan in the 1800s. Then for a hundred years, as one reporter put it, "their boats were battered and blown, stranded in ice packs, one went down, and another blew up. But despite storm or season, year after year, most docked on time." To this summation by a newspaper reporter, I can add only that they were the last of their kind to serve Fish Creek.

After the demise of the Hill Steamboat Line, other ships continued to compete with land transportation. One of these was a car ferry crossing Lake Michigan commanded by Captain Eugene L. Hill, a son of Wallace E. Hill. Another son was first mate on one of the big ore ships. My own grandson is now serving aboard an aircraft carrier, and I will always remember his excitement after returning from a boat ride on Green Bay when he was only seven or eight years old. "Grandpa," he said in all sincerity, "when you kick the bucket, who gets the boat?"

# Martin Kinsey
by
*Ann Thorp*

Martin Kinsey was one of about a dozen commercial fishermen who worked the shores in the Fish Creek area from the late 1800s until well into this century. The father of Fish Creek residents Roy and Neil (Pat) Kinsey and of Mrs. Jessie Crommel, he was born in Juddville around 1870, one of seven sons, and learned his trade from his father, Ingham Kinsey.

Mart's first boat was a Mackinaw, possibly built by Larson Brothers of Marinette, Wisconsin. For many years it was sail-powered, but later converted to a gasoline engine. Mart made his living as a fisherman, supplemented by farming. For most of the year, except at mid-summer, he fished herring with pond nets set along Cottage Row shores. His sons Roy and Pat worked with him as they grew up. His enterprise was not one of the big ones and didn't bring in large profits. The work was extremely hard.

Herring were then the fish in demand. The market for whitefish was almost non-existent, and perch were considered trash fish. The pound-nets, which were traps, were forty feet square, varying in depths from twenty to fifty feet. The nets were suspended on tamarack stakes which had been driven into the bay bottom. Nets were lifted and fish scooped into the boat. Back at the fish shed, the fish were headed, gutted and split flat, then salted and packed into wooden kegs known as packages. The kegs were bought from local coopers; John Brown was one, with a shop located at what is now the Fish Creek swimming beach. Peter Weborg had another cooper shop just north of Weborg's point. Later, wooden boxes were to replace kegs. They were less expensive, costing about fifty cents each.

The herring were shipped to wholesale markets by steamboat, often the Hills Brothers or Hart Brothers lines. The biggest buyer for a time was the Seidel Fish Company in Marinette. From there, the fish were shipped by rail, and, for many years, most of them were sent on to the coal-mining areas of Pennsylvania, where

Staner Olson (third from right) and fellow anglers. The individual hanging from the ropes is descended from the illustrious Door County family for which Sturgeon Bay is named. This photograph was taken in about 1915.

the inexpensive fish were welcome in a depressed economy. Commercial fishermen often got as little as one to one-and-a-half cents a pound for salted herring. It took about one hundred sixty pounds of fresh herring to make a package, which brought about two dollars and seventy five cents.

Winters presented a different and even more rigorous routine. Nets were suspended in the ice through hand-sawed openings. At each lift, the ice was removed from the "pot," and the blocks of ice hauled away from the hole to make room for lifting the net. Fish were scooped out of the net, hauled to shore, dressed, and shipped by horse and sleigh to the Seidel Fish Company. In later years, a Chicago market developed, and the fish were shipped in the trucks of the Anderson Transportation Company of Ellison Bay, Wisconsin. The Chicago markets bought large shipments of herring. Trout were also marketable in the 1920s and were speared or hook-caught through the ice.

There were few restrictions by the state in Mart's early career, but it was illegal to take sturgeon. One winter Mart landed a huge strugeon through the ice, weighing about 135 pounds, and loaded with about thirty pounds of valuable roe. He "pirated" it with a load of herring to Seidel's in Marinette. Seidel bought it gladly, then took it into the fish shed, unrolled the tarp to expose the big fish, and jokingly announced, pointing to Mart, "There's that outlaw, Mart Kinsey!"

Fishermen are exposed to many perils on the water and ice, and occasionally on shore as well. As a young man, Mart was once fishing at Fayette, Michigan with another Fish Creek family, the Jones brothers. He set out one night for Sack Bay on his bicycle, perhaps to see a girl. There was a "gut dump" on the road, where fish remains were discarded, and it was a favorite haunt for bears. In the black of night, returning on his bike, he literally bumped into a bear, which let out a loud "WOOF". He said later that he bent the pedals on that bike getting away!

Mart lived to be eighty-four, and fished for over sixty years. On one of his last fishing trips in March 1942, he, Roy and Pat left in an open truck to lift a net set west of the Strawberry Islands. About a quarter of a mile from the net, Roy spotted open water, but Pat, who was driving, was unable to avoid it. The truck and all three men went into the icy water. The men struggled in heavy wet clothing for a hold on the ice. Mart began to tire. Roy supported him, while Pat succeeded in getting on top of the ice, and both assisted in their father's rescue. Their clothes froze like armor as they walked toward Friedmann's Point, a distance of over a mile. They were picked up by Ray Chambers in his home-made, gas-powered sleigh, a forerunner of the snowmobile. Arriving home with the assistance of his sons, after a hot bath, dry clothes, and a couple of brandies, he was none the worse for the experience. The truck was later salvaged in open water.

In Mart's lifetime, the herring market provided a living. By the 1940s, the fish were scarce and the commercial herring market was gone. Whitefish then became the target for commercial fishermen. One era had ended, and another begun.

# The Ingham Kinsey Family
by
*Roy Kinsey* and *Virginia Kinsey*

A marriage certificate in our home tells us that it was April 25, 1862 when Ingham Kinsey of Fish Creek took Elrissa Minor of Fish Creek as his bride. Besides this record, we also have a genealogy of the Minor ancestors dating back to the landing of the Mayflower at Plymouth, Massachusetts on November 11, 1620. These ancestors signed the Mayflower Compact before they landed, and it was not until March 21, 1621 that the group left the Mayflower to live in Plymouth, Massachusetts.

Elrissa Minor was the daughter of Martin Minor, a man of English descent, whose family became Wisconsin pioneers when they moved in 1845 from Jefferson County, New York, to Milwaukee, residing there until 1858. Minor was a ship calker by trade, and he moved his family to Door county in 1858. In July of that year he took a half-section of government land in Fish Creek and began to farm and harvest the timber. Cutting cord wood was the first step in clearing the land for agriculture.

Martin Minor was the father of a true pioneer family. He took an active part in establishing schools, was progressive, and in politics stood as a stalwart republican. Besides a son, Edward S. Minor, who became a U.S. Senator, Minor's family consisted of a daughter Elrissa and sons Augustine and Grant.

Ingham and Elrissa Minor Kinsey resided in Fish Creek for their entire lifetime. They had eight sons and two daughters: George, Sherman, Sanford, Martin, Archie, Alson, Earl, Ingham, Jr., Belle, and Jessie. The eight sons were hardy, adventurous, "fiddle-footed" frontiersmen, who partook of various occupations, and some of them were lured west. Four remained bachelors. George prospected for gold in the Black Hills, went on to the California gold rush and then to Oregon, where he died, never having returned to Wisconsin. Arch also prospected for gold in the Black Hills and then moved on to Butte, Montana, where he worked as a laborer in the copper mines.

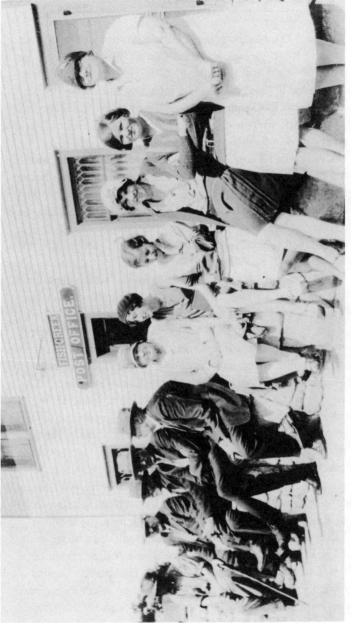

This gathering at the post office (now the Roy Kinsey home) in about 1930 included, left to right: Dan McKnee, Roy Thorp, Sam Kinsey, Harry Churches, John Melvin, Emma Milvia, Everil Kinsey, Hazel Kinsey, Doris Melvin, Jessie Kinsey, and May Thorp Kinsey (postmistress).

About 1900, Martin homesteaded a government land grant of 160 acres in Rock Springs, Rosebud County, Montana, where he raised crops of wheat and flax. Many of his Fish Creek neighbors also homesteaded in that general area, including Robert Noble, Bert Barringer, Herman Rockendorf and Gus, Herman and Emil Krause. After twelve years, Martin and his family returned to Fish Creek where he engaged in fishing.

Alson staked a copper claim in Port Arthur, Canada, where he spent a portion of his life until returning to Fish Creek to engage in trapping and fishing. Sanford also lived in Port Arthur and worked as a fisherman on Great Slave Lake. Upon leaving Canada, he likewise returned to Fish Creek to fish. Sherman remained in Fish Creek and worked as a carpenter; he supported his mother after his father, Ingham, died in 1900.

This family of sons loved the water and related occupations; those who returned to Fish Creek found their livelihood in boat building, fishing and sailing.

The Mackinaw, an 18th-century sailing craft built before steam, was the fisherman's workhorse. Many fishermen built their own boats. Double-ended and thirty to forty feet long, Mackinaws were lean and fast. On one occasion Martin Kinsey left Garden Bay, Michigan, for Fish Creek in a moderate northwind, sailing a Mackinaw with both sails set wing and wing. He had planned to stop at Washington Island, but the wind increased steadily and by the time he got into the Door Passage he was moving so fast he was afraid to tack or touch the sail, being alone in the boat. Sailing with the sheets cracking and the rigging groaning, he looked back at his wake to see a rooster tail behind the rudder. He never forgot that six-hour record run from Fayette, Michigan to Fish Creek as long as he lived.

Like many of her brothers, Belle also ventured west for many years of her life, and she married there. Jessie Kinsey remained in Fish Creek and married Freeman F. Thorp. The marriage ended in tragedy when Freeman drowned, along with many other Fish Creek residents, in the sinking of the *Hackley*, a steamboat. Jessie continued to live in Fish Creek sharing her home with her brother

Sherman and an adopted niece, Everil Kinsey. Jessie lived until 1934. Earl and Ingham Jr. died in their teen years.

In about 1905, brothers Alson and Martin Kinsey married sisters May and Bertha Thorp respectively, daughters of Fish Creek residents Matilda and Roy F. Thorp. Increase Claflin, the first settler of European descent in Door County (1836), was Roy F. Thorp's maternal grandfather, and the marriage of these descendants from Minor-Claflin ancestors thus united two pioneer families who have lived in Door County since the early eighteenth century, where the fifth and sixth generations of these families still reside.

# The Herr Doktor
by
*Ann Thorp*

Strict disciplinarian, health and fitness enthusiast, gourmet, and lover of art, music and nature; vigorous, stubborn, domineering, frugal, and snobbish: this was Hermann Welcker, a German physician who fell in love with Door County and established a unique health spa and resort in Fish Creek.

Welcker was born in Germany in 1849 and graduated in medicine from Leipzig University in 1877. He came to Milwaukee in 1894. On his first visit to Fish Creek two years later, he was so delighted with the area that he proceeded to acquire property from Asa Thorp.

From four cottages at the site of the present White Gull Inn, the Welcker establishment grew to more than 300 acres and consisted of twelve cottages, a dining hall, bath houses, the imposing "Casino" (now the Whistling Swan), the family cottage, and laundry buildings. He later bought the large Sunrise Farm behind the present Irish House as well as some bluff acreage in the Peninsula Park area, some of which eventually was given to the state and is now known as Welcker's Point.

The Doctor presided over his exclusive realm with great pride and a firm hand. An early guest once witnessed this portly, bearded figure standing on the porch of the Casino, gazing over his resort, and announcing *Das ist alles mein!* (This is all mine!).

The history of the casino is as remarkable as its owner. Built around 1889 in Marinette, it was called the Lumberman's Hotel. Due to economic problems in the region following the Peshtigo fire, it evidently was built at bargain prices. Welcker had planned a large building to serve as the center of his resort, and in 1906 he bought the hotel.

It was dismantled and brought across the bay – whether on horse-drawn vehicles across the ice, on scows and barges, or both is not clear. After it was reassembled, he opened it as Dr. Welcker's

"Casino" –the word being his expression for play –a place with game and card rooms for his guests' pleasure.

The furnishings arrived by steamboat from Sheboygan and Milwaukee for six weeks. They included ornate and elegant pieces of furniture, oriental rugs, plush draperies, and a Bauer baby grand piano. It must have been an exciting time for the people of Fish Creek, then a small village with no electricity, telephones, or automobiles. There were only a few other summer hotels – the Thorp Hotel, the Central Hotel, and the Nook Hotel – all quite modest in comparison to the accommodations provided by Welcker.

His early guests were often German friends from Milwaukee, people of refinement, perhaps personally chosen by Welcker. They arrived by steamer, a rigorous trip then, and stayed for the season. The Doctor reserved the right to refuse rooms on whatever basis he chose: attire, personality, or attitude. One story claims that he turned away a young member of the Pabst family and his party because of their racy clothes and forward manner.

He organized his program in the manner of European health spas of that era. He believed in exercise, hearty meals, rest, and cultural stimulation. A day's schedule might begin with a hike along the shore to Ephraim with stops along the way at little rest areas named for trees in the vicinity; there was a birch bench, a balsam bench, and others, with water fountains nearby. After returning by boat, perhaps aboard the *Thistle*, the large noon meal was announced by a big iron bell, and everyone was required to be on time. The table was laden with huge platters of roast pork or wiener schnitzel, potatoes, noodles, baked cabbage and other vegetables, smoked fish, and fresh bread. All this was follwed by rich desserts such as a three-layer cherry *kuchen* liberally crowned with whipped cream.

A two-hour silent period followed and was strictly enforced. Herr Doktor strode through cottages and hallways shaking a small hand bell, calling *Ruhe, Ruhe* (quiet, quiet).

Swimming was a favorite pastime and form of exercise for the Doctor and his wife Henrietta, and guests were encouraged to join them for an afternoon dip at the bathing beach (now the Town

Beach). Bathing costumes were of dark wool. Men wore two-piece suits, knee length, and one rather imperious man was seen entering the water with his Phi Beta Kappa pin fastened to his bathing suit. Women wore voluminous skirts and bloomers, often with a white hat pinned to their hair, creating a merry picture of white dots floating and bobbing on the water.

After another hearty meal, evenings were devoted to music, games, and socializing at the Casino. Women had a sewing room and a card room for bridge or Mah Jong. Game and billiard tables were set up in the basement for the men, and there were ping-pong tables and other amusements for children. There were ice boxes stocked with beer and other beverages, available on an honor system.

Plays starring some of the guests or visiting actors were presented, and concerts by professional musicians from Chicago and Milwaukee were performed. The great opera singer Madame Schumann-Heinck once sang at the Casino, and its Great Hall was hung with paintings by famous artists. Guests sometimes went to the Town Hall to see the flickery movies of that time.

At ten o'clock sharp the day was over and all the kerosene lamps were extinguished. Herr Doktor patrolled the walks and would shout up to a lighted window, *Abdrehen!* (Turn it off!).

Welcker had his office in his home, across from the Casino. Guests went there to pay their weekly bill and were amazed at his collection of snake skins, butterflies, antlers, a boar's head, stuffed fish, and stacks of books and sheet music.

Evidently he gave up medical practice when he established his resort, but he occasionally would prescribe for a mild illness. He had once studied virology, and when a smallpox epidemic threatened the village, he undertook the task of manufacturing a vaccine. At the time, he didn't have the breed of cattle necessary for the production of the vaccine. Instead, he used a local boy, Merle Thorp, then about eleven years old. Merle was vaccinated over and over, and the Doctor used his blood to make vaccine for the rest of *die Kinder* in the town.

Herr Dr. Hermann Welcker in about 1915.

Throughout the warm summer days the figure of Herr Doktor prevailed, a sometimes romantic image. There is an old photo of him, on a boat trip to Chambers Island, with a lovely young lady on each arm, his bright eyes showing pleasure and admiration. His old-world sentimentality was evident when he named the cottages for the women in his life – the Henrietta, the Matilda, the Hermine, the Tina, the Minna, and the Else. Hermann and Henrietta had one daughter who died at the age of twenty. Hermann's brother, Kurt, was an ear, nose, and throat physician who also had property in Fish Creek.

Henrietta died in Chicago in 1920. Hermann died in Fish Creek in 1924, and the hotel was then managed by a niece, Martha Fahr, until her death in 1939.

The Casino changed ownership many times during the next three decades, and for a time it was sadly run down and shabby. Its two most recent owners, the Harts in the 1970s and now the Coulsons, restored it with great care in the original manner.

Jan and Andy Coulson are now proprietors of the first Welcker holding (the White Gull Inn and Cottages) and the Casino (the Whistling Swan). The Herr Doktor undoubtedly would be delighted to see his dream living on once again.

* * *

Acknowledgement is hereby made to the following sources for historical information and photographs: the late Elsa Carl; Ellie Hart; Victor Welcker; Edward Schreiber; H.R. Holand's *History of Door County*; Duncan Thorp; Alice Clark Peddle; Andy Coulson; Clare Adele Schreiber; and William Guenzel.

# The Duclon Family
by
*Vivian Duclon Shine, Grace Duclon Lefebvre,*
*Lucille Duclon Hays,* and *Clyde J. Duclon*

Claudius Duclon immigrated from France via Scotland to Canada and settled in Alexandria Bay, New York, about 1826, where he worked as a fisherman. There he married Sophia Curler, who bore him six children. The eldest, William Henry moved to Mackinac Island, Michigan, where he took the position of Assistant Lighthouse Keeper. The Keeper was Ambrose Davenport, a full-blooded Ottawa Indian. In May of 1867, Willaim married Ambrose's daughter Julia. Eight sons were born to them: Ambrose, Albert, Frank, William, Charles, Joseph, James, and Walter. Albert died in infancy.

In 1882 Grandfather Willaim Henry Duclon was transferred to Eagle Lighthouse as Captain and Keeper of the Light. The state of Wisconsin later purchased the land, and it became part of Peninsula State Park. The lighthouse was a family project. From early spring when the ice left Green Bay until the bay froze over again, some years as late as December, Captain Duclon kept the light lit from sundown till sunup every night. It was a very particular job; the light had to be cleaned at midnight because carbon formed on the prisms of the light from the use of lard, mineral oil, and (later on) kerosene.

We grandchildren were allowed to climb the winding staircase to see the light. Grandpa would take us outside and walk around the base of the light. If we touched anything we were not allowed to go there again, so of course we were all very careful. There were 100 steps from the shore to the lighthouse.

The government boat brought supplies of kerosene, staple foods, and barrels of paint. The buildings were painted inside and out whether or not it was necessary. The government expected the paint to be used. The boys helped their father to keep the grounds clean, to work in the garden, and, later on, to build a barn to house horses and a cow. Captain Duclon was awarded many citations for having the best looking grounds in the area.

Grandma Duclon cooked and sewed. It was nothing for her to bake twenty loaves of bread and a dozen pies and to prepare delicious meals, not only for her family but, in later years, for many visitors. A summer kitchen built about fifty feet from the house was used in summer for cooking and eating, but also to keep the lighthouse cooler. Grandma made dozens of cookies and stored them in large crocks, which were always kept full, one with sugar cookies and the other with molasses cookies. In the winter, Grandma pieced and quilted quilts by hand. She made clothes for seven boys, starting each suit to a certain point to be sure they were all done at the same time. As her sons married she made a quilt for each family. Some of the grandchildren still have their original quilt.

In the winter, the boys had less work to do and, to fill their spare time, they acquired musical instruments and learned to play. Uncle Frank got a Stradavarius violin trading with a sailor. Grandpa bought a grand piano that was so large they couldn't get it into the house; he had to return it and get a smaller one. By removing the legs and tipping it on its side, they got it into the house through a window. That piano is now in the museum in Sturgeon Bay.

They began the Duclon Band, which played at dances, round or square. When they played out of town, the piano was moved with the legs and pedals removed; they put it on a sleigh or wagon wrapped in quilts and returned home the same way. In those days they played all night. The Duclon boys and the Baileys Harbor boys had a feud going. One night it developed into a fist fight. Of course the Duclon boys won.

Soon the boys married and each daughter-in-law stayed for a short time in the lighthouse, helping with the housework. The sons built small homes at Shanty (now Nicolet) Bay. Afterward, when the state bought the property, Joseph and Charles were given $100 each and asked to relocate. Charles moved his house across the ice to Fish Creek and Joseph moved to Fish Creek and rented. The rest of the boys already lived in Fish Creek.

Captain William and Julia Duclon

Many happy days were spent at the lighthouse. In the early years, we walked from Fish Creek to "the light" as it was fondly called by Grandpa. In later years, a road was cut and we traveled by wagon or horsedrawn sleigh. Thanksgiving and Christmas were very special times. The wives and granddaughters slept in the house, the men and grandsons slept in the barn on the hay covered with grandma's tied quilts.

Grandpa built a house in Fish Creek just before he retired, after forty years of service with the government. Our holiday reunions continued, with relatives coming from Green Bay and Black Creek. In summer, especially on the 4th of July, we made ice cream and everyone brought food. Walter and William Jr. became engineers on tugs that guided ships into the harbor of Green Bay. Jim lived in the Black Creek area working at various jobs. Joseph was a barber, a rural mail carrier, and, for forty years, caretaker of the Friedmann estate, now Hidden Harbor. Charles was caretaker for the Maltman family on Cottage Road. Frank lived with Grandpa after Grandma died, and he worked with Joseph at Friedmann's. Ambrose lived in Green Bay and worked in a paper mill.

Grandpa Duclon fought in the Civil War. He was fighting on land when the Monitor and the Merrimac were in combat on the water. He was with a group who were watching the engagement and cheering the ships as they fought. Eventually he was wounded, and for several months he was listed as a deserter, but he was later found in a hospital. Grandpa was a jolly man and loved to tease. We lived next door and our fruit and vegetables were stored in Grandpa's basement. Mother would send us there to get an apple for lunch at school. Grandpa always came upstairs with anything but an apple to which Grandma would say, "Paw, they don't want a carrot or potato - - they want an apple". With a twinkle in his eye he would say, "I thought this was an apple."

Uncle Walter and Aunt Gustie were riding in a horse-drawn buggy when a bear (then very numerous in the park) decided to cross the road in front of the horse. The surprised horse bolted, thereupon taking off and giving Gustie and Walter the ride of their life.

This Duclon family gathering in about 1912 included, left to right: Charles, Walter Chambers, Captain William, Gertrude, William Jr., Ruth (Mrs. Wm. Jr.), Edith (Mrs. Wm. Jr.), unidentified boy, Helen, Julia (Mrs. Wm. Sr.), Augusta (Mrs. Joseph), 2 unidentified people in back, Louis (baby), Edith (girl sitting), Augusta (Mrs. Walter), Frank (behind post), Walter, Clyde & Walter Jr. (2 boys in front), and Joseph.

All of our aunts and uncles are now deceased though there are a few cousins living. Grandma Duclon died of tuberaculosis in September of 1922. Grandpa Duclon died in September of 1926 at the age of 81.

Grandma had a recipe of beaten egg which she put on pancakes. It consisted of two eggs beaten until they had the consistency of cream; then a quarter-cup of sugar was added while beating constantly until the sugar was disolved; next, sliced bananas and a half teaspoon of vanilla was added. The recipe has been handed down for generations and the great-great-grandchildren love it. Grandma also made her own syrup browning two tablespoons of white sugar in an iron skillet, adding two cups of boiling water, and two more cups of sugar, then simmering the mixture to the consistency of syrup. It was delicious used hot or cold on pancakes, corn meal bread, or french toast. Try it sometime!

# The Thorp Family
## by
### *Duncan Thorp*

### Asa Thorp

The first person to bear our name that I ever heard about was one Jacob Thorp, an Englishman who landed in Essex County, New Jersey in 1776. His descendants appear later in Pennsylvania and still later in upstate New York near Oswego. One of them, Truman Thorp, was a lock tender on the newly opened Erie Barge Canal. He and his three sons, Jacob, Asa, and Levi, drove their mules along the tow paths of the canal, moving barges and flat boats loaded with eastern Americans hungry for free western lands. All were headed west. Many returned with stories of forests where three great trees were enough to build a cabin; of rivers where fish were so dense in the spring runs that they forced each other out of the water, and could be picked off the rocks and ledges of the rapids in whatever size and variety one preferred; of flights of doves that darkened the sun for days; of soil so fertile you could raise potatoes that weighed two pounds each; of fat livings to be made with a rifle, marketing buffalo and deer.

All the Thorp boys took the hook. Asa, the oldest, went first. One day he coiled the reins and hung them on the hames of the off-mule and left the team standing as he jumped onto a lake schooner just clearing the last lock. He was off for the magic *west,* and the famed happy hunting ground beyond the cabins and camps of men.

Asa landed in Milwaukee in due course. He had learned the cooper's (barrel maker's) trade from his elders, and he moved on to Rubicon in Dodge County, Wisconsin, where he had heard the free land began. There was land, but no flocks or herds for the taking. Earlier settlers had already plowed the prairie and set up their fences. He filed on a piece of farmland and wondered whether to go home or farther west. At this point he met a traveler from the north, a rambler like himself, a trapper and fur trader who had spent three years exploring the margins of Lake Michigan.

The man told young Asa he could make a fortune making barrels for commercial fishermen who came each summer to an almost barren rock in the lake called Pilot Island to fish for lake trout. The fish came so fast on their hand lines that the crew had to halt fishing every few days and make barrels in which to pack their catch in salt for shipment to Chicago. A cooper would be worth his weight in gold in a Lake Michigan fishing camp. Asa rolled his blanket and set out early the next morning. He got to Fort Howard (now Green Bay) by hitch-hiking on freight wagons with ox teams, then boarded a side-wheel steamer and headed for the magic islands. He got there, too.

None of the fishermen were settlers. All were natives of Chicago, up for the summer and anxious to catch and sell several tons of fish before winter drove them off the water. Each fisherman had a shack and a boat. The boats were oar-powered, about seventeen or eighteen feet long, with a single mast and a sail to ride the wind when it was fair. On a good morning, twelve to fourteen of these heavy boats scattered over the straits between the islands and the mainland, dropped their baited lines to the bottom, and jerked them steadily up and down in a motion called "bobbing". One would jerk his line high in the air and drop it several feet to bottom. Another would raise it in a series of small jerks and lower it the same way. Occasionally one of the fishermen, bored with inaction, would leap upright on a thwart or tiny foredeck and dance violently to activate his "bob".

At any moment at least half of the boats were landing fish, all gray trout averaging eight pounds. Often one of the men would signal with a piercing whistle and display an unusually large trout between fifteen and twenty pounds. Each pair of boats shared a single "bait net", a fine-meshed gill net which they lifted first thing in the morning to remove the small chubs and bloaters that they used for bait. Some of the men used wobbling spoons and spinners in the

Asa Thorp with grandchildren (left to right) Harold, Mildred and Leland in about 1902.

water, but hardware produced as many fish as live bait. By high noon the "lucky" boats were heading for the beach to dress and salt their catch. Asa worked all summer making wooden half-barrels for salting fish.

Soon the old hook-and-line fishermen turned to linen gill nets which caught more fish. Then, little by little they used smaller mesh nets, until all the trout were juveniles which had never spawned. The age of specialization had dawned on Pilot Island, and the fishermen reorganized their operations. They built a cooperative salting shed with salting benches, fish hoppers, and washing facilities, so all hands could work at the same tasks of dressing and salting. The trout fishermen of Pilot Island had discovered the assembly line.

The new system allowed them to process many more fish, but the resource was not limitless. They put in longer hours in the boats, brought in more fish and processed them faster, but the fish seemed to quit after yielding up a couple hundred pounds. The fleet of dories was catching lake trout at or near the total reproductive rate of the adjacent spawning grounds. If they had continued "bobbing," the trout fishery would have kept up with human predation.

A few years ago at Gills Rock I saw an angler bobbing from a drifting boat at the foot of Table Bluff. Later I saw three nice trout in his boat. Hook and line had produced a catch 150 years after Asa's time, though those trout were raised in a hatchery and planted. The native fish had become extinct.

Asa took time from the cooperage to learn to sail, row, and bob. He still hoped to become wealthy and successful harvesting fish and game, as in the "pie-in-the-sky" stories he had thrilled to on the tow path of the canal. But he was a practical Yankee, and he realized that every man on Pilot Island had the same ambition. From time to time one of the crews sailed farther offshore hunting new ground and a lake-trout bonanza, but few of the explorations paid off. If a boat came back "loaded," the new ground was immediately over-run by competitors and stopped producing extraordinary catches within a few days. Nature imposed limits on men –generous limits, but not unrestricted mother lodes.

There were men on the larger islands and on the mainland – red men, Potawatomi Indians. Asa learned their language and listened to their stories, the same kind of stories he had heard from pioneers returning from the west - of bonanzas of fish, meat and timber, of fertile lands where corn grew higher than a horse's ears by the 4th of July.

But Asa stuck to his cooper's forge. Special bolts of wood had to be cut from timber to make staves, and ash withes for hoops were steamed or simmered in a tank until they were almost as pliable as ropes. Staves were split from an oak bolt with a hoe-like hand-adze called a "froe," and hardened in the fire. A barrel was assembled on a model form, with staves stuck upright between a starter hoop, and then the hoops were driven down snugly around the outside with a wooden mallet and a hardwood block. Then the new barrel was filled with water and left to swell tight in a corner of the cooper shop. When a packet ship came from Fort Howard, the fishermen took their bank drafts from the wholesalers and cashed them at the General Store and Post Office on Washington Island. They paid Asa so much for each of his barrels, and Asa saved every penny. He still wanted that corn field higher than a horse.

Fall came, and the calms of August blew away in vicious north gales and snow squalls. Fishing slowed, and the first fishermen left for the cities. In time, Asa rolled his blankets, nailed shut the door of his cooper shop, and took ship for Fort Howard.

In the early 19th century, most boat traffic followed the shores of the Great Lakes, and an expansionist federal government had begun building lighthouses and coast guard stations at capes and shoals of particular menace to encourage settlement of the Great Lakes area - a military vantage point. En route back to Fort Howard, Asa noted how the little side-wheeler outran its fuel supply of cordwood every few days and the ship and crew would moor in a cove and go ashore to cut more wood for the ever-hungry boilers. At one cove with a pretty creek at the head there was a lone cabin and chimney marking the home of a settler named Clafflin, a downeaster veteran of the War of 1812 who was originally from Massachusetts.

Asa wondered why Clafflin didn't build a pier and make a fortune selling wood to steamboats. As soon as he got back to Fort Howard, Asa headed for the Federal Land Grant Office at Appleton and filed an application for all the shorelands around the cove which he called Fish Creek. He went back to Rubicon around Christmas and found a buyer for his prairie land claim. With money in his pocket he headed for home and his waiting fiancee, Eliza Atkinson, in Lockport, New York. On arrival, Asa poured his tales of the happy hunting ground into the ears of his brothers. Brother Jake was the most susceptible. He was becoming a bit of a Rip Van Winkle, roaming the woods with rod and muzzle-loader and neglecting his mules and towpath duties to hunt, fish, and camp with Indians. Jake headed for Asa's claim in Fish Creek and suckered his kid brother Levi into going along.

The Thorp brothers hired two more men and started felling trees. They decked the thirty-foot long cribs on the beach and built a cribbed pier by spiking together a series of log crates, each a little deeper than the last, to fit the deepening bottom at the site selected. When the harbor was plated with two feet of ice in February, they sledded the big clumsy cribs out in a row, chopped holes in the ice, and sank them. Then they hauled innumerable sleigh-loads of coarse rocks and dumped them in the cribs, which sank to bottom. By the time the ice broke up and left the harbor in early May, the Thorp pier was ready for business.

During the winter, Asa went to Rubicon and engaged in his favorite activity, "trading". With a man named Sellick he traded a location on his dock at Fish Creek, the only one between Sturgeon Bay and Washington Island, for Sellick's sawmill and the sawing of thousands of feet of lumber at no charge. By the summer of 1840, Asa had a pier, a warehouse, a sawmill, and a stockpile of pine lumber ready for a flood of settlers.

The settlers were slow in coming. They arrived on steamboats and looked, but frowned at the heavy timber and rock outcrops and decided to keep going west or south. Jake and Levi moved to Egg Harbor and built stout log cabins. Levi subsequently built a home of milled lumber with a cupola on the top, the first house of "finished" lumber ever built on the Door Peninsula of Wisconsin.

## The Thorp Hotel

The hotel was almost an accident. Uncle Asa, founder of Fish Creek, never planned a big establishment. He just had some extra rooms in his large house that he was willing to rent to a teamster, a "drummer" (salesman), or whoever else got left on the dock in a county that had no inns for travelers in the 1860s.

That was the start. The first tourists came on the "Chicago Boats," excursion steamers of the Goodrich Line, in the 1880s. At first they were only a trickle, and they became a flood after highways were built and motor cars became common. The railroad came later but ended at Sturgeon Bay, terminus of the Green Bay and Western (GB&W), which locals called the "Grab Bag and Walk Line". Thorp Hotel was the second summer tourist hotel in Wisconsin. The oldest, a place on trout Lake in Vilas County, was an abandoned lumber camp favored by fishermen and was in operation two years earlier.

Asa's main building was built about 1850 and was added to many times. Other buildings were moved onto the land and became cottages. Asa added an orchard of apple trees and a grape arbor. His first guests paid $3.75 a week for board and room. Some of the very earliest cancelled and moved out –to Sturgeon Bay, where they found cheaper accommodations.

Asa sent his son Edgar (Ted) to Eastman College in Poughkeepsie, N.Y. for a business course, and he managed the hotel on his return in 1895. He established a new service. Uncle Ted's livery stable offered a horse and rig for a sight-seeing tour or a picnic. Later you could rent his Model-T with a driver. Uncle Ted had a Ford agency at his stable and sold some of the first horseless carriages in Door County. As kids we liked to walk through Thorp's barn and admire the tourists' shiny automobiles, cars you don't see now – Kissels, Willys St. Clairs, Studebakers, Marmons, Jewetts,

Stevens-Duryeas, Chalmers, Maxwells, and others gone to limbo with Edsels.

There were two autos with drivers in Fish Creek, one owned and operated by Bill Vorous, the other, Ted's, driven by my father Merle Thorp. They would meet tourists coming off the train and bring them to the Thorp Hotel. Quite a few of these early visitors were settlers themselves, having bought land from Asa and built summer homes. They lived at the hotel for a year or two and when their mansions were built, they brought in their friends.

At peak capacity, Thorp Hotel and cottages had room for about 125 guests, and it was usually packed in July and August. The dining room did a big trade among the guests and among Cottage Row residents and their visitors. Ted bought a farm in the creek bottom and raised much of the produce consumed in the hotel. His wife Matilda worked long hours keeping the rooms clean and doing much of the cooking.

My cousin, Evelyn Thorp Baraboo, youngest daughter of Ted, has these memories:

> I was born in one of the downstairs rooms of the main house, with Dr. Egeland and Mrs. Lundberg assisting. I did cleaning and other work, and lived there until I was married. For a time we also owned the Nook Hotel, which was on the corner, now Bunda's Hutch. We had a very short tourist season. In winter it took us two days to get from Fish Creek to Sturgeon Bay, going over fields at times and staying overnight in Egg Harbor. We had a covered sleigh with a little pot-bellied stove. In summer, Indians used to come to the village. They would peek into our windows and ask for food. There was a very close relationship among the village people then. We called the adults "Aunt" and "Uncle". We had sleigh rides, and square dances at the Town Hall with the Duclon Family playing. The Ladies' Aid had quilting bees and other social functions for many years.

In the late 1920s, when Ted grew old, his son Leland came home from Milwaukee where he had been a buyer for the Schuster Stores, and he then managed the hotel. Leland was astute in his dealings with devotees of the newly popular sport fishing; he often

The Thorp Hotel in about 1906.

made arrangements for fishing parties out of Fish Creek. He invited sportswriters from Chicago and Milwaukee as his pampered guests. If any of them wanted a reservation, his wish was Leland's command. They were honored guests and the best was none too good. Their fishing articles attracted more business to the hotel.

Originally, the hotel had two motor launches and two guides: Harold Thorp, Leland's brother, and Clyde Helgeson, his brother-in-law. They maintained a friendly rivalry. Both preferred a particularly choice bass-fishing spot off the gravel bar on Middle Strawberry Island, and they would race their engines to get a jump on the other. Timing was everything! The first to arrive would anchor squarely across the end of the bar facing into the south current and load up with bass. The second might anchor within ten feet or less and get nothing but a few runty fish. Since both boats had ancient two-cylinder motors, and neither could whack off more than a dizzy four miles an hour on a good day, it was often a dead heat.

As the fishing trade grew, Leland added a third launch with an old Straubel engine. I acquired my guide license and on rare days with an early start I would even get to their bass hole first. On one occasion, I filled up the limit for all hands and then yielded my hot spot to Harold, who also filled up. What happened to all those small-mouths? A favorite use for them was to have Henderson, the hotel chef, fry them for dinner and invite friends for the feast. There were other boats out of Fish Creek run by Les and Elmer Anderson, Fred Wesner, and Harry Schuyler. Eventually the hotel added a fourth guide boat run by my father, Merle Thorp, and on very busy Sundays might even have another, piloted by my brother Jim.

At the peak of the fishing frenzy it was hard to find a "Fish Cricker" who didn't sometimes serve as a guide. Sheldon Doughty, Warren Baxter, and Ray Chambers fished every day, as did such private boats as "Doc" Apfelbach's *Night Crawler*. Bait was scarce. My cousin Roy Kinsey and I crawled for hours on hands and knees over dew-soaked lawns catching worms to sell to the guide boats for one cent each. Worm sales kept me in the University for two years in the 1930s. The fishing business helped preserve the hotel.

The Fish Creek pier and warehouse in about 1912. The steamship at the dock was one of those that carried passengers and freight on Green Bay, the two-masted schooner was a freighter.

I also worked as a night clerk for Leland during the Depression. Sometimes I handled checks for well over a thousand dollars for an entire family, parents and children, who had been guests for the whole summer. Hot water to the cottages came from coal-fired heaters located in separate sheds. At night I made the rounds to fire up the heaters and make reservations for fishermen. Boats provided a cane pole and bait for $3.00 per person.

Leland hired a professional chef in the 1940s and his wife Sylvia ran the dining room and did much of the interior decorating. The business was sold to Polyventure Incorporated, in 1968. At that time it consisted of six shops and eleven cottages. Charles Pelletier, who did some carpenter work there, began a restaurant business in one of the small buildings, and did fish boils in the front yard. Later he took over the west end of the main building and established a larger restaurant.

In February, 1984, the large building burned down in a spectacular early-morning fire. It was rebuilt in the original style, and Founder's Square, with its stately trees, broad walks and porches, and a variety of shops and food establishments continues to be a highly popular tourist attraction.

Leaving Fish Creek by small steamer in about 1906. The crowd that saw the boat off can be seen standing on the newly repaired and extended pier.

# Ferdinand Hotz
by
*G. Leonard Apfelbach, MD*

Ferdinand Hotz first visited Fish Creek in 1905 somewhat by accident. He was on a business trip from Chicago to Marinette by train to visit a client, and he had extra time. To use his time he took an excursion boat from Marinette to Fish Creek. He had heard of the beauty and delights of the area, though we should remember that many areas such as Peninsula State Park, Newport, etc. were not as beautiful then as they are now because they had recently been logged. This visit began a long association between Fish Creek and Mr. Hotz and his descendants which persists to today.

He next visited Fish Creek in 1908 and brought along his wife and children; his youngest, Ferdinand L. Hotz, was only one year old. They stayed at Welker's Resort in a cottage north of the main lodge (the Casino). Another visit was made in 1911, and again they stayed at Welker's resort. After 1912, they came annually to Door County, and he began the acquisition of property which eventually resulted in his being the largest private land owner in Door County.

His first purchase was the Gibraltar Orchards on Cottage Road, now part of the Slaby property; in 1912 he also purchased land at the top of the Fish Creek hill, then known as "Noble's Pasture," from the Noble family, where he built a series of cottages. Soon afterwards, he bought land along the present Spring Road in Fish Creek, including the present Fish Creek Condominium development and half the valley below; that land included the oldest Door County log homestead north of Sturgeon Bay (at 3993 Main Street). That building previously owned by Captain Joseph Vorous, who went down on the *Hackley*, is now hidden by clapboard and additions.

By 1915, Hotz had purchased a large tract of land which later was sold to the DNR and became Newport State Park, as well as a tract at Mud Lake. He also purchased the entire Juddville Bay land and bluff, extending from the present Peninsula Players to beyond the south point of Juddville, as well as the presently wooded tract

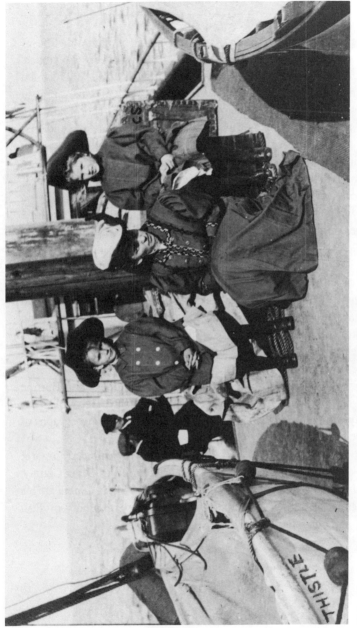

This photgraph of Ferdinand Hotz' daughters Helen (left) and Alice and of his sister Mary Hotz aboard the *Thistle*, one of the Hart Transportation Company steamers, was taken ca. 1908.

between Hwy 42 and Spring Road just north of Peninsula Player Road. Two of his children, Ferdinand L. Hotz and Alice Apfelbach, laid out the roads above and below the bluff in Juddville and divided the land. He had other acquisitions in the Clarks Lake area, at Ellison Bay Bluff, and 600 feet of Fish Creek harbor shoreline north of the public beach, part of which is still owned by his descendants. Over the years most of these lands were sold. The Hotz offspring continued in his tradition of love of land and preservation of its original state resulting in the preservation of the large tract for Newport State Park. Hotz also built a log retreat overlooking Europe Lake, which has since been removed by the DNR, as well as three cottages and a garage on the east side of the top of the Fish Creek hill.

Mr. Hotz was born in Wertheim, Germany, in 1868 and came to the United States in 1884 after learning the trade of designing fine jewelry. He became an international diamond merchant and designed the finest custom jewelry for an elite group of customers from coast to coast, often traveling across the country to cater to their needs. He lived in Glencoe, Illinois, and had his private office in downtown Chicago.

He died in 1946 and his ashes were scattered upon Europe Lake, as he requested, because of his love for the land of Door County and that area in particular. Some of his early photographs of the area appear in this book.

His four children, Alice Apfelbach, Helen Schmidt, Margaret Klok, and Ferdinand L. Hotz, all have summered in Door County, and his son Ferdinand L. Hotz survives to this day. Some of his grandchildren and great-grandchildren are now residents of Fish Creek and carry on his traditions.

# Sketches From Life: Fish Creek Voices
by
*Duncan Thorp*

## Horsehide

Uncle Ed was spooky. He was scared to walk through a graveyard after dark, and he didn't like to join in "waking" a dead relative or friend. Knowing this, his drinking pals would fill him full of ghost stories and as a result often had to walk him home.

Uncle Ed ran a livery stable in Fish Creek, and some of his horses were old enough to vote. One of them just plain fell down and died one cold winter day, and when Uncle Ed went to the stable, there lay his oldest horse, Henry, dead in his stall. No help for it; and Uncle Ed was a most practical Yankee. You couldn't make a dime renting a dead horse, but the hide was worth a few dollars. So he contracted with George and Tim to skin the animal. Then he hitched up Blackie to his cutter and drove south to find consolation at the tavern of Jerry LaMere, five miles hence.

George and Tim, meanwhile, got the hide off Henry, and the icy gale from the north was freezing the carcass stiff before they were finished. Once skinned, the old horse looked frightful with bulging eyes and great lipless teeth gleaming like knives. Tim got an idea!

They dragged the frozen corpse into one of the stalls, stood it up, put the harness on, and departed. The hour waxed late. Uncle Ed found his way home, unhitched Blackie and led him to the stable. Inside, he groped and found his coal oil lantern hanging on a nail, lighted it and held it high.

The light reflected from the great eyeballs and wicked teeth of old Henry, standing stark and harnessed in the next stall. Uncle Ed bolted for the house, lantern swinging wildly.

"Nellie," he howled at his wife. Aunt Nellie was in a bad mood as she always was when Uncle Ed was out late drinking - let alone when awakened by a howling drunk.

"What ails you," she growled.

"Come and see!" cried Ed. "There's a ha'nt in the barn, a devil horse, harnessed and hitched and standin' right in old Henry's stall. You'll shiver when you see it! Come on Nellie, I'll show you the demon."

Aunt Nellie followed, grumbling, to the barn, enumerating the evils of strong drink that muddled the brains of men lucky enough to have any. "There, Nellie," he cried. "If you see what I see, I'll never take another drop as long as I live!"

Aunt Nellie had the whip hand but lost it before she knew that fate had placed a powerful reform tool in her hands. She looked and then looked again.

"Ye danged old fool," she said. "That's the dead horse Tim and George skint today while you was gettin' drunk. It's been rigged up to scare you!"

Uncle Ed's pledge of abstinence vanished. He gazed on the apparition and realized Nellie was right. "By damn," he said, I need a drink NOW!"

✤ ✤ ✤

## Ghost of the Black Hand

When old man MacLamon died, he was laid out in Auntie Rachel's living room on Main Street, and half a dozen neighbors showed up for the wake. Among the "wakers" was Archie Mack, a somewhat alcoholic grandson with built-in radar for occasions that offered a bottle of cheer. This was one such, and Archie and several of the boys killed the bottle of "moon" in jig time. As the night wore on, the temperature dropped (it was March), and a false spring had melted all the drifts and opened the creeks. Auntie Rachel's house grew colder and the men sitting up with old Mac began to shiver and beat their arms to gain a measure of warmth. Alvin Smith fiddled with the draft of the chunk heater and cursed the stove.

"Damn thing won't draw," he complained. "Probably never cleaned that there stove pipe since the Civil War." And so saying he hauled the stove pipe out of the chimney and took it to the window to look inside. He saw a lot of black soot and it gave him ideas. He covered his palm with soot and planted a black palm print on the wall next to the casket. He kept making more palm prints around the room to a point beside the old horsehair sofa where Archie Mack snored loudly.

Smiling to himself Alvin planted a black palm print on Archie's cheek, then carefully blacked the palms of the corpse of old Mack lying with his palms crossed upon his chest. The rest of the watch party were alert now and grinning broadly. They woke Archie rudely. "Time to have another nip," they said and Archie agreed, rubbing his eyes.

"What ya got on your face," they asked. Archie went to the mirror over the sofa and looked. He saw the black palm print and shook his head.

"Same as on the wall," he observed and all the mourners sat down and began telling ghost stories. They told of the ghost of Black Ash Swamp and the other village yarns of the occult. Al told about a black-handed demon who visited funerals and marked his visits with a "black hand." Archie went back to the mirror and holding the kerosene lamp began inspecting the prints on the plastered walls.

He swiftly followed the prints around the room to the casket and when he saw old Mack's hands he screamed and bolted out the door. Alvin followed him down Main Street, urging him to come back. "It was all a joke," he cried, but Archie ran into his own house and stayed there until the sun came up.

✛ ✛ ✛

## Deer Hunter's Camp

In the long years that Door County was closed to deer hunting, native hunters trekked each fall to northern Wisconsin to hunt, while burgeoning whitetails frolicked on their lawns and gardens back home on the peninsula.

Dozens of deer were poached every month by normally law-abiding citizens to save money on the meat bill in the Depression years of the thirties. Wardens and courts kept busy.

The gang from around Fish Creek who got together for a November cutting in Forest County each year often spent more time playing practical jokes on each other than in hunting. Each could remember a recent season in which he had been the butt of a joke and this was the time to get even.

Uncle Ned was spooky and could be scared by a ghost story or a weird sound so he came in for a lot of pranks. One late afternoon as the woods were darkening to dusk one of the boys found Ned resting his legs and sitting on a down log after plowing through a thicket of spruce and willow in a nearby hollow.

"Hello, Ned," said Herb. "Did ya hear that bloodthirsty critter yowling last night, like this?" and Herb demonstrated with a shriek that make Ned's hair stand on end.

"Thought I heered somethin' like that," said Ned, "but it was kinda far away and faint."

Ned picked up his rifle and made for camp. Herb followed and took a parallel track through the swamp.

"Eeee-yow!" The hideous shriek of the terrible critter echoed between the gloomy pines along Woods Creek. Ned hiked a notch faster. Keeping pace Herb yowled again. Ned walked faster and broke into a sweat. The howling cat followed closer and closer all the way to camp.

Ned burst into the cabin and told all the hunters about the howling. Herb arrived and supported Ned's story by describing the ferocious animal that followed him back screeching its call every hundred yards.

"I know that critter well," said one of the men.    "It's downright dangerous."

"What do they call it?" asked Uncle Ned.

"I think it's called a dire cat," said one of the nimrods.

The hunters outdid each other with stories of the wild cat. Uncle Ned kept his rifle within reach when he went to his bunk. Often in the night the Dire Cat howled outside the cabin. But all the hunters except one slept soundly.

✤ ✤ ✤

## The Retired Horse

Old Frank, our black gelding, grew tricky in his old age. He did no more hard work, but stood most of the day in the meadow with the milk cows, which he regarded as his harem and under his protection. He would rest his big head on a cow's back and stand still in a guardian pose. When we kids came to drive the cows to the barn to be milked, throwing hard green apples at his cows, he would come galloping straight at us, teeth bared, rearing up on his hind legs with his forelegs suspended like hammers over our heads. When we ran back into the orchard, he would return peacefully to his harem and resume his guard.

He learned to bump his soft nose against the corn crib door until he loosened the wooden peg that held it shut, then nudge the door open and reach in to steal an ear of corn. He would stalk around the grounds all day, proudly holding the corn cob in his lips until he tired of carrying it, and drop it any old place. He just enjoyed stealing it.

He developed a taste for vegetables. When mother appeared on the back step and gave a shrill whistle, he would gallop up to her and relieve her of the potato peelings, onion skins, cabbage leaves or pea pods, and guzzle them down with great relish. Then he would dash off with a sportive flirt of his tail, a flick of the heels, and an impertinent passing of wind.

Old Frank reached the venerable age (for a horse) of thirty years, and he had been scheming for most of his years how to get out of work. When hitched to a team with the stout mare, Nell, he would imperceptibly ease off on the collar and the tugs of his harness, shifting the main burden of the wagon load to Nell. Granddad would keep a fishy eye on Frank's whippletree and when he caught him malingering he would yell "Hi-yah," and give him a cut with the whip. Frank would then lean into his collar and assume the whole load for six or seven paces, acting as though he had just aroused from a dream and remembered why he was there, harnessed to a wagon load of limestone.

A few years before his retirement Frank began to go on strike. Granddad was using him with a light cart to haul dry wood from a nearby tract of forest. He would march the wagon cheerfully up the tote road and stop beside one of the stacks of dried poles we had gathered. Granddad and I would toss the poles onto the rack of the wagon, building a load. When the poles were piled just so high Frank would snort or whicker, a sound suspiciously like a Bronx cheer. It was his first warning. Add one more pole, no matter how light, and Frank would heave a sigh and lay down on his belly. No coaxing, beating, cursing or other persuasions known to teamsters would ever get him to stand again on his feet. Finally Granddad and I would walk sulkily back to the load and throw off two or three of the poles we had loaded last. Having won the argument, Frank would rise and march briskly home to the woodpile. He had made up his mind to pull just so much and no more. No one ever won an argument with old Frank.

❖ ❖ ❖

## Golf as Income

We became caddies at about twelve to sixteen years of age for pocket money. A caddie at Peninsula Park golf course got 35¢ for a nine-hole job and 75¢ for eighteen. New balls sold as high as one dollar cash and resold for fifty cents, or three good balls for a buck. So we searched the roughs of the course fairways for balls and sometimes we hit a jackpot.

Squirrels had the curious habit of retrieving the balls and burying them in caches in the ground or in hollow trees. If we saw a squirrel with one, we followed him to see where he hid it and then excavated the site, at times finding more than a dozen balls.

Back in the 1920s, golfers would ask their caddies if they had any golf balls to sell, and a good day selling them was better than lugging bags of clubs around the course.

Caddies were assigned a spot on a side hill near the clubhouse and kept keen eyes on each car that drove into the parking lot – Pierce Arrows, Stearn's Knights, Marmons, Cadillacs, Franklins, Kissels, Huppmobiles, and perhaps a Willys St. Clair or two. Every regular golfer was known and his generosity or lack of it thoroughly indexed.

One well-known bank president drove a Lincoln Phaeton and would tip us a penny or two plus a lecture on the virtue of thrift saving. When he drove into the club, all the caddies fled into the woods. He was a Scotsman and all the caddies called him "Old MacDonald." The caddies sometimes let the air out of the tires on his Lincoln while he was playing a round. It cost $5 to call a mechanic from the village and changing a tire was something Old MacDonald would not do. But the caddies would change the tire for him – for $2.50.

I took my kid brother Kenny to the golf links to break him into caddying. In came the old Lincoln touring car, and the brush cracked as all available caddies, including me, bolted into the woods. All, that is, except my greenhorn brother who sat on the caddie bench like a gopher at his burrow.

"Where are the other caddies?" asked Old McDonald of the lone twelve-year-old on the bench.

"They all ran off when you came," said Kenny with childish candor.

"You want to carry my bag?"

"Okay, I guess."

The result was Kenny carried Old McDonald's heavy bag regularly. They got on famously. Old McDonald even tipped him a quarter and gave him a ride to the county fair at Sturgeon Bay. Old McDonald was a reformed golfer due to my kid brother's becoming frankness.

The day of the caddie closed and we became a threatened species as motorized golf carts replaced farm kids sweating under the heavy bags. But caddie fees and the resale of lost golf balls kept us in small cash through the 1920s.

✛ ✛ ✛

## A Sailboat Race

In the days when almost everyone was a fisherman and owned a sailboat, there were strong feelings about whose boat was the fastest, or was the handiest, or sailed best into the wind. Fish Creek fishermen were no exception. One day when a sleek new boat from Sturgeon Bay pulled into the dock sporting a broom at the foremast – a symbol of a clean sweep of her competitors – there was much scratching of heads and beards. After lengthy and profound discussion it was learned that the craft recently launched had indeed outdistanced several boats well known for speed and canny skippers.

The challenge was irresistible, and a wager was soon staked that a Fish Creek boat could out-sail her on a course from the town dock around Chambers Island and back, thus testing both boats on head winds, cross winds, and fair winds. The betting was hot, and considerable money was laid on both sides.

The Sturgeon Bay boat had a bevy of well-heeled sports aboard when the boats left the harbor. The challenger was a lean sloop built by one of the Weborgs, and Roy F. Thorp, the skipper, was a most redoubtable sailor.

They rounded Chambers Island to the north, which made it necessary to swing wide to avoid the dangerous northeast point and its two-mile rock reef on which many a craft had come to grief. The Fish Creek boat lost a half mile of lead on this leg. As they approached the reef, Roy Thorp took a range on two high pines on the shore of the north harbor, and, sailing by the seat of his pants, zipped through a cut in the reef with six inches to spare under his centerboard.

The shortcut gave him a lead he never lost since the more cautious Sturgeon Bay skipper took an extra three miles to round the reef in safety. Reaching in a beam wind, the boats came back to the dock, and bets were paid. An excited squad of men on the dock demanded, "You boys take that damn broom down now!"

Years later, when bass fishing, I learned to negotiate that same cut in the reef and to take my bearings from the same twin pines on the north shore. The cut was a treasure chest of big bass and jumbo perch, and it did save time rounding the island, whether under canvas or a two-cylinder Straubel.

✛ ✛ ✛

## Ducks

Driving about the country roads of Door County's heartland, we note the presence of many farm animals, unchanged for half a century or more. Calves, colts, chickens, geese, pigs, sheep, bulls, and even a rare guinea fowl or two are commonly seen, but seldom ducks, which used to be prevalent.

What happened to the ducks? I know what happened to ours. They changed the law so that hunters couldn't use live decoys. The hunters are gone and with them their beloved mallards, the glossy green-headed drakes and the busy brown hens followed by little flocks of yellow and black ducklings.

We made a pool next to the pump house for our ducks, a square six feet filled with water eight inches deep and refilled when needed from the same well we used for our stock barrels and orchard sprayers. The ducks enjoyed it hugely, and the hens led their squadrons of ducklings to their pond where they splashed and peeped like kids always do when you give them water. I could never get over how fast those little ducks could swim. They actually could scoop flies from the air as they scooted across the duck pond!

We raised ducks to eat and to sell to hunters, and if there was a slight surplus we sold them to proprietors of "shooting matches" who gave them to the winning marksmen.

I remember the first time I was allowed to go on a duck hunt. We drove before sun-up to Rowleys Bay and got a cabin from Jay Rogers, a rowboat for ourselves, and one for our friends from Green Bay. The boat with the old Elto twin motor on behind towed the other one, so we all sailed up Mink River in style.

In a blind built many days before, the reeds and cedar boughs had aged like the ranks of brown weeds on all sides. We opened our lumpy grain sacks and took out our call ducks, lovely garulous creatures from our very own farmyard. To each was fastened a small bead anchor with a shot mooring line and a tiny ankle strap.

We set the call ducks in a shallow vee in front of the blind, facing the prevailing wind. The callers immediately got busy chewing at their anchors, heads under water. Suddenly the tame hens threw back their heads, pointed their bills at the sky, and quacked with strident enthusiasm.

Here came the wild ducks! The guest hunters from the city rose to their feet and blasted the air over the decoys. No luck. When they were done and busy reloading, my dad took his old Ithaca double and knocked down two of the wild ducks at extreme range. We retrieved them with the boat. It was the same the rest of that day and for many days after that.

Once a precocious call duck picked her ankle strap loose and escaped. We chased her with the rowboat all over "Roger's Lake" and the rest of Mink River. Finally, worn out from diving and escaping, she allowed herself to be captured and returned to the bag in the boat.

Yes, the ducks are gone, and with them went the pattering squads of ducklings, the duck pond by the well, and the brown call ducks that trumpeted Judas quacks to their wild relatives. They're gone along with the hacked-down trees, the drained swamps, the vanished butternuts, and thickets of chewy hazelnuts to join the Door County yesterdays.

I miss the ducks in the dooryards!

✠ ✠ ✠

## The Day of the Trident

A favorite sport of boys in the Fish Creek graded school in the 1920s was to spear the fish that swarmed up our village stream to spawn, both suckers and pike. The suckers were not highly prized, although a few thrifty families pickled and presumably ate them, but the northern pike were four or five feet long and regarded as trophies.

Spearing season could begin in winter if you could talk your old man out of a pitchfork with one or more of the tines broken. Then you took the busted tool to George Schuyler's blacksmith shop and he would straighten the bent and twisted rim, then put sharp points on the three tines and beat sharp barbs into them to hold your fish once speared.

With the melting of the snows, the creek swelled and became a torrent. The current chewed a lane into the ice of the harbor, sometimes reaching a couple hundred feet into the vast Green Bay ice field before the thawing weather overcame all the ice. Under the ice, the suckers and pike felt the call of the meltwater and headed upstream on their urgent business. We were ready.

En route to school in the morning and in the late evenings, we patrolled the creek banks, jabbing with our long-handled gigs at anything that moved. Suckers were often discarded on the banks, but big pike were carried in triumph down the main drag and across the school yard so that our success might "shine more brightly in a naughty world." I remember once when the smallest kid in the school marched in one morning with a pike longer than himself slung over his shoulder and dragging on the ground behind him.

Alas for our sports careers. They changed the law. Spearing was outlawed and game wardens even arrested some kids caught in the act. We countered by making our spear handles longer and stouter out of hardwood saplings. My spear had an ironwood handle. Then when a warden with a big flashlight came snooping up the bank, we used our spears as vaulting poles to cross the creek. We hid our fishy trophies in the willow thickets.

Then the wardens violated the code. They patrolled in pairs, one on each bank, and no one was safe!

Eventually, we grew up and stopped spearing altogether. Hook and line was more fun, and a catch carried more prestige. So passed the age of the boys who carried the trident on the squashy banks of old Fish Creek.

✠ ✠ ✠

## Colt

The old Colt cap-and-ball five-shot revolver was issued about 1838. It came down to our family through an in-law of my grandfather, once a cavalry colonel in George Custer's regiment.

The old pistol had a romantic name –Old Neverfail. It had seen the Black Hills and was fired at the Sioux many times, but there is no proof of showdowns, slain Indians, rustlers or claim jumpers. It just lay there gathering dust on a closet shelf.

Once in the last century, when my dad was a small boy, he charged it with black powder from an old shotgun shell, whittled an old .38 rifle slug until it would chamber, and used the heads of several Norwegian sulfur matches for caps. All set for a blast to wake the sleeping centuries, Daddy cast about for a suitable target. On the rear wall of a backyard three-holer (Chick Sales design) hung a rusted and battered washtub that was used to carry wood ashes to the privy. Dad leveled the old Colt at the tub. Snap went the hammer, Ziss-s-s went the match heads, boom went the Colt, down went Daddy flat on his kiester in his mother's day-lily bed, and down fell the target with a clang. Out from the privy precipitately issued Great Uncle Ted, who had been enjoying a tranquil session when all hell broke loose and the thin boards over his head blew apart in a clap of thunderous noise. Uncle Ted left the outhouse without "standing upon the order of his going." He was across the backyard and about halfway over the rail fence with his overalls down around his knees before he realized he was unharmed.

Another uncle borrowed the Colt from Granddad to go and try his luck mining gold at Sutter's Mill, California. But my forebears found no gold in the Dakotas or in California, and the only depredation credited to Old Neverfail was blowing off a rattlesnake's head in some remote and long-forgotten trail camp.

Certainly a fearsome, five-shot, .31 caliber Colt that had helped win the West deserved a better reputation than that provided by scaring the pants off a lame elder of our clan, and I give it a bloody history whenever I have the chance, now that it's mine.

The pistol now rests in our bank deposit box. Its spring is broken and unable to snap even a match head. Several screws are missing, and the stock is loose. I doubt if Old Neverfail can survive another century, and I must try to conjure up more colorful tales of its exploits for my grandchildren.

✤ ✤ ✤

## The Great Smelt Rush of 1939

Half a century ago in April, Fish Creek smelt dippers were arming themselves for the annual smelt run which had been getting heavier for each of the previous several years. Some of us made big wire-mesh scoops and others made four-foot-square dips on long poles. My father Merle and I bought a new seine, fifty feet long. We were not sure what the DNR (then called the Wisconsin Conservation Commission) limit was.

A light rain was falling in the dark, and the waters of Fish Creek ran warm into the harbor where the smelt waited under the last ice cakes of winter. We pulled our big seine across the mouth of the creek and got about two dozen smelt. That was poor. We wanted hundreds of pounds! We waited and watched. Upstream, Clarence Byers, a friend of mine, had pre-empted a good spot where the current ran between two boulders. He had a crew of little kids armed with wire basket dips on poles to help him, and they were beginning to stack up a pile of smelt!

We pulled our seine again. More smelt, perhaps fifty this time. The rain increased, then stopped. The creek waters grew warmer, and we tried again. As I dragged one end of the seine across the creek, I could feel the little fish bumping against my boots. The smelt were moving in!

When the seine was circled, I brought my end in to shore on a sandbar. The seine stopped cold, as though we had snagged a wrecked car. I dropped my end of the seine and walked backward lifting the lead-line with my toes. As I did I could feel solid fish oozing out of the seine. It was full of tons of smelt and two men couldn't pull it an inch. A third man helped us pull.

With two ends of the seine still several feet from shore, a great solid wad of smelt was being forced up onto the sand. We had less than a dozen fish boxes on the truck, and we dipped and filled six or seven boxes to the brim. Then we arranged the full boxes in a crude square and filled that space with more fish. Upstream, the kids with dippers were piling their heaps of smelt higher and higher.

This rustic bridge over Fish Creek was removed in about 1940, just about the time the Great Smelt Rush of 1939 took place. The photograph was taken in about 1919.

We made another haul and got somewhat less smelt. A
burly figure with a big flashlight waded out and followed the corks
of our seine to the end.

"How long is that damn net?" said Hallie Rowe, the game
warden. Our smelt season was over. Next day we went to the court
house and paid our fine. Warden and judge made sure we
understood the legal size limit of smelt gear, and gave us back our
seine with a stern warning.

Earlier that morning a local fish buyer had guessed our catch
at forty-two hundred pounds and offered us 1¢ a pound. We took it
– $42 for our night's work – a veritable fortune in 1939!

The kids who had dipped and dumped all night had an even
bigger pile, estimated later at seventy-five hundred pounds. I have no
idea how many smelt were taken that night, perhaps ten tons. The
Anderson Transportation Company of Ellison Bay hauled truckloads
of smelt to Chicago for two days.

The great smelt run of 1939 was over. We retired our illegal
seine and thereafter used it for seining minnows. As the April sun
came up, it reflected on silvery heaps of fish along the banks of Fish
Creek. The smelt never came that thick again.

✤ ✤ ✤

## By-Gone Bands

Door County is the home of many musical groups. Does
anyone remember Patzke's Nite Hawks, Bill Carlson's Band, Hogan's
Little German Band, Brault's Canadians, or The Red Raven Polka
Band? Or, even further back, the Duclon Family Band of Fish
Creek?

They played the first dance music I ever heard, following a
Men's Club venison stew dinner. In they came, Joe Duclon with his
fiddle, Charlie Duclon and his stand-up bass, Edith Duclon playing
her long sweeping chords on the piano, and someone else with
drums. Al Doolittle, chef for the supper, called the squares, and

around they went, the staid parents of us all. "Do-si-do, alleman left, and grand right and left, then swing when you meet!" We kids loved it. It was just noisy and rowdy enough to be great fun, and the old Gibraltar town hall rocked on its underpinnings.

Who else remembers some of the pick-up groups of bygone days? There must have been quite a few of them to serve the public dances at Koepsel's in Sister Bay, at Fernwood Gardens (then Elmer Gabler's), the Nightengale, and the Grasshopper in Sturgeon Bay, and at the Concord and La Mere's in Egg Harbor. Dance halls were a big part of our social life when we were in our teens.

We never tired of the music – *Tiger Rag, St. Louis Blues, Carolina Moon, Elmer's Tune, Me and my Shadow, Show me the Way to Go Home, Bye Bye Blackbird,* and *Goodnight Sweetheart* to end the evenings.

Girls wore 1920s-style clothes –short skirts with fringy hems, made popular by the Charleston. Boys wore bell-bottom trousers whose 22-inch cuffs were considered barely ample, white shirts (sometimes with French cuffs), four-in-hand ties, and short, short haircuts.

We danced tirelessly –the Lindy, the Shag, the Indiana Hop, and an occasional waltz (very clumsily). Dance styles were jerky before WW II and sometimes led to fractures and sprains.

The horns of the 1930s died out as the Big Band era waned, and the jazzy rhythms of the dance halls faded out. The generation who danced the Charleston and the Big Apple gave way to the loud beat of Rock, and the great bands died like the last dinosaurs.

✣ ✣ ✣

## The Photo Contract

My friend Lenny Reinhardt found an old camera in a farm house and got the farmer to sell it to him for almost nothing. As usual, he boasted of his acquisition as though it were a rare and valuable instrument worth a fortune, and from this ownership he expanded in all directions.

At a hardware store's closing-out sale, he found a large bin of photo chemicals and acquired them for a pittance. To make room for his developers, fixatives, and washes, he converted a small chicken coop in his father's yard, swept out all the chickens, feathers, straw, and droppings, and made some deep tanks for his chemicals out of three large clay tiles.

The tiles were upended and set in bases of concrete, one full of developer, one full of fixer, and one filled with water. The last had a spillover drain rigged so that we washed films by putting the garden hose in the washer and opening the valve.

I became fascinated with watching the images appear on the film and seeing the prints develop in the bath after a brief exposure on the antique enlarger. In a short time, Lenny tired of developing and printing the few pictures he was able to capture on film.

I was one of eleven seniors on the committee charged with collecting material for the 1932 Gibraltar High School annual and obtaining bids from a printer and photographer.

Lenny and I submitted a bid for the photo contract, and, for closure we took a group picture of the annual committee ranked closely together on the school's front steps. After we distributed all eleven prints to the committee members (they accepted this bribe with the dispatch of Mexican border guards), we were a shoo-in for the contract and we had all those kids at school to photograph.

We ran that ancient camera hot, and slaved long hours in the gurgling chicken coop to produce scores of prints. The toughest part was the individual photos of juniors and seniors. Our classmates were fussy. Some of the more affluent students ordered photos from real "pro" photo shops and then compared our prints with theirs. What made the "pro" shots preferable was the retouching, which eliminated wrinkles, shadows, and moles from faces, making each look as nearly as possible like all the rest. Lenny developed some skill at burning and dodging, or controlling the light from the enlarger to over-develop some areas and under-develop others. Night after night, we sat in that odoriferous chicken coop and dodged the mugs of 125 upperclassmen. Then, Lenny hit on a short cut. Most of our portrait shots were taken with one of his mother's bed sheets for a background. If taken in weak shadow in late afternoon, there was much less retouching needed. All the features came out slightly blurred and even gray. So Lenny posed our subjects before the bedsheet, aimed the old camera, and waited for the sun to get behind a cloud before making the exposure.

When the annual came out, the entire population of our high school looked leprous and moribund. Perfidious to the end, both Lenny and I sneaked off to a pro shop for our class photos!

\* \* \* \* \*

Staff for *The Rock* that year was: Herbert Uhlemann, editor in chief; Frank Eberlein, assistant editor; Arni Olson, athletics; Alice Jischke and Vivian Olsen, pictures; Richard Woerfel, business manager; Harvey Grasse, humor; Helen Wilson and Vivian Duclon, alumni; Caroline Becker, calendar; Duncan Thorp, senior class reporter; Rita Newberry, junior class reporter; Dorothy Casperson, sophomore class reporter; Evelyn Eckert, freshman class reporter; Bernice Kihl, art; Virginia Magnette, typist; Mr. O.E. Massey, faculty advisor.

✛ ✛ ✛

## Fire In The Park

Fires in the far west during the long, hot summer remind me of a raging fire in Peninsula Park in the 1920s, when I was a young boy.

No one knew how or where the fire started. The weather had been so dry that the earth was cracked, allowing oxygen to reach the smoldering and sinuous roots of pines and hemlocks. Fire traveled underground to erupt without warning at some distance from an area where flames had just been beaten back.

All available men living anywhere in the vicinity were mustered to fight the spreading blaze. The park had only primitive equipment – shovels, pails and a water tank drawn by a team of horses. My father and grandfather camped out to watch the park for flash fires.

As the threat to houses and buildings grew, we and many others hitched up our teams to plow and till a strip of cultivated earth around our houses and outbuildings to create a firebreak. We were all scared stiff. Our buildings, just across the highway from the park, were wooden and dry as tinder, and the firebreak seemed pitifully narrow.

The little crew of park hands and volunteers fought the flames day and night. Wives and mothers provided gallons of coffee and many sandwiches for the men, who shouldered thick blanket rolls and slept in the park to watch the sneaky flames that kept blazing up.

The fires went on for over a week and many acres were burned clean until a change in the weather finally brought a welcome rain. No homes were lost and no one was injured. The fire didn't burn to the bay, and the houses in the park were not threatened.

Today, sightseers who drive Highway 42 from Fish Creek to Ephraim will note the dense stands of planted pines, now fifty feet tall, which come toward the road in even rows. These reforestation plantings were done by Superintendent A.E. Doolittle and his park crew after the fires were out. One such plantation of pines stands behind Gibraltar School.

As a fringe benefit, when I was still a youngster, the old burned-over fields grew bumper crops of wild strawberries, raspberries, and blackberries. We picked gallons and gallons, converted them to sauces and jams, and ate them during the long winters, while the planted pines prospered and persevered on the scorched acres.

✤ ✤ ✤

# A Nice Sunday Drive

When we switched from horses to a Model T it was considered obligatory for Dad to take the family for a Sunday afternoon drive around the neighborhood. No one else in the family could drive the car but Dad.

One particular Sunday, Dad was sleeping off roast chicken and mashed potatoes and was completely oblivious to Mother's demands to be chauffeured.

"If you don't get up and take us for a drive," Mother threatened, "I'll drive myself, even if we smash that car to pieces."

"Humph," snorted Dad. The idea was obviously preposterous.

Mother's short fuse was burning low. She marched to the old touring car and climbed into the driver's seat. I climbed in beside her. Car driving was a fascinating process, and I had watched every move Dad made behind the wheel.

"How do you turn this thing on?" asked Mother. I was hugely flattered.

"Here," I said and clicked the switch on. "Now stamp on that button," I directed her. She started the engine and I let go of the choke to rev the throttle a time or two. Mother got the idea, and revved the engine time after time, expecting Dad to come bursting out of the house to prevent her suicidal attempt to drive. The dogs and cats disappeared and the cows looked uneasily at each other. But Dad continued to snore, and Mother grew grimly determined.

"How do you make it go?" she asked me. I was delighted to be appointed coach. It was almost as good as driving myself.

"Shove that pedal down all the way with your right foot, and take off the emergency brake," I advised her from my vast knowledge and seven-year-old observation.

Mother's lower lip protruded, a sure sign that her determination had peaked.

"Hang on," she cried. We lurched into motion with a clatter of gravel and a cloud of dust. Rounding the barn we met a hen mallard with a flock of ducklings, and drove through them at a smart clip. The ducks were able to fly short distances, and they all took wing, but they couldn't steer themselves, and ducks were bouncing off the fenders and windshield.

"I'm glad that's over," said Mother when we had run out of ducks. We drove gaily north on Highway 17 toward Ephraim.

"Why is everyone blinking their lights at us?" asked Mother. I looked around. That model Ford had three doors that opened against the wind and hence stayed that way, unless forcibly closed.

"I think they're telling us our doors are open," I said. "It takes up too much room on this road."

"Can you close them?" she asked.

"Of course I can," I said loftily, and I scrambled to the back and slammed all the gaping doors.

We got to the four corners on County A and managed to back and turn around. We got back to the farm in one piece. Mother was swollen with pride.

"Nothing much to driving," she snipped. "I'll do it every time I want to take a nice Sunday ride."

We went into the house. Dad was gone. "Down town," said Dan, the hired man. "He thought you'd likely be stuck somewhere."

"Oh he did, did he?" said Mother. "I'll just run down and pick him up!" So off we went again, this time with Dan and our collie dog in back and without hitting any ducks. Dan was wary of Mother's driving talents and kept one back door open and one foot on the running board, prepared to bail out if danger loomed.

When we got down to the village of Fish Creek, the main street was stuffed full of parked cars, the sidewalks were crammed with tourists, and a gang of local men, including Dad, were standing in front of Pelke's Pool Hall.

"How do you stop it," Mother cried, beseeching any authority, most likely Providence. She had forgotten how she managed to do it at the farm.

"I think you push that", I said, pointing. It wasn't the right pedal. Our car leaped past the curb like a rabbit and crunched into the back of a parked car, fortunately one belonging to one of my uncles. I cannot remember a Sunday drive for the next fifty years in which Mother drove and Dad didn't.

✤ ✤ ✤

## The Roads

More than anything else it was the building of roads that opened Door County. When I was two years old, our town had five miles of road surfaced with "macadam," a combination of oil, tar, and crushed stone. The edges of every field along the highways were lined with piles of loose limestone, patiently picked from the cultivated area and piled there, so this raw material was very convenient to the highway workers. Tom Carmody was a road builder from Egg Harbor, and his rock crushers ground our limestone walls to pebbles and powder and spread them on Highway 42 between Fish Creek and Ephraim.

The highways came abruptly. There were no roads at all before 1872, and after that even the main roads were often impassable. Hjalmar Holand's *History of Door County* records that the roads were often in wretched condition, with stumps left in them and deep mudholes like Plum Bottom, where the water was breast deep on the horses. But, by 1917, the county was building twenty miles of new macadam roads annually.

Plum Bottom was a melt-water lake in spring. Early drivers tried to pick their way through, but their cars drowned out and stalled, hub deep with their floorboards floating. On one trip my father and I left our Model T on the north side of the lake and hitched a ride in my uncle Al Kinsey's big 4-cylinder Dodge. When the Dodge gasped and died, Al put it in low gear and stepped on the starter. We were only a few feet from crossing and that old car's twelve-volt battery pulled us out of the water. We were across Plum Bottom!

Another hazard was a mud hole on Highway 57 between Little Sturgeon and Green Bay, where many cars bogged down and a neighboring farmer made a fine extra income towing them out with his powerful team of stout Belgian horses. One time, some motorists from northern Door were stranded there and called on the farmer, who in turn called his fourteen-year-old son to bring the team for a tow. The driver noted the boy seemed to be staggering with fatigue as he hooked the team to the front axle.

"What's the trouble, son?" he asked. "Are you sleepy?"

"You'd be sleepy too," answered the boy, "if you had to stay up all night and haul water to this mudhole!"

It seemed the owner of the tow team wasn't about to let his little gold mine dry up.

✛ ✛ ✛

## Oswald's Baby

Oswald was our high-school science teacher, and he was nothing if not literal-minded. Early in the new year, his missus presented him with a new-born baby, and Oswald decided to test his textbooks. He told his science class how it was.

"The books claim babies are born with only two fears," he said. "One, a fear of falling, and two, fear of a loud noise."

Accordingly Oswald put his child to the test. His missus was startled by a great thunderclap as Oswald fired a shot into the air just outside her window. She then saw him lift his newborn high into the air and drop it abruptly to the bed.

"The books were right!" he told us next day. "Babies are terrified by loud noises, and scream their little heads off if dropped more than two feet. So do their mothers, apparently."

Oswald's experiments with his baby ended there. But most of us in the class of 1932 remember that he could make science interesting like no other teacher we ever had, because he was so interested himself.

Rural Free Delivery (RFD) revolutionized life in many rural communities, including those in Door County. This photograph of a rural postman was taken in about 1912.

# Vlad W. Rousseff – Depression Artist
by
*Duncan Thorp*

Vlad W. (Walter) Rousseff came to Fish Creek in the early depression years of the 1930s with his wife and elderly parents. He was a Chicago artist, born in Bulgaria, and had studied art in Paris and Chicago.

He entered some of his oils in an artistic competition and was winner of the Frank G. Logan prize of a few thousand dollars. With this small stake he built a house on a high wooded hill on Gibraltar Road, now owned by the Pat Spielmans. When the house was finished Walt installed his family. His father would often walk to the village, check for mail and trudge home again. As a teenage neighbor boy, I often borrowed books from Walt's considerable library and thus encountered such dubious influences as Karl Marx, Ben Hecht and Anatole France.

Walt was a slightly pudgy, short man with a fringe of brown hair and a mustache. He painted exclusively in oil colors, working painstakingly in front of his big northlight window to get just the right tone. Sometimes he would scrape off the canvas and paint it over a dozen times. He admired such artists as Manet, Modigliani, and Gauguin.

Walt began teaching art classes in Fish Creek and attracted many students from Cottage Row. In those years, we often saw young princes and princesses of "millionaire's row" proudly displaying their splotches of spilled paint on smocks and shirts.

The grim depression years rolled on. Walt was appointed to the New Deal's Public Works Art Project (PWAP). His studio bulged with great canvasses of fishermen, lumbermen, farmers, and harvesters and striking scenes of Door County life, intended for use in such public buildings as the post offices then being built with Federal funds. Walt's canvasses were unmistakable. All men and women, whether hoers or lumberjacks, looked distinctively Middle-European, as though Door County were inhabited by bands of gypsies. Walt sometimes would use me as a model for a detail like a tensed muscle while pulling a boat up onto a beach.

Walt's first wife, Min, was also an artist and many persons who were regular readers of the popular kid's magazine *Child Life* will remember "Bertram and his Animal Friends," a series that ran for a long time, always handsomely illustrated by Min Rousseff, who thus had a steady income as an illustrator.

Mama Rousseff, a sweet-faced old lady of sturdy Bulgarian peasant stock, liked to baby me with big slabs of feshly baked bread and huge cups of coffee.

Walt had some off-beat friends, including political radicals, labor organizers, and left-wing writers. We spent hours discussing my reactions to one of his books by Anatole France. I'm sure he was too cautious by nature to ever have aligned himself with the Communist Party, but he liked to lurk around the fringes of the iconoclastic groups of society.

Times changed and Walt left us to become head of the art department of a private girl's school in Illinois. We heard later that the post office in Kaukauna, Wisconsin, displayed some of his murals. His smaller works were a regular feature at Dr. Welcker's Casino (now the Whistling Swan) in Fish Creek during his time here. But, though some of his paintings are in private homes, none of his originals were hung publicly in or near Door County – a significant loss to our community.

✠ ✠ ✠

# Ella Weborg's Travels
by
*Duncan Thorp*

When old Peter Weborg the cooper died, he left his three daughters his log cabin (with cooper's forge), forty acres of scrub land with ten acres cleared, and a handful of gold and silver coins wrapped in a calfskin and hidden under a loose board in the floor. The girls lived on in Peter's old cabin. Vida went to the Normal School and became a teacher; Joanna followed her, but Ella stayed at home. Vida traveled to remote places like Waco, Texas, where their brother Alfred lived.

The sisters divided the spoons and napkin rings and the little store of coins. Finally, Joanna went away to live in the big town of Chicago. "Ella Pete" stayed home, leaner and more querulous with the passing years. The cabin was four miles from Fish Creek, and Ella often walked to town for mail and groceries.

In 1912, before Ella knew the forty acres was to become part of the new Peninsula State Park, a man from the Mountain Land Company came and offered her $900 for her property. Ella shook her graying head. "Worth more," she said.

"To who?" asked the speculator. "Gotta clear it first."

"Rich people moving in," said Ella, "from Chicago. They like land with trees on. Funny folks in Chicago, my sister lives there."

But in the summer of 1913, Ella's two sisters signed over to her their share of the forty and Ella sold it to the land agent for $800 and put the money with the coins in the calfskin under the loose board. She didn't trust banks.

Ella had a way of looking frail and pitiful standing in heaped snow by the roadside and clutching her battered man's felt hat as icy winter gales swept over frozen Green Bay and assailed her thin stick figure. Any passing car would stop and offer a ride. She only walked in bad weather, and only until a car passed going her way.

She like to visit my Grandma and always arrived a few minutes before lunch. I remember she used to spread butter on her wedge of apple pie, a mannerism I felt was quite unique. Sometimes she stayed for supper and I watched to see if Grandma would serve apple pie, but it was cinnamon rolls with the tea, and Ella lavished lots of butter on her rolls. Then, when it was time for her to leave, Dad would go out and crank the Model T and drive her home through the drifting snow to her log cabin in the middle of the state park. Ella seemed to travel always accompanied by a blustery, cold wind, from the north. When I pointed this out to Dad, he said, "that's because she's a Norwegian, and they all carry the North Wind in their pocketbook." Ella packed a big purse of red and white calfskin with the hair on it, and I thought it bulged like the cheeks of Boreas, the Greek god of winds.

In the late 1920s, Ella got the wanderlust herself and decided to travel. Her sisters, she told Grandma, had been just everywhere, Texas and Chicago, and it was time she saw some of the country. So she climbed on the highway bus right in front of the general store one morning and said she was "agoing to look at the west coast."

In her calfskin bag she had her life savings and a printed business card given to her long ago by the land agent who had bought her forty for $800 and sold it six months later to the state of Wisconsin for $1100. The card read "Abel Hansen –Mountain Land Co., 541 Figueroa Street, Los Angeles, Calif."

Ella finally got to Los Angeles and Figueroa Street. She found Mr. Hansen, who, as she suspected, was a Dane, and Ella grew wary.

Ella said she was sick and tired of the cold winters and would like to "look at some nice proppity around southern California." Abel Hansen threw himself into gear. He drove Ella around in a Willys St. Clair Phaeton to Glendale, to Burbank, to San Pedro, to Balboa, to Mount Palomar, and even to Pasadena and San Diego.

At last Ella said he sure had a nice bunch of "proppity," but she didn't want to "plunk down $10,000 in hard cash until she had seen how things looked around San Francisco." Mr. Hansen drooled at the words "hard cash" and bought her a ticket to San Francisco.

In San Francisco, she was met by a Mr. McAdam, also from the Mountain Land Company, and he drove a nice Maxwell sedan. They looked at "proppity" in Monterey, Marin County, Alameda, Oakland, and Berkeley, but Ella at last shook her gray locks.

"Nope," she said firmly. "The more I see here, the better my cabin looks to me. I'm goin' home tomorrow." And she did.

# Places and Institutions

# The Peninsula Players
## Theatre-In-A-Garden
by
*Tom Conners*

The Peninsula Players came into being the night of July 25, 1935, when a small and friendly audience of Door County summer residents saw Noel Coward's play *Hay Fever*, with Caroline Fisher, Gertrude Needham, and Kevin O'Shea.

The original setting for the theatre was a natural amphitheater located between the Bonnie Brook Motel and a scenic area next to the creek in Fish Creek, a very picturesque locale for the new enterprise. That summer, four plays were produced by the Peninsula Players: *Hedda Gabler, Criminal at Large, The Second Man*, and *The Mad Hopes*, with an original musical revue closing the summer.

Talented and energetic producers Richard and Caroline Fisher were convinced that a permanent summer theatre in Door County could work, and they came back for a second summer which was even more successful.

In 1937, the Fishers purchased the Wildwood Boy's Camp and made it the permanent home of the Peninsula Players. Under the guidance of the Fisher family, the twenty-two-acre dell was to become one of the most beautiful summer theatres in the nation.

Mama Fisher ruled the company with an iron hand and could often be found in the kitchen preparing hearty meals. She also designed and sewed the costumes for all the plays. Papa, known as C.R. Fisher when he acted, was the mad genius of the company who was also our Mr. Fixit.

An exciting part of an evening's performance was to watch Caroline, who acted as hostess as patrons entered the seating area; she led them to their seats, often taking time to sit and chat for a moment before greeting the next group. One got the feeling that it was a special privilege to be part of the evening and the enjoyable experience that followed. With her beauty and dynamic personality,

Caroline was a natural actress. Her brother Richard directed, wrote reviews, and designed the surrounding gardens. Her sister Margo was a voluptuous beauty who acted when called upon, and she eventually made Hollywood her home.

For the first few years, the audience sat under the stars watching plays on the proscenium stage. More than a few of those early theatre-goers remember running for shelter or joining the cast at the foot of the stage during a sudden Door County thunderstorm, or sitting it out under sodden blankets during inclement weather. Mama Fisher and her excellent coffee were especially important on such nights.

In 1946, the company finally acquired a huge canvas that was slung out over the audience with the help of local shipbuilders and riggers. Unfortunately, in strong winds, it had a tendency to flap loudly unless a dozen or more people clung to its edges, and windy nights often found apprentices, audience members, and even actors in makeup hanging onto the canvas for dear life.

Heavy rains beat loudly on the canvas, forcing the cast to project their voices much more strongly than the average actor ever does, and in really bad storms, they would halt the production and wait for the storm to pass, then continue as though nothing had happened. The audiences loved it.

Caroline had long envisioned a permanent pavilion which would retain the atmosphere and beauty of the Theatre-In-A-Garden, but which would also provide more secure protection. In 1957, her dream became a reality, and the season opened under the new laminated oak structure designed by Neenah architect Frank Shattuck. (Caroline later married Basil Rathbone's son to become Mrs. Rodion Rathbone.)

The new shell is acoustically excellent, with no posts or other obstructions. It replaced the canvas top, and was built directly onto the original stage house of the theatre. Much attention was devoted to planting colorful beds of flowers and shrubs throughout the theatre grounds, and different parts of the grounds are connected by stone pathways that meander among the stately old trees. Wandering through the gardens while chatting with friends during the intermissions thus became part of the thrill of the evening and helps to maintain the original feeling of Theatre-In-A-Garden.

But, nothing can survive without change, and, after more than twenty-five years of running the company, Caroline and Richard Fisher decided for both business and personal reasons to sell the theatre. In 1961 it was purchased by a New York City attorney who engaged James B. McKenzie as producer. McKenzie purchased the theatre in 1978. Since 1966, the theatre has been operated by the Peninsula Players Theatre Foundation, Inc., a small group of Door County residents and professional theatre people who have undertaken to maintain the legacy of living theatre in Door County.

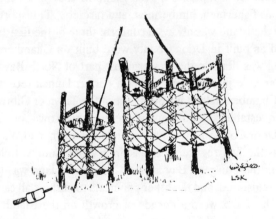

# Chambers Island
by
*Joel Blahnik*

Through centuries of Indian and French occupation, Chambers Island was known as a place of plenty and hospitality. Ceded by France to England in the Treaty of Paris of 1763, and then by England to the United States in the Treaty of 1783, Chambers Island acquired its present name in 1816 when Colonel John Miller named it for one his officers, Captain Talbot Chambers. This same expedition named Washington Island after George Washington.

Chambers Island was occupied by various native American groups as they were pressed westward by European settlement in the East. They left burial mounds on the island that were studied in the middle 1850s. Aside from French explorers and missionaries who passed through the area in the mid-17th century, the first Europeans who came to Chambers Island were a band of hardy souls from the British Isles who entered Wisconsin via the northern Great Lakes. They established a foothold on the island in 1847 and eked out an existence as fishermen, lumbermen, and farmers. Transportation to and from the island was always a concern; three of the first five ships registered as built in Door County were built on Chambers Island. Launching was done in the westernmost part of North Bay where a deep water hole just offshore makes a perfect launch receptacle.

Chambers Island is now a part of the Town of Gibraltar, but it was an established community before the Town of Gibraltar existed. Door County settlement began in the north, and Washington Island was the first registered township in Door County, followed by Otumba in the Sturgeon Bay area. Chambers Island was the third township registered, and the other peninsula townships all came later.

The 1860s were a decade of growth on the island. A post office was established for a community of 250 people with no fewer than three Justices of the Peace. Accounts by visitors to the island reflect a wonderful vitality and spirit among the islanders. Visiting preachers were paid with chickens, corn, and fish products.

In 1867, Lewis Williams sold a 40-acre tract on which he had a sawmill to the U.S. Government as a future sight for a lighthouse. The price was $250. In May of the following year, construction began on the Chambers Island Lighthouse, and it was completed by mid-September. Its sister, Eagle Lighthouse in Peninsula State Park, was constructed in the same year. The only difference between these two structures is that the 40-foot tower of Eagle Lighthouse is square, while the Chambers Lighthouse is octagonal. Both were built with Cream City brick manufactured in Milwaukee. The government lighthouse inspector who came through to inspect and accept the building said "it was of the finest construction of any lighthouse he had inspected in Lake Michigan." The light was lit for the first time on October 1, 1868, and Lewis Williams was appointed the first keeper, at an annual salary of $420.

The Williams name was extremely widespread on the island. Lewis Williams had eleven children, so there were thirteen people named Williams living in the lighthouse, and there were eight other Williams families living along the western shore of the island. Homer Williams, one of Lewis' sons, was a commercial fisherman. He had a dock on the south end of Chambers Island in Homer Bay, which is named after him. Homer is credited with supplying Lake Mackaysee, the larger of the two inland lakes on Chambers Island, with its sturgeon. Members of the Williams family still reside in the Upper Peninsula of Michigan as well as on Mackinaw Island.

As communities developed on the peninsula, some families moved off Chambers Island, though other families kept arriving from Britain on their way to more permanent homes. The O'Brien and Cunningham families were among them. These families lived principally by harvesting trees, and stands of red oak, maple, and white pine were of premium quality. Leathem Smith from Sturgeon Bay owned a sizeable part of the island at this time, and he harvested over 20 million board feet of white pine. In the middle 1890s there was a general exodus from the island, for life on the mainland seemed more promising. But, in 1898 came the most unique man and family in Chambers Island history −the Fred A. Dennett family.

After Leathem Smith had harvested the white pine, Dennett purchased most of the island.  By 1898 he owned all 2,800 acres except for the 56-acre lighthouse tract.  Dennett was president of the Wisconsin Chair Company of Sheboygan and was interested in the island's hardwoods for his business, but he also had a dream of an island utopia.  He erected a series of beautiful buildings on the north shore of 540-acre Lake Mackaysee, which stands six to eight feet above the waters of Green Bay which surround Chambers Island, and has two islands in it.  The lodge, the largest of Dennett's buildings, had a gorgeous view of Lake Mackaysee and its islands.

Dennett employed a large crew of men during the warm-weather months.  From 1904 until 1916, his caretaker was Edwin Casperson, who later established the Casperson funeral home in Sister Bay.  Casperson's daughter, Mildred Johnson, was born on the island and lived there until she was eight years old.  She now lives in Sister Bay.   She has a wonderful store of memories and photographs from that era and has told me a great deal about the Island.  The caretaker's home, now called the "farm house," still stands and was recently remodeled.

Dennett was a man of considerable means, and he had many celebrity friends who visited him on the island.  His tenure was a time of wonderful elegance.

Dennett was a great lover of Shakespeare; the walls of the lodge dining room were decorated with murals of Shakespeare's dramas.  His passenger launch was named *As You Like It*, though his freight vessel, a forty-foot craft designed for gill-net fishing, was named The *Islander*.  The lodge was called *Woodmancote*, and the following lines are inscribed on one of its walls:

> And this our life,
> Exempt from public haunts
> Finds tongues in trees,
> Books in running brooks
> Sermons in stones and good in everything.
>                         Shakespeare

Dennett tried raising 8,000 White Pecan ducks on Lake Mackaysee, which was assumed to be a good natural duck habitat, but the venture did not succeed. The next year he tried raising other poultry, but that also proved not to be profitable. With Dennett's death in 1922 the property passed to his daughter; she ran an elegant Chambers Island Camp for Girls from 1922 to 1926. However, upkeep was costly, and the Dennett family sold the island to the Chambers Island Land Company, a Chicago investment firm. They set up the Chambers Island Association, comprised of the island property owners, which still exists today.

The Chambers Island Land Company proposed to develop the Dennett estate into a sophisticated and very exclusive community. The restrictions set up by this organization filled a 40-page book and are absolutely bizarre by today's standards. The idea was to provide summer homes on the island with mother and family vacationing there, while father would fly up on Friday and return back to Chicago on Sunday. Consequently, they laid out an airstrip on the island, but they built only three structures during their three-year tenure.

In 1927 a beautiful log home was erected by the late Sam Erickson of Sister Bay for a Mr. Drake who was president of the Union Steel Tank Company in Chicago and whose family was connected with the Drake Hotel in Chicago. This building still stands as a part of the Holy Name Retreat House which is in operation during the summer. Mr. Drake's caretaker was Ernie Steinseifer, now of Detroit, Michigan, who has been a wonderful source of information about Chambers Island at that time.

In 1928, the present Thenell cottage became the second building put up by the Chambers Island Land Company. It was built on the northwest shore by Sam Erickson for the Nelson family, who owned laundries in the Chicago area. This building still stands as an elegant masterpiece of that era. In 1929, the Kates cottage was erected just north of the Nelson cottage near the north tip of the island, but it was destroyed in the great fire of October 1947, and all that is left is the chimney and foundation.

The Chambers Island Land Company was thought by many people to have been a syndicate of questionable merit backed by Samuel Insul, the famous financier of the 1920s  To clarify this matter, I quote from a letter to me dated August 28, 1985 from Robert S. Lynch, of Loves Park, Illinois:

> Samuel Insul Jr., who recently passed away, lived in Geneva, Illinois. He had an office in the Loop of Chicago and was also in the insurance business. I called him one morning (he was very cordial) and asked if [we could] . . . discuss the history of Chambers Island. His answer was:
> "I never set foot on Chambers Island and my father never set foot on Chambers Island. I have heard this rumor [of Insul's involvement] from many people. Where the rumor came from was in fact that a man named Thompson, who I befriended when I was in the electric railroad business," (Insul controlled the Chicago North Shore and the Chicago and South Bend urban lines) "approached me on buying a 5 percent interest for a recreational development to be put up on Chambers Island in the late twenties. He also approached the son of then Vice-President Dawes who likewise invested in this development. Using our names as investors he solicited funds in that Dawes and Insul (using only last names) were heavily investing in this project. That is the only connection that the family of Insul had with Chambers Island.
> "Many years have elapsed since the name of Insul was in prominence. For those who do not recall, Mr. Samuel Insul Sr. was the controller of the majority of electric power in the United States (36 of the then 48 states) with the ownership of a very small percentage of stock. The Commonwealth Edison Building (which is now the Kemper Building) in Chicago was built under his direction as president of the Commonwealth Edison and the Chicago Civic Opera was sponsored by Mr. Insul. (He was an early partner with Thomas Edison). Insul later fell victim of the Depression when so many, many leading industrial magnates lost out."

Insul exiled himself to Greece to escape his financial failures, and was later tried for "financial crimes." He returned to America a broken man. The Chambers Island Land Company folded, for it had no real financial resources, and, by 1932, everything on the island except the lighthouse was vacated.

There was a great deal of vandalism on the island during the 1930s and 1940s. The Dennett buildings were gutted, and by the end of World War II, only the naked walls of Woodmancote were left. The Dennett buildings burned when a sudden wind blew sparks from a campfire into dry grass and fanned the fire which then engulfed them. That fire burned all the way to the shore, destroying the Kates cottage but missing the one owned by the Nelsons. The scarred oak trees near where the old lodge stood are present-day reminders of that destructive fire.

Many people believed that Insul had a hotel on the island, and the old Dennett lodge was used as a residence for prospective buyers during the years of 1927-29 when the Chambers Island Land Company was hosting prospective investors. However, to my knowledge, the lodge was never operated as a commercial hotel and served only as a guest house.

There was not much activity on the island during the 1940s except a few logging operations. The deer herd multiplied from about 200 to more than 600, and starvation was a real threat. In 1947 the Wisconsin Conservation Department (forerunner of the Department of Natural Resources) harvested 429 deer, donating them to charity, and the island herd was brought back into balance. During the 1940s there was no hunting season on the island and poaching activities made little dent in that large herd. As of October 1989, there are no deer on the island, probably for the first time in its history.

During the ups and downs of the island's history, only the lighthouse has remained constant, focusing its vigil on water safety and traffic rather than the exploits of land barons.

The late 1940s saw new investment on Chambers Island. Much of the property was bought for delinquent taxes at prices averaging a dollar an acre. Considerable acreage was purchased by the Algoma Lumber Company with Reinhard Krause as its director. Commercial logging operations now take place there about once every fifteen years, with millions of board feet of red oak being harvested.

Another purchaser of land was George Baudhuin of Sturgeon Bay. His purchase took in the old Drake cottage, the old Nelson cottage, and the farm house, in addition to other acreage on the north section of the island. However, these buildings were too much to maintain, and in 1951 he and his wife donated about 60 acres, including the Drake cottage and the farm house, to the Catholic Diocese of Green Bay for the purpose of establishing a retreat house. It was a perfect setting and the donation was met with great enthusiasm. Fr. John Mueller was the first Retreat Director, and the retreat program has grown significantly during the ensuing years.

From 1951 to 1957 the old Drake home and the farm house were used to house religious retreats for laymen of the diocese, and in 1957 a beautiful chapel was annexed to the Drake home. Much of the timber for its construction was sawed at the Matt Theis sawmill on the island, and at the active age of 90, Matt Theis still maintains that sawmill. I consider him the "governor" of the island.

In 1961 a dormitory wing was added, and the retreat can now house sixty-eight people comfortably. The Retreat House serves as a wonderful guiding spirit for present day islanders who exist today as a community of people who work together in pioneering their summer residences on the island without public utilities, much as their island predecessors did 140 years ago.

The retreat has special programs for men, women, younger and senior couples, singles, widowed, etc. and is open to people of all denominations, though its credo is based upon the Roman Catholic faith. Retreats run from mid-May to mid-September and are made possible by a network of volunteers who lend their talents as skilled craftsmen and/or financial backers and who believe in the unique values of the program. Since 1976, I have been captain of the *Quo Vadis*, the 52-foot vessel that transports passengers to and from the island. As of the end of the 1989 season, I had logged more than 1,600 crossings between Fish Creek and Chambers Island.

In the bicentennial year of 1976, my family and I became caretakers of the Chambers Island Lighthouse Park. The lighthouse was last manned in 1955 when the light was automated. The building was vacant, and the grounds were being swallowed by wild sumac and poplar trees. A couple of the buildings had been removed to other parts of the island and the lighthouse stood hollow. In cooperation with the Gibraltar Town Board and its chairperson Harvey Malzahn Jr., the 40-acre tract (what happened to the other 16 acres?) was deeded by the Federal Government to the town as a day park. We immediately registered the building on the National Registry for Historical Buildings.

There was a real need for this day park because all other property on the island is privately owned, and visitors were not especially welcome. Part of this situation was a carryover from the 1940s and 1950s when thievery was commonplace, and a good deal of resentment had built up on both sides. Establishing a public park on the lighthouse property was a perfect solution. Now the island can host visitors on the lighthouse property and on the seven miles of town roads, and the 1980s has witnessed a friendly welcome for island guests, whether they be boaters, retreat guests, or island families.

Each summer the lighthouse is open daily, with certain exceptions for supply runs and mainland commitments. Guided tours of the building include an ascent to the top of the tower. The structure now has a new roof and has had an interior face-lift. It stands tall and proud in great shape more than 120 years after it was built, and with care it will stand for another 120.

My family and I love the island and its history. A history room in the building presents the island story from different standpoints. I hope to write a full-length history of the island, and I have researched almost a century of the daily logs kept by the lighthouse keepers. I would welcome any information about the island, especially old photos which could be copied, though we already have more than 300 photos from the 1890s onward, and I am grateful to all the people who have supplied me with materials over the past twenty years.

The island's essence beckons and nurtures its visitors. One only needs to set foot on the island, listen, and take in its energies for a very special touching to take place. In the words of one of my students, "When the Earth was created, certainly God started here on Chambers Island." It does possess that presence of Eden. Even the

friendly ghost at the lighthouse who takes care of the premises during
the winter is a very special spirit going back to the Native Americans
before us. No one really can own any of the island, for it has a spirit
that cannot be captured. Its naturalness, innate beauty and power are
beyond taming. The families who have summer cottages there can
attest that the island is a sanctuary, a beautiful garden that beckons
us to live from our innermost beings. We are only stewards in time.
It is our wish to share that unique spirit with our friends.

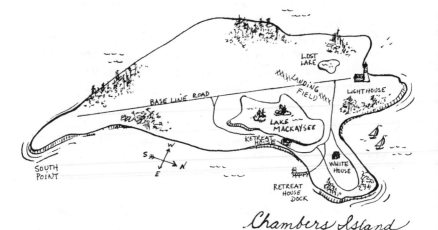

Chambers Island

# How We Were Almost Killed By An Icelandic Cod, And Other Tales of The Heritage Ensemble
by
*Gerald Pelrine*

"What happened at the *end* of the play?" the woman demanded. Clad head to toe in yellow rain gear, she stood at the edge of our stage, streams of water pouring from the brim of her rubber hat. A rain of nearly biblical proportions was falling, and the wind was bending ancient pines almost to splitting, as a creek formed in the center aisle of the theatre. "Did they get married or not?" she cried. Patrons cowered beneath blankets and umbrellas, as a few lucky ones fumbled with the gizmos on their inflatable rafts. Actors dashed to cover sound equipment while trying to avoid being electrocuted. In the woods, squirrels were donning snorkels, skunk families jumped into tiny boats with outboard motors, and raccoons stretched sideways from trees like flags on flagpoles.

In a storm like that, any sensible person would have been worried about personal safety, but no Wisconsin thunderstorm was going to prevent this particular Heritage Ensemble fan from knowing what happened at the end of that play.

As the storm approached on that August evening in 1984, we had struggled toward the climax of *Flaxen*, a musical comedy based on a short story by Wisconsin author Hamlin Garland, and we had hoped to reach its conclusion before the storm broke. If you joined us that season, you may recall that it is a tale of two Norwegian bachelor farmer buddies engaged in the unlikely activity of raising as their daughter a young girl whom they had rescued from a neighboring farmhouse after her parents had frozen to death. Now, near the play's climax, one of the farmers was hoping to marry her. However, on this particular night the marital fate of young Flaxen seemed doomed to remain unresolved, and our brave patron demanded to know the outcome. At last cast member Tim McNurlen took pity on her. "No," he explained, "she didn't mary Bert at first, because she fell in love with a guy at school and married him, but he

later died in a bizarre skating accident, and I think she marries Bert
eventually, but in a different story." Satisfied, the lady in yellow
turned and trudged off into the gale.

To me, this event illustrates the deep devotion our fans have
shown the troupe over the years. It is but one story of many that
come to mind of our summer days in Fish Creek. Another that I
recall is embarrassing to me personally. One night during the run of
the same production of *Flaxen*, I was so overcome by fits of laughter
that the performance was ruined. I'm so sick of hearing that story
that I can't even tell you the details. Nonetheless, each year, I hear
it told to newcomers to the cast, while I sit there with a pain gnawing
at my stomach. I am saddened that alleged friends would shamelessly
exaggerate to the point that the story no longer even resembles what
actually happened. Before they tell it to you, let me.

Just before going on stage one night, I said to Fred Heide
that I couldn't believe he had studied so hard at Penn State, become
a psychologist who published in *Psychology Today*, and then travelled
2600 miles at his own personal expense to portray one of the
Norwegian farmer buddies. We had a laugh about it just as the
lights were going down, and then walked onstage to our places. Well,
the lights came up and there he stood: Dr. Frederick J. Heide,
Ph.D., wearing bib overalls, a tattered flannel shirt, a straw hat which
had been smashed in a trunk for ten months, oval granny glasses, and
with a corn cob pipe hanging out of his mouth. Even he seemed a bit
doubtful just at that moment, and I became overwhelmed with silly
laughter and could not control myself throughout that evening's
performance. I regret to say that seated among the capacity crowd
that evening was Peninsula State Park Superintendent Tom
Blackwood, apparently in the company of DNR dignitaries from
Madison who reportedly were dismayed by the proceedings. I regret
the whole unfortunate incident, but I more strongly regret that I
apparently will be hearing about it for the rest of my life.

*Flaxen* was unique for us in that it is a play with continuous
characters throughout. Most of our shows have a revue format of
songs and stories ranging over a topic in American folklore, such as

whaling as a metaphor of the *Great Quest of Life*; the Civil War as a tale of the *Reuniting of Great Psychic Forces*;  or the founding of Milwaukee as the *Tale of Three Overweight Guys Who Occasionally Rammed Each Other's Bridges With Barges Out Of Spite.*

Not all performances of our summer troupe are presented in Fish Creek.  Throughout the 1970s and 1980s, our merry band regularly packed our banjos, hats and props and performed all over the countryside, even touring to such distant spots as Marinette and Green Bay.  In 1983, a true show-business disaster occurred when we hit the road to Minneapolis to perform at the American Theater Association's national convention, at which the keynote speech was to be given by Burt Reynolds.  Utterly convinced that we would be "discovered" and swamped by lucrative offers of bookings across the country, we cheerfully set of one steamy August morning for the long ride across northern Wisconsin on highway 29.  The day grew blistering hot, but we pushed forward thinking of the glory to come.

Our first intimation of trouble came as soon as we arrived and read the description of our show in the program:

*Research and Creation of a Folk-Historical*
*Documentary Theatrical Presentation: An Exploration*

We were horrified by this hopelessly tedious title;  we had hoped to see something like:

*A Wonderful Performance of a Well-Rehearsed*
*Show On a Subject You'll Love!*

but it was too late.  Of the thousands of people at the convention, our audience consisted of but one patron.  As if that wasn't bad enough, the UW-Madison Children's Theatre was performing in the room adjoining ours, and their play required the entrance of a four-foot-high, fifteen-foot-long, giant worm about ten minutes into their show.  Therefore, instead of beginning on time, we cooled our heels while three actors inside an enormous slug waited for their cue to enter, which was hard to hear because of the peals of laughter and room-shaking applause coming from thc huge crowd next door. *Their* program description must have been something like

*A Wonderful Performance of a . . . .*

An annual touring event has been our August trek to Old World Wisconsin in Eagle. In 1987, the trip resulted in a major fiasco which found both Fred Heide and Fred Alley the closest they've so far come to wearing gossamer wings and playing folk songs on harps. The day before the company was to travel, they had performed at a birthday party near Sister Bay. This was not so strange, I suppose, except that the party was for a sheep. Fred and Fred stood on the back of a flatbed truck at Ek Tradet and sang out toward a field where a number of sheep were grazing, the guest of honor presumably among them. As Doc (Fred Heide) tells it, about halfway through this performance, the critters got up and sauntered off. That evening the two Freds played a post-Ensemble club date at the Blue Iris in Egg Harbor, and, as is usual on such occasions, they were up until 3 AM packing guitars, wrapping up cords, and carrying on engrossing late-night consultations with kindred folk-music enthusiasts.

The next morning, they set off for Eagle, exhausted, with less than four hours sleep. The trip takes over four hours, one way, and, once the company arrives, two hours of setup follow. Then both shows are performed, and all the equipment gets stowed for the long drive back to Fish Creek. This experience has always wiped us out under the best of circumstances, but given the sad condition our Freds were in at the start of the day, the stage was set, as they say, for disaster.

The fellows can't remember exactly what they both ordered at the restaurant on the way home. It may have been some sort of deep-fried icelandic cod burger, or it may have had something to do with chicken. One thing is certain, however; that thickly sliced food substance, fried to extinction and all but obliterated under great gobs of mysterious sauce, made our boys as sick as they have ever been. For days they only got worse. According to Doc (Fred), Young Fred was so ill during one performance that he "looked like he was ready to be embalmed, or perhaps already had been," propped there against his stool. That night, at 2 AM, as Young Fred lay sick in his cabin, he heard a car drive up. For what seemed an eternity, no further sound was heard, but then the screen door slowly whined open. In a touching moment somewhat reminiscent of Custer's troopers at Little Big Horn, one Fred, clutching his stomach with one hand, reached the other toward his fellow Fred, who lay sick upon his bed, unable to move. "Here," he said, "drink half this can of Point Beer, and I guarantee you will feel better." And it worked.

Ghost stories are a stock in trade in any resident theatre company, and ours is no exception. During the 1970s, members of the troupe lived in the Victor Welcker mansion, high on the bluff overlooking Fish Creek. Most of the troupe was dancing one night at a local nightclub called the Rock, when one member of the company who had stayed home alone in the mansion burst in with a strange tale. Fred Heide tells the story:

> You remember the Rock; it was the place that eventually became Charlie's. Kelly was this very tall, perfectly down-to-earth guy who was in the Ensemble that year. Well, he showed up at the Rock while we were dancing and came right out on the dance floor, still wearing his pajamas. He had heard something like chains dragging across the floor of the attic of the Welcker mansion – chains and thumping. He was as white as a sheet.
>
> I found this interesting because it had always seemed to me that there was something unusual about the Welcker place. A sign just above the door – I don't know if it's still there or not – said "You're Welcome Here If Your Thoughts Are Kind; Leave Horror Tales To A Weaker Mind." Poor Kelly was scared to death, but nothing ever came of it.
>
> This incident scared us all. One night Steve Weitz awoke to the feel of a hand over his face; he was horrified, turned on the light, but no one was there.

✣ ✣ ✣

To trace the history of the Heritage Ensemble, one must look back through the mists of time to dust-bowl Kansas in the 1930s and acknowledge at least a couple of interesting coincidences that occurred along the way. Robert Gard, who graduated from the University of Kansas in the 1930s, went off to do graduate work at Cornell and worked there with a visionary theatre professor who preached something unusual: America should create its own regional drama (at that time our popular drama consisted mainly of musicals and British imports). Gard was inspired by this notion, and when World War II ended, he was asked by the UW Department of Agriculture to come to Wisconsin and create his own vision of Regional Arts. The department recently had created the first-ever position of Artist-In-Residence for painter John Stuart Curry, who, along with Grant Wood and Thomas Hart Benton, were known as Regionalists. It was to be Gard's responsibility to collect folklore, create drama, and oversee creative writing projects.

For the next fifteen years, Gard wrote books, created a popular radio show, and had one of the very first Wisconsin Public Television programs, featuring storytelling and folk singing. He also operated an important predecessor to the Heritage Ensemble troupe called the Wisconsin Idea Theater, which produced original plays drawn from Wisconsin lore. In 1960, the first important coincidence occurred. The Wisconsin County Fair Association contacted Gard with a request for a show about Wisconsin lore to be performed at county fairs; at precisely the same time, our director David Peterson, then a high-school teacher, contacted Gard about a musical he had written based on one of Gard's short stories. One thing led to another, and before long, Dave's troupe was tramping to county fairs all over the state. By 1965, having spent a year in New York observing the Broadway scene, Dave accepted a permanent position at the University of Wisconsin, having established himself as a brilliant interpreter of Gard's writing.

Soon thereafter, Dave began work on a show that might be described as the missing link between Gard's earlier work and what was to be the Heritage Ensemble format for many years. Called

*Badger Ballads*, it was inspired by a show Dave had seen off-Broadway in New York called *In White America*, which dealt with black history. The format alternated historical figures making speeches, dramatic scenes involving small groups of people, and songs that tied the whole thing together. *Badger Ballads* made the rounds of county fairs in 1965 and 1966, also performing one-night stands in schools and community halls.

At this point, another fortuitous coincidence occurred. Dave had a troupe of players travelling the state performing one of the musicals he had written. Camping at Peninsula State Park with his wife Joan, Dave discovered a pretty amphitheater deep in the woods that didn't seem to get much use except for an occasional natural history program. Our future home had been discovered.

Mrs. Hazel Buchbinder was a longtime summer resident of Fish Creek with an active interest in the arts. She had been a strong supporter of the Peninsula Players since its inception and had also supported the Peninsula Arts Association, which created the Peninsula Music Festival. She was acquainted with Carl Sandburg, the poet, and had worked with him assembling his wonderful collection of folk songs, *American Songbag*. Mrs. Buchbinder had been a composer in the 1920s and apparently enjoyed catalyzing interactions between artists. For example, at a party held at the Buchbinder's Chicago residence many years ago, Sandburg became acquainted with Andres Segovia, the great classical guitarist. By the end of the evening, they had become pals enough to exchange pledges of lessons for one another; in return for guitar lessons from Segovia, Sandburg was to provide lessons in writing poetry.

Just south of Fish Creek at a summer home called Roadstead, Mrs. Buchbinder was hosting a conference on regional theatre. The Guthrie Theater of Minneapolis was represented, and Robert Gard was there as well. Somehow word got out that Dave's show *Ice Cream 7 Times A Day*, about the Ringling Brothers was out and about, and the conference promptly arranged for Dave's company to give a Monday-night performance in Fish Creek on the Peninsula Players' stage. At a reception following the performance, Dave

Peterson met Mrs. Buchbinder and subsequently became a Roadstead Fellow, one of the group of artist-composers she invited to live and work at Roadstead. With her support, Dave travelled all around the Great Lakes and wrote *Song of the Inland Seas*, which would become one of the most popular Heritage Ensemble shows. At about this time, Dave Peterson met Tom Birmingham, the managing director of the Peninsula Players and then superintendent of the Gibraltar area schools, and many other Door County people interested in the arts.

Having written *Song of the Inland Seas*, having discovered the amphitheater in the park, and having developed a personal connection with Fish Creek, it was only a matter of time before Madison-based Professor Peterson would establish his folksinging-storytelling troupe at Peninsula State Park. The opportunity came in January 1970. A group of students at UW-Green Bay conceived a project in which they would develop a performance piece to include the type of material that Dave had been creating for years. The project was to be conducted under the auspices of the UWGB Office of Lectures and Performances, run by Tom Birmingham. Tom brought Dave and the students together, and they became the first troupe to perform *Song of the Inland Seas*. Through an agreement with the Wisconsin Department of Natural Resources, they did the show for two weeks that summer at Peninsula State Park, and in 1971 the Heritage Ensemble was established as a resident summer theatre company, performing from the 4th of July through Labor Day.

In the years since, the group has developed significantly, especially in the late 1980s. The troupe of college students singing folk songs in the park during their summer vacations has become a much more professional company performing in the beautiful park amphitheater. Fred Heide, a member of the troupe since 1973 and company manager since 1978, has authored shows of his own, performed on alternate nights with Dave Peterson's shows since 1984, and the two have guided the company to become the third largest summer theater company in Wisconsin.

During his years at the University of Wisconsin, Dave Paterson has created innumerable shows that have toured the state, the region, and even around the world.  In 1985, The *Milwaukee Journal* called him "Wisconsin's musical historian".  Ensemble shows are now routinely recorded in multi-track Dolby stereo for distribution, and Wisconsin Public Television has broadcast several University of Wisconsin Heritage Ensemble works.

As we look ahead, we see new shows, more television projects, and national tours on the horizon.  In future, the Heritage Ensemble at Peninsula State Park will be known as the American Folklore Theatre, but we remain located in and identified with our beautiful summer home in Fish Creek.

# The Peninsula Players
by
*Tom Birmingham*

It is said that theatre in its simplest terms is two planks and a passion. The two planks are easy to come by; the passion is rare. Yet it was the passion of the Fisher family that accounts for the existence of a professional theatre company in Fish Creek.

Charles R. (Papa) Fisher was a marine design engineer who made frequent business trips to the Sturgeon Bay shipyards. It is said that one of his inventions was an improved dredge capable of quickly removing sand and silt from canals. It is further reported that much of the debris removed from waterways in northeastern Wisconsin was transported to Chicago to become the fill for the Outer Drive along Lake Michigan. On occasion, C.R. would bring his family from Michigan, and after a day of business in Sturgeon Bay, they would travel north to vacation at the Bonnie Brook, which was a small house at the time. It is now the Bonnie Brook Motel.

Richard Wylie Fisher, the oldest of the three Fisher children, was a student at Northwestern University. His talent for writing scripts and directing was recognized at Northwestern, and at other midwestern colleges. He viewed the natural terrain in the back yard of the Bonnie Brook as a natural amphitheater for plays.

Caroline Fisher, the second oldest child, was not an accomplished actress. In fact, early accounts of her association with the Players referred to her as a business manager. However, Richard had great affection for his sister, and perhaps he saw some talent, for he cast her in various roles. She became the Players' first leading lady. Her business sense combined with dogged determination and a personal flamboyancy mesmerized people. She could get practically anything for the theatre –usually at no cost –all the way from planks for a stage, to day-old baked goods to feed the company, to a monkey procured from the primate lab at UW-Madison for *Inherit the Wind*.

The company never knew if the monkey would be a part of the show each evening. Surreptitiously it would get out of its cage each day and sit among the tree tops, defying recapture. Yet, when the pre-show music started, and in response to Caroline's coaxing and commands, the monkey would scurry down and take its place backstage. Caroline had a way with animals.

Caroline's flamboyancy was not pretentiousness. On light ticket sale days, she could often be seen standing at the entrance of the bookmobile parked in front of Schreiber's store on Fish Creek's Main Street, hawking tickets. Dressed in a coat that looked more like a bathrobe, with her hair put up under a bandanna, and with a box of Ritz crackers under her arm, she would offer "two-fers" for that evening's performance. When special deals didn't work, she might give tickets away, hoping that the people would have the graciousness and generosity to buy a couple tickets to a later show.

Margo was the youngest of the Fisher's three children and was an actress of rare talent. Richard wrote original plays as vehicles for his beautiful sister, including, for example, *Undine* in 1940. In 1939, Margo played the title role in Oscar Wilde's *Salome*, which lead a critic to state: "Miss Fisher performed the title role perhaps as well as it has ever been done." Margo left the Players to take up permanent residence in Hollywood. Her first big notice came when she played the female lead in the west-coast premiere of Maxwell Anderson's *Eve of St. Mark* at the Pasadena Playhouse.

Lydia (Mama) Fisher was a graduate of Pratt Institute and of the Emil Alvin Hartman School of Design, and she was crucial in the Players' climb to fame. She took over the entire job of costuming the performances.

The first season was an artistic success and convinced the founders, Richard and Caroline, that their idea of a theatre colony and outdoor playhouse was sound and that the concept would have the cooperation and patronage of the people of Door County, of people from nearby cities, and of summer visitors. The tourist business seemed bound to grow.

Financially, the first season was not unlike any other summer theatre. It closed with a lot of satisfaction, a lot of hope, and a lot of debt, and those debts made a second season in 1936 impossible.

However, the idea had been proven, and, instead of being discouraged, Richard and Caroline were filled with even greater zeal and enthusiasm to establish a permanent theatre in Door County. With financial help from Papa and Mama, a larger and permanent property was found. The Wildwood Boy's Camp, the site of the present theatre, was purchased in 1937.

The early companies were drawn largely from long-time friends and associates of the Fishers. Most were from midwestern university theatres and from the Goodman Theatre of the Art Institute of Chicago. Leo Lucker, Gertrude Needham, Kevin O'Shea, Helen "Casey" Bragdon, Stacy Keach, Richard Lederer, Fred Randolph, and Bob Thompson helped write the scripts of the Players.

The idyllic Wildwood Camp setting is twenty acres of cedar, pine, and birch forest set along a quarter-mile of Green Bay shoreline. In the early days, the audience sat in the open air; in the mid-1940s, a large canvas tarp was strung over the audience, and on windy nights the audience sometimes had to leave their chairs to help hold down the canvas flapping in the wind.

After a hundred plays under the noisy, leaky, cumbersome canvas, Caroline (now Mrs. Rodion Rathbone) lost her patience and commissioned Neenah architect Frank Shattuck to design an unusual laminated oak pavilion. This produced an acoustically perfect and beautifully protective shelter with roll-down canvas sides to shield the long-suffering audiences. The cost of the pavilion, erected in 1957, exceeded available income, and this capital expense began a series of seasons of financial difficulties.

When the theatre opened on its new site in 1937, talented but eccentric Papa Fisher named himself handyman. He particularly liked to do plumbing because he could hide his beer from Mama in the toilet tanks scattered about the property; he even installed a toilet tank in his office – now the general manager's office – to provide ready access to his beer, but Mama soon discovered the cache and made him remove the commode. Richard occasionally put Papa on stage under the name C. Raeburn Fyfe, but C. Raeburn was a better plumber than actor.

The Players went "dark" during the war years 1942-1944, but reopened in 1945 in time for just one play – *Wuthering Heights* – which then toured to Sturgeon Bay, Green Bay, Wausau, and Chippewa Falls.

During the war years, Caroline married Rodion Rathbone, son of Basil and Marion Forman Rathbone, both distinguished actors. Basil created a legendary Sherlock Holmes, and Marion toured with the famous Benson Company from England. The meeting between Caroline and Rodion was by chance, almost like a Hollywood script. Carolyn was one of the top models for the John Powers Modeling Agency in Chicago. She was discovered by Hollywood, and was signed to a seven-year contract with the agency on the west coast. Caroline and several other models from the agency were invited to attend a function in honor of Basil Rathbone, and Rodion was in attendance, but was about to leave for Canada to join the RAF. Presumably it was love at first sight, for they were married and left for Canada together. After the war, Rodion became a navigator for TWA Airlines, and Caroline returned to the midwest and the Players. Rodion was never around the Players very much during the summer because of his flight assignments. During the war, Richard became a naval officer, complete with sword.

In his autobiography, Basil Rathbone's only reference to his son was that he was involved with a theatre in northern Wisconsin. Basil's dream had been for his son to become an actor, and Rodion's going off to fly airplanes was beyond Basil's comprehension or forgiveness.

The early seasons usually ended with an original musical revue about Door County written by Richard Fisher and Casey Bragdon. Maggy Magerstadt would do her rendition of *Tip-Toe Through the Tulips*, and Bill Munchow would end the evening with his sweet *Mona Lisa*.

In 1946, a full resident company was assembled, and the Players began a schedule of ten plays in ten weeks, playing in semi-repertory, with some early-season plays repeating in August.

Madness was rampant that summer;  it was a season of creative explosion and Eva Klingbile's homemade dandelion wine.

Marion Forman Rathbone joined the company in 1948 as an actress and to establish a theatre school. The "southern mansion" at the north end of the property, replete with Corinthian columns and other finery, became her home. The dwelling had formerly been a garage on the Roadstead property and was moved to the Players. Marion is said to have arrived with at least a thousand steamer trunks.

One of the communal bathrooms and showers on the property was declared off-limits to everyone for a half-hour each morning and again in the evening; these were Marion Times. Part of the school training included the apprentices each morning meeting with Marion on the beach. With pebbles in their mouths, they would speak and recite poetry to Hat Island, Marinette, and Chambers Island.

Richard left the Players in the late 1950s to become a member of the artistic and production staffs of CBS-TV in Hollywood. He became head of production for the Burns and Allen Show, and he was a writer and assistant director for the Jack Benny Show.

A group of company stalwarts known as the "golden dozen" emerged in the late 1940s and the 1950s; they had a great loyalty to the Players and to one another. In addition to the Fishers, they included the late Leo Luckner; Jean Sincere, who occasionally comes back for "just one more show" and is presently a TV and film personality; and Casey Bragdon, whom the Fishers wooed away from some of the best summer theatres in the East, including the Cleveland Playhouse, and who is now living in North Carolina. Other members of the "golden dozen" are: the late Jeanne Bolan McKenzie, who was to become associate producer with her husband James B. McKenzie, now owner and producer of the Players; Bob Thompson, presently one of the Players' directors, who is probably one of the best character actors on any stage today; Paul Ballantyn, who was associated with the Guthrie Theatre; Jean Leslie, now teaching voice and movement in New York City, who recently bought a retirement cottage in Cannes; Maggy Magerstadt, who started as an apprentice at age seventeen, and who now has a home near the Players; Harvcy Korman, Carol Burnett's sidekick; Bill Munchow, still active in Chicago theatre; Dan Scott, who became the hospital administrator on "Trapper John, MD;" Ted Baird; Ray Taylor; Judy Haviland; Frances McVey; Edith Dunn; and Maurie Ottinger.

With increasing expenses, small weekly grosses, Caroline's declining health, and the debt of the new pavilion, the Fishers finally had to put the Players property up for public auction after twenty-five years of total dedication to theatre in Door County. Kenneth Carroad, a New York City tax attorney, bought the theatre in 1960 in homage to his wife and Caroline Fisher, who were friends. At Caroline's request, James B. McKenzie became the acting producer, with Caroline as theatrical advisor. McKenzie began his association with the Players in 1946 and has worked in every capacity from apprentice to master carpenter to press agent. Jeanne Bolan, McKenzie's wife, served as associate producer, actress, and director until her death in 1976.

Caroline Fisher died in 1985, and Richard's death followed in January 1987. Caroline and Rodion had three children, all now living in the east. Rodion, Sr. lives with his daughter Heloise in Brooklyn. Heloise is married and is teaching special education. Second daughter Dounia, at one time an actress with the Players, is also married, has two children, and founded and operates one of the most prestigious catering firms in New York City, "Remember Basil." Son Rodion, Jr. lives in Hamden, Connecticut, is married, has several doctorate degrees, and does research in robotic medicine at the Yale University Medical School.

For the fiftieth anniversary souvenir book of the Players, Heloise wrote a piece that shows the family's relentless love and dedication to keeping the theatre going during its financial crisis. Heloise wrote the article about the 1959 season, the year before the bankruptcy took place; she was in high school at the time.

In the summer of 1959, I ran the theatre. Caroline (mother) had been in a serious car accident on Memorial Day. Being afraid she wouldn't be able to open, she let the company she'd hired find other jobs. Two weeks later, she was somewhat better and couldn't bear to see the theatre closed, so she and I and my brother headed for Fish Creek. From New York, we got as far as Chicago, where mother became very ill. From her hospital bed, she asked me to hire a company and open the theatre. I believed then that she would lose her will to live, if the theatre didn't open. (She has lived another twenty-five years.) She gave me her clipboard and told me a few people to call and then I was on my own. I had no way to handle the task but to imagine that I was she and try to do what she would do.

It was mid-June and we wanted to open for the July 4th weekend. I arranged with several actors and a director and a scene designer to arrive at the Players in about a week. We decided that the only way we could open in so short a time was to stage a play with a small cast. We decided to open with "Champagne Complex" because it had a cast of three. I had no idea how this would work out. I was taking one step at a time and didn't let the size of the undertaking enter my consciousness.

After a couple of days I took my nine-year-old brother Rodion up to Fish Creek. I remember being aware that we had enough money for the train and bus up there, but not enough to get back to Chicago. I didn't dwell on it. Going back didn't seem like an option.

We got to the theatre and broke into the main house. There was no electricity. I contacted a high-school classmate working in Ephraim, who drove down with some food. We cooked our meals on a campfire on the beach. The weather was warm and we sank the milk in a pail in the bay to keep it from spoiling. We were proud of our ingenuity.

Three days later, while Rodion and I were sitting on the beach, the family dog, Armand, came bounding toward us. I was greatly relieved. I knew my father, sister, and Roger Hamilton had arrived. I knew I had help now, and the family car to get around in. In opening up the buildings we found a coffee can full of change worth $72.16; I have never forgotten that number. That was all the money we had to open the season with.

In the early 1960s, reorganization became necessary. Tom Conners, with the Players since 1959, was appointed general manager in 1963. He left in 1977 to purchase a flower shop in Sturgeon Bay.

Due to heavy snows in the winter of 1962, the ridge pole of the lodge gave way. Only the great stone fireplace on the north wall was left standing. A new recreational lodge and dining room with a completely equipped kitchen to feed the company was rebuilt around the fireplace by Walter Kurth of Sturgeon Bay. The lodge's magnificent windows face the "sea."

The Peninsula Players Theatre Foundation, Inc, was formed as a not-for-profit corporation in 1968 and entered into a lease with Kenneth Carroad for the operation of the theatre. The first foundation officers were: Jeanne Bolan McKenzie, president; Chan Harris, vice president; Tom Birmingham, secretary; and Thea Hercules, treasurer; with board members Cliff Herlache, Frank Butts, Tom Conners, Jim McKenzie, William Parsons, and Tom McKenzie.

The 1967 season grossed the unheard-of sum of $50,000; fiscal daylight could be seen.

The exhausting summer schedule of one play a week for ten weeks finally gave way in 1975 to a more sane schedule of five plays, each running two weeks. The tourist turnover in the county allowed a play to be sustained for a two-week period.

On March 15, 1978, James B. McKenzie became the third owner of the Players when he purchased the property from Kenneth Carroad. McKenzie's theatrical career has included management experience as a former partner in New York's Producing Managers Company, an organization known for its production of Broadway and touring shows. From 1969 to 1986, he was executive producer of the American Conservatory Theatre (ACT) in San Francisco in addition to his Players responsibilities. Through ACT, he presented theatrical tours through Russia, South America, Japan, and Hawaii. He currently also serves as executive producer of the Westport Country Playhouse in Westport, Connecticut. McKenzie's association with New York theatre has provided the Players with many plays while they were still playing Broadway and off-Broadway, prior to national tours and general release to other theatres across the country.

McKenzie is a native of Appleton and graduated from St. Mary's High School in Menasha, Wisconsin, from which he received an Outstanding Alumni Award in 1986. Jim met his wife, the late Jeanne Bolan, at the Players in 1949; she was a student at the

Goodman Theatre of the Art Institute in Chicago. He graduated from the University of Iowa in 1950.

After Tom Conners left the Players, I became the general manager, having served the theatre for ten years prior to that as press representative. During part of my tenure with the Players, I was also district administrator of the Gibraltar Area Schools in northern Door County. In 1969, I gave up the job of general manager at the Players to join the academic staff at the new University of Wisconsin-Green bay as theatre manager and director of lectures and performances.

Even before the Peninsula Players, there was summer theatre in Door County. This photo, taken about 1910, shows the cast of the Operetta "Prince of Night", including Henrietta Welcker (far left), Emily Netter (fourth adult from left), and Edna McLeod Thorp (in black hat).

# Index

Adventist Church 27, 49
Adventure Island boys camp 36, 78
Airplane landing 97
Aladdin mantle lamps 22
Algoma Lumber Company 245
Algonquin Glacier 1
Allen, Helen Schreiber 98-125
Alley hill 104
Alley, Fred 252-253
Alwes family 29
Alwes market 19, 47
*Amelia D.* 81, 84
*American Songbag* 255
American Conservatory Theatre 265
American Folklore Theatre 257
Amphitheater in the park 255, 256
Anderson, Carl 31
Anderson, Lester 35, 100
Anderson, Les and Elmer 198
Anderson, John and Andrew 54
Apfelbach,
　Alice x, 203
　"Doc" 198
　G. Leonard 202-204
　Helen Hotz 204
Apples 102
Arnol, J.P., Company 126
Art Institute of Chicago 260, 266
Artists and craftsmen 40
Artists-In-Residence Program ix
*As You Like It* 242
Atkinson, Eliza 194
Auditorium 40-41
Automobiles, early 96, 142, 179,
　　195, 211
Bach, Mrs. 33
*Badger Ballads* 255
Baird, Ted 263
Ballantyn, Paul 262
Baptist church 15
Baptists 49
Baraboo, Art 68
Baraboo, Evelyn Thorp 196
Barber shop 112
Barrel-making (see Coopers) 52
Barringer, Bert 176
Barringer family 12, 49, 134

Barringer, Lawrence & Edna 130-135
Barringer Hotel 12, 17, 19, 47-48,
　58, 72
Baseball 85, 121
Baudhuin, George 245
Bauer piano 179
Baumgarten, Dr. 68
Baxter, Warren 53, 92, 198
Baxter family 5
Beaver Island 128, 153
Becker, Caroline 223
Becker family 55
Becker, Hugo 55
Belgian horses 229
Bell, Josh x, 26
Benson Theatre Company 261
Benton, Thomas Hart 254
Berquist, Gus 59
Big hill 87, 104
Big Band era 221
Bill Carlson's Band 220
Birmingham, Tom 256, 258-267
Black Creek 186
Blackfield, Henry 121
Blacksmith shops 22, 48, 102, 122, 215
Blackwood, Tom 250
Blair, Dr. 68
Blakefield, Frank 129, 131-136
Blizzard 111
Blossomberg Cemetery 134, 164
Bobsled, horse-drawn 18
Bolan, Jeanne McKenzie 263
*Bon Ami* 55, 141-142
Bonnie Brook Motel 237, 258
Bonville, Earl 93
Bonville, Ethel 102
Bonville family 102, 108, 110, 119
Boon Company Dock 126
Boyd, Richard 126-137
Boyd, Sue 126
Bragdon, Helen "Casey" 260
Brault's Canadians 220
Bronsdorf Beach 42
Broodie, John 59
Brown, James x
Brown, John 5, 170
Brungraber, Art 23, 118

Brunswick, Blanche 115
Buchbinder, Hazel 255
Bunda's Hutch 50, 196
Burda, Jeanette 126
Burda, Michael 126-137
Buresk, Martin 59
Burnesky, Stanley 59
Burr, Frank 93
Butts, Frank 265
Byers, Clarence 218
C & C Club 17, 19, 47, 48
C.H. Hackley 48, 49, 126, 127, 131
Cadwallader family 64
Camp Meenahga 32, 78
Campbell, Captain Peter D. 127
Card parties 109
Carl, Elsa Bertelda x, 138-142, 182
Carl, Foster 72
Carlson family 34, 54
Carlson, Ole 59
Carmody, Tom 227
Carolina 55, 68, 138
Carroad, Kenneth 263-265
Casperson, Dorothy 223
Casperson, Edwin 242
Casperson Funeral Home 242
Catholic Church 16, 49
Catholic Diocese of Green Bay 246
Cecelia Hill 5, 55, 154, 162-167
   destroyed by fire 163
Centennial 127
Central Hotel 179
Chalmers 196
Chamber, Annie Pat 72, 109
Chambers,
   Captain Howard 166-167
   Captain Talbot 240
   Don 81, 92
   Mrs. 74
   Ray 198
   Ray and Don 83
   Sam 167
Chambers family 54, 153, 167
Chambers Island 36, 91, 131-132, 136,
144, 149, 182, 212-213, 240-248
   Association 243
   Camp for Girls 243
   Land Company 144, 243-245
   Lighthouse 241
   Lighthouse Park 246
   Retreat House 243, 246

Charlie's (cf. The Rock) 253
Charnetski, Ignatz 59
Chase, Marian 74
Cheese factory 59, 60
Cheeseville 44
Cherry harvest 146
Cherry picking 35, 122-123
Cherry, Martha Hochmeister x, 2, 69
Chicago North Shore RR 244
Chicago Civic Opera 244
Chief Blackhawk 156
Chief Kahquados 30
Children's diseases 108
Christjohnson, Ole 59-61
Christmas 106-108, 186
Christmas trees 32, 144
Church family 5
Churches, Frank 66
Churches, Harry 38, 66 94, 175
Circus 97
City of Marquette 154, 165
Civil War 186
Clafflin, Increase 2, 160, 177, 193-194
Clafflin-Thorp family 2, 134
Clark,
   Alice 32
   Eunice x
   Robert 44, 164
   George M. 13, 14, 44, 63, 64, 164
Clark family 14, 123
Clay Banks 42, 46
Cohn, Abraham 40
Cole, Dr. 68
Coleman mantle lamps 22
Commercial fishing 6, 18, 50, 52, 54,
62, 81, 110, 190, 192
Commonwealth Edison Building 244
Communist Party 231
Community Church 15, 106
Community building 16
Concord 221
Conners, Tom 237-239, 264, 265
Coopers 5, 52, 170, 189, 190, 193, 232
Cornils, Thade 32
Cottage Row 13, 62-70, 170, 230
Coulson family 41, 182
Cracks in the ice 56, 57, 111
Crommel, Mrs. Jessie 170
Crunden family 14
Crunden, Frank P. 64
Cunningham family 241

Curler, Sophia 183
Curry, John Stuart 254
Custer, George 216
Davenport, Ambrose 183
Dawes, Vice-President 244
Deer hunting 208, 209
Deer herd 245
Dennett family 241-245
Detroit Harbor 128
Devil's Pulpit 142
Diamond merchant 203
Doolittle, Alfred E. 34, 35, 142,
      220, 224
Door County Advocate 159, 166, 167
Door County Auditorium 38
Door County Country Club 31
Door County Republican Party 61
Doughty, Roy 92
Doughty, Sheldon 198
Douglas, Archibald G., Jr. x, 62-70
Drake family 92, 243-246
Drake Hotel 243
Dramatic productions 24
Dressing fish 52, 54
Drinking water 23
Drummond Island 157, 160, 167
Ducks 213-215, 243
Duclon,
      Ambrose 186
      Captain William 31, 122, 183
      Charles 186, 220
      Claudius 183
      Clyde 38, 183-188
      Edith (Mrs. Charles) 72, 220
      Frank 186
      Grace 183-188
      Joseph 186, 220
      Jim 186
      Lucille 183-188
      Vivian 183-188, 223
      Walter and William Jr. 186
      Willaim Henry 183
Duclon family 54, 110, 183-188
Duclon family band 196, 220
Dunn, Edith 263
Dutch cheese 12
Dyer family 34
Dyer, Lilia 76
Eagle Lighthouse 183, 241
Eastman College 195
Eau Claire 74

Eberlein, Frank 223
Eberline, Mrs. 33
Eckert, Evelyn 223
Eckert family 58
Edison, Thomas 244
Egeland, Dr. 68, 196
Eldred, Howard 64
Electric power 22
Episcopal Church 15, 50, 51, 72
Erickson, Sam 243
Erie L. Hackley 55, 126-137, 176, 201
Europe Lake 203
Eva M. Hill 164
Eva's store 59
Evenson family 54
Fahr, Martha 74
Fairchild, Charles 158
Fairchild family 153
Fairchild, Percy 39, 49
Fairchild, Skip x
Falck-Pedersen family 27
Federal Marine Inquiry Board 136
Fernwood Gardens 221
Fire 25, 74, 77, 90, 91, 100, 101, 200,
223, 243, 245
      in Peninsula Park 68
Firecrackers 119
Fire-fighting equipment, 24
Fischel, Dr. 68
Fischer, tugboat 132
Fish nets 83
Fish-packing 5, 6
Fish Creek
      dock 7
      garage 48, 75
      graded school 105, 215
      library 26
      Men's Club 25
      pier 67
      post office 75-78
Fish Creek Hotel 62
Fish Creek Transportation Company
127
Fish   Creek   Volunteer   Fire
Department 25, 101
Fish Creek Yacht Club 65
Fish boil 6
Fish sheds 83
Fisher,
      Caroline 26, 237-239, 258-263
      Charles R. (Papa) 237, 258-260

Fisher (continued),
Lydia (Mama) 237, 259
Margo 238, 259
Richard 237-239, 258-261
Fisher family 258-263
*Flaxen*, a musical comedy 249-250
Floating store 54
*Flora M. Hill* 166
Folklore 254
Fordson tractor 147, 148
Founder's Square 48, 117, 200
France, Anatole 230
Franke, Mrs. Alfred x
Franke family 58
French explorers 1
Friedmann, Albert 24
Friedmann estate 186
Friedmann family 24, 64, 119
Frost damage to cherries 146
Fruit Growers Cooperative, 61
Fruits, small 146
Fuhr, Alta 71, 74
Fuhr, Erwin 24
Fyf, C. Raeburn (cf. Papa Fisher) 260
Garage, Lester Anderson's 100
Gard, Robert 254-2555
Garland, Hamlin 249
Gartman, Wilmer x
Gatter, Miss 33
Gauger family 58
Gauguin 230
*Georgia* 55, 68
German prisoners of war 35
German settlement 58
German-speaking people 64
German cuisine 179
Gibraltar Orchards 201
Gibraltar High School 12, 38, 40,
61, 222, 224
Gibraltar Historical Association x, 26
Gibraltar, town of 59, 240
Gill nets 18, 81, 82, 190, 242
Gilliam, Erna Carl 138-142
Gogats, James 78
Going through the ice 92, 93
Golf 211-212
Goodman Theatre 266
Goodrich Transportation Company 5,
8, 10, 11, 55, 66, 67, 99,
138, 195
reorganization of 166

Grab Bag and Walk (GB&W) 195
Graham, Anna I 159
Graham family 5, 54
Grasse, Harvey 223
*Grasshopper* 221
Great Slave Lake 176
Green Bay and Western (GB&W) 195
Green Island 128
Green, Bennie 72
Green's farm, 84
Greene family 104
Grey, John 59
Grimmer, Merton 96
Griswold, L.M. 153
Guenzel, Betsy x
Guenzel, Paul x, 69
Guenzel, William (Bill) ix-x, 182
Guinea hens 84
Guthrie Theater of Minneapolis 255
Gypsies 116
Hackley family 126
Halloween 102
Haltug, John 129, 135
Hambleton family 64
Hanover shoal 131
Hansen, Abel 233
Hansen, Sulie Anderson 116
Hanson, Milton 129, 135
Hanson, Thor 59
Hardin, Adlai 30
Harris, Chan 265
Harris, Sidney 14
Hart, Fanny 55
Hart, Ellie 182
Hart, Eugene 55
Hart Brothers 170
Hart Transportation Company 55,
141, 204
Hartman, Emil Alvin, School of
Design 259
Haskell, Grant 46
Haviland, Judy 263
Hays, Lucille Duclon 182-188
Hecht, Ben 230
Heide, Fred 250-256
Helgeson, Clyde 50, 198
Henry family 183
Hercules, Thea 265
Heritage Ensemble 41, 249-257
Herlache, Cliff 265
Herman family 58

Herring 53, 170
Hidden Harbor 119
Hill,
    Captain Eugene L. 162, 165, 1
        64, 169
    Captain Ludlow Leonidas 158, 165
    Captain Wallace E. 157, 169
    Cecilia Seaman 156-161
    Duncan and Roland 162
    Floyd Stevens 159
    Harwood ix, 153-169
    Jedediah 155, 158
    L.P. 153-160
    Ludlow Leonidas 164
    Wallace 28
    William Seaman 158, 159
    William Wallace 5, 160
Hill Brothers pier 165
Hill family 5, 29, 54, 153-169
Hill store 19, 28
Hill Steamboat Line 153-169
Hillsdale Farm 160
Hirthe, Professor Walter 126
*History of Door County* 153, 160, 182,
    227
Hodgin, Elliott 76, 78
Hogan, Joe 93
Hogan's Little German Band 220
Holand, Hjalmar R. ix, 30, 33, 153,
    160, 182, 227
Homer Bay 241
Hotz, Ferdinand x, 100, 153, 202-204
Hotz, Mary 204
Hotz family 104, 202-204
House cleaning 112
Howe, Gertrude x, 48
Huber Theater 36
Hunting 88, 89
Hypothermia 131
Ice-boating 88
Ice boxes 65, 109
Ice-cream 89, 90
Ice fishing 18, 82, 84
Ice houses 20
Insul, Samuel, Jr. 244
Irish House 74, 178
*Islander* 92, 160, 242
Jarman family 58, 123
Jarman, Will 56
Jensen family 93
Jerasick, George 96

Jerasick, Gretna 96
Jewetts 195
Jischke, Alice 223
John Powers Modeling Agency 261
Johnson, Captain Fred 132-134
Johnson, Mildred Casperson 242
Johnson, Thor 41
Johnston, Captain Asa 132
Judd, Vet 82
Juddville 59, 76, 170, 203
Kalms family 59
Kates family 243
Kazmarek, Andrew 59
Keach, Stacy 260
*Kenosha* 169
Keuchler, Agnes 33
Kihl, Bernice 223
Kihl, Claude 76
King Edward VIII 74
Kinney, Charles 36, 78
Kinsey,
    Al 227
    Alson and Martin 177
    Everil 175-177
    Hazel 175
    Ingham 170, 174-177
    Jessie 175-176
    May Thorp 175
    Martin 170, 172, 173
    Neil (Pat) 170
    Roy 170, 174-177
    Sam 175
    Sherm 58
    Virginia 26, 174-177
Kinsey family 12, 23, 28, 92, 93, 112,
    119, 153, 174-177
Kissels 195, 211
Kita, Roman 59
Klingbile, Eva 262
Klok, Margaret Hotz 203
Knuppel, John 24
Kodanko family 31
Koepsel's in Sister Bay 221
Korman, Harvey 263
Krause family 29, 58
Krause, Gus, Herman and Emil 176
Krause, Reinhard 245
Kurth, Walter 265
*L.P Hill* 162
La Mere's in Egg Harbor 221
Lake Mackaysee 241-243

Lambeau, Curly 64
LaMere, Jerry 205
Larson Brothers 170
Larson's Mill 143
Lasaa, C.M. 30
Lauerman Brothers 54
Lautenbach family 123
LeClair, George 131, 134, 135
LeClair, Meta 49, 122
Lee, Captain Seth 126-127
Lefebvre, Grace Duclon 183-188
Leipzig University 178
LeMere, George, barber shop 112
*Lena Delta* 162
Leslie, Jean 262
*Lily Chambers*, tugboat 128
Lippmann, Dr. 68
Livery stable 195
Long Arch, the hired man 148
Lovekin, W.R. 31
Luckner, Leo 260-262
Luke Hill 154
Lumbering 62
Lumberman's Hotel 178
Lundberg,
    Alexander 17, 28, 48
    Alice 106, 196
    Alma 17, 44, 48, 166
Lundberg family 15, 29
Lundberg store 19, 28, 47, 117, 166
Lutheran Memorial Building 59
Lynch, Robert S. 244
Mack, Archie 206, 207
Mackinaw boat 170, 176
Mackinac island 55, 241
MacLamon family 206
Madame Schumann-Heinck 180
Magerstadt, Maggy 261-263
Magnette, Virginia 223
Mah Jong 180
Mail 16, 45
Maltman family 186
Malzahn, Harvey 247
Manet 230
Manitou Island 127
Maple Tree Cafe 12, 49, 113, 121, 140
Maple Grove 27, 58, 59
Marinette 110
Marmons 195, 211
*Marquette* 159
Mason, Helen 61

Massey, O.E. 223
Matheison, F. 130, 135
Maxwells 196
Mazur, Roman 59
McClathlan, Robert 2
McCummin family 5
McCummings, Tim 82
McGee, Mrs. Caa x
McKenzie, James B. 239, 262-265
McKenzie, Tom 265
McKenzie, Jeanne Bolan 262-265
McKnee, Dan 175
McLeod, Christy 160
McLeod, Duncan 165
McLeod family 28, 29, 77
McLeod store 48
McSweeney, B 130, 135
McSweeney, Blaine 121
McSweeney family 5
McVey, Frances 263
Melvin, Doris 175
Melvin, John 54, 175
Menominee 128
Melvin, John 175
Menominee River Brewing Company
    48
Mentor, Mary M. 127
Miller, Hugh 129, 134, 135
Miller, Colonel John 240
Milvia, Emma 175
*Milwaukee Journal* 257
Mink River 214-215
Minor family 174-177
Minor-Clafflin family 177
Modern Woodman Lodge 50
Modigliani 230
Moeller's Garage 147
Moravians 59
Morley Murphy Hardware 54
Morning Star 81
Mountain Land Company 232-233
Moving pictures 23, 118
Mueller, John 246
Munchow, Bill 261-263
Musical groups 220
Muskegon 126
Mystery Ship Seaport, 136
Nash, Mrs. Kenneth 167
National Cherry Growers Assn 61
National Registry for Historical
    Buildings 247

Needham, Gertrude 237, 260
Nelson family 243, 245
Nelson, Nels 129, 133, 134, 135
Netter, Emily 267
Newberry, Rita 223
Newhall, Benjamin and Franklin 127
Newport State Park 201, 203
Niagara Escarpment 1
Nightengale supper club 221
Noble, Alex 27, 122
Noble, Charley 166-167
Noble, Robert 176
Noble family 27, 48, 201
Noble's pasture 201
Nook Hotel 9, 23, 62, 113, 179, 196
North Muskegon Ferry Line 127
Northern lights 123
Norton, Rachel 123, 124
Norton, Steven 16
Norton family 27, 102, 123
Norz, Gary 165
Norz family 28, 29, 48
Norz store 19
Nygaard, Ralph 44
O'Brien family 241
Ohman, Eugene 89
Ohnesorge family 58
*Old Peninsula Days* ix, 33
Old World Wisconsin 252
Olsen, Vivian 223
Olson,
     Arni 223
     Annie Carl 72, 109
     Carl 54
     Lany Resler 160
     Martin 129, 135
     Milton 129, 135
     Nels 59
     Ruby 160
     Staner 12, 53, 138, 171
     Willie 59
Olson family 60
Olson, Foster x
Oneson, Barnt 91
O'Shea, Kevin 237, 260
Ottinger, Maurie 263
Otumba 240
Pabst family 179
Parsons, William 265
Patzke's Nite Hawks 220
Peddle, Alice Clark 182

Pelkey, Carl 129, 134, 135
Pelkey, Rose x
Pelke's Pool Hall 226
Pelke's Tavern 49, 102
Pelletier, Charles 200
Peninsula School of Art ix, 40
Peninsula Music Festival 38, 40-41, 255
Peninsula Players 27, 41, 237-239,
     255-267
Peninsula Players "golden dozen" 262
Peninsula Players Theatre Foundation
     239, 265
Peninsula State Park 30, 41, 71, 76, 92,
     134, 164, 179, 183, 201, 223,
     232, 241, 250, 255, 257
   golf course 31, 211, 212
   lighthouse 31
Pequot Indian War 158
Peshtigo 110
Peshtigo fire 178
Peterson, Dave 254-256
Peterson, Peter 59
Peterson, Theodore 59
Petscheider, Robert 30
Pilot Island 190, 192
Pleck's Dairy 114
Plum Bottom 162, 227
Poirer family 28, 29
Polish settlement 59
Polster family 58
Polyventure Incorporated 200
Pond net 50, 53, 170
*Port des Mortes* 2
Potawatomi Indians 1-2, 30, 193
Potter's Wheel 40, 72
Pratt, Delando 156
Pratt Institute 259
Public Works Art Project 230
Putnam family 48
Putting up ice 94, 95, 109
Quarantine 109
Quilting 109
*Quo Vadis* 246
Radio 95, 96
Raft fever 115
Raiza, Leo Stanley 59
Randolph, Fred 260
Rathbone,
     Basil 238, 261
     Dounia 263
     Heloise 263

Rathbone (continued),
  Mrs. Rodion (see Caroline Fisher)
    238, 260
  Marion Forman 261-262
  Rodion 261-263
Ray family 58
Red Raven Polka Band 220
Red Barn 153
Regionalists art movement 254
Reimer family 133
Reinhard family 58
Reinhardt, Lenny 221-223
Retreat Dock 83
Revivalists, religious 49
Reynolds and Rickles Pea Canning
 Company 45
Ringling Brothers Circus 255
Roadstead fellowships 256
Robertoy, Frank 60
Robertoy, Henry 127, 131, 134, 135
Rock, The 253
Rockendorf family 5, 54
Rockendorf, Herman 176
Rogers, Jay 214
Rogers, Sam 142
Rogers, Will 153
Root beer 118
Rousseff family 72, 230-231
Rousseff, Vlad W. 230-231
Rowin, Orin 130-135
Rowleys Bay 214
Ruckert, Charles 56
Runquist, Dick 59
Sacketts Harbor 155
Sail-sleigh 20-21
*Sailor Boy* 55, 142
Salona 44-46
Sandburg, Carl 255
Sawmills 5
Sawyer (west Sturgeon Bay) 42-46
Scandinavian settlement, Juddville 59
Schmidt, Alice Hotz 204
Schmidt, Helen Hotz 203
School Christmas play 107
Schooner, two-masted 199
Schreiber,
  Allen 81-97
  Bob 70, 94
  Clare Adele 182
  Edward v, ix-x, 5-41, 94, 182
  Ella 101

Schreiber (continued),
  Helen 71, 98-125
  Hollis 101
  Lester 28
  Lois ix-x, 26, 71-74
  Lottie 108
Schreiber family 29, 48, 97, 103
Schreiber store 28, 117, 259
Schulz, Anita 75-78
Schutz family 46
Schuyler,
  Albert A. 42
  Bob 85
  Fred 102, 115
  Francis 44
  Frank W. 42
  Harry 42-61, 85, 91, 198
  Helen 61, 71
  George 22, 48, 215
  Mrs. 56
Schuyler's orchard 123
Scott, Dan 263
Seaman, Caleb 158
Seaman, Captain John 158
Seaman, Daniel Murry 157
Seaman family 158
Seaworthiness of the Hackley 134
Segovia, Andres 255
Seidel Fish Company 170
Seiler, Carl 28, 75, 78
Seiler family 58
Sellick family 5, 194
Seventh Day Adventist Church 15,
    124
*Shamrock* 128
Shattuck, Frank 260
*Sheboygan* 132, 169
Shield, Ben 60, 61
Shipbuilding 62
Shine, Vivian Duclon x, 183-188
Simmons, Rouse 127
Sincere, Jean 262
Singing 74
Skating 110
Slaby family 201
Slaby, Ray Sr. 85, 98, 100, 106
Sliding on the alley hill 86
Smallpox, vaccination for 68, 180
Smelt 6, 218-220
Smith, Alvin 206, 207
Smith, Gilbert 64

Smith, Kate 74
Smith, Leathem 241, 242
Sneeberger, Dr. 109
South Bend Urban RR 244
Spielman, Pat 230
St. James Harbor 128
Stearn's Knights, 211
Steamships 67, 199
Steinseifer, Ernie 91-92, 243
Stenzel, Henry 28, 75
Stenzel family 58
Stevens, Myron and Hulda 159
Stevens family 13
Stevens rooming house 13
Stevens family 153
Stock, Mrs. 106-108
Strang, James 154-156
Strawberry island 36
Sturgeon 171
Summer theatre 267
Summertime Restaurant 113
Sunrise Farm 178
Sunset Beach, 81
*Tales of the Sea* 166
Tank, Otto 91
Taylor, Ray 263
Telegraph wires 47
Telephones 68, 120, 179
Templeton, Jenny A. 42
Tennison, Joseph 54
Tennison Bay 31, 92
Thanksgiving 103, 186
Theatre-In-A-Garden 238
Theis, Matt 246
Theis sawmill 246
Thenell family 243
*Thistle* 55, 142, 179, 204
Thompson, Bob 260-262
Thorp,
    Ann 26, 170-173, 178-182
    Annie Roy 26, 72
    Asa 16, 62, 178, 189-190
    Edna McLeod 267
    Duncan ix, 1-2, 143-150, 182,
        189-200, 205-234
    E.T. 127
    Edgar (Ted) 26, 120, 195
    Edna McCleod 71, 106, 145
    Freeman 27, 131-135, 176
    Harold 2, 198
    Jacob 2, 189

Thorp (continued),
    Jake and Levi 189, 194
    Jess 77
    Jim 198
    Kenneth 92
    Leland 196, 198, 200
    Maria Clafflin 2
    Matilda 196, 177
    May and Bertha 177
    Merle 2, 145, 180, 196, 198, 218
    Mildred 48, 105
    Roy F. 2, 54-58, 133, 143, 158-177,
        213
    Sylvia 200
    Ted and Tilda 120
    Uncle Ed 205
Thorp family 5, 8, 48, 50, 143, 153,
    189-200
Thorp Hotel 8, 13, 23, 48, 64, 102-103,
    117-119, 138-140, 179,
    195-198
    fire at 9
Thorp House Inn 27
Thorp pier construction 194
Thorp plat 8, 62
Timble, Miss 85, 100
Totem pole 30
Tourism 70
Tourtelot, Madeline ix, 40
Town Hall 50
Tractor, 1020 Titan 59
Transport by water 55
Traveling evangelists 39
Tree culture 144
Tufts pier 42
Tugboats 128, 132
Turkey shoot 102
Turnbull Boiler Works 126
U.S. Lifesaving Service 132
Uhlemann, Herbert 223
Uhler, George, Inspector General 136
Union Steel Tank Company 243
Universal Shipbuilding Company 157
UW-Madison Children's Theatre 251
Valquarts, Henriette 106
Van Vorous, Hudson
Victrola, portable 106
Vincent, Edna and Ethel 130-134
Volquartz, Henriette 71
Von Briessen, Ralph x

Vorous,
  Bill 142, 196
  Captain 128, 129, 134, 135-136
  Captain Joseph 127, 201
  Levi 127
  Mabel 48
  Vorous family 29
  Vorous store 28, 48
Waldo, Alma Lundberg x, 110
Walker, Mary Ann 2
Wallace, Captain William 158
Walloping Window Blind.  37
Warrens Corners 44
Washdays 116
Washington Island 128
*Waukegan* 169
Weborg,
  Alfred 232
  Ella 33, 76, 232-234
  Joanna 232
  Olaf 59
  Peter 170, 232
  Vida 30, 33, 232
Weborg, boat built by 213
Weborg family 54
Weborg Point 96, 114
Wedepohl, William 78
Weisgerber, Dick 60
Welcker,
  Dr. Hermann 26, 48, 62, 74, 138,
          140, 178-182
  Henrietta 179, 182, 267
  Hedwig Enger 138
  Henrietta 267
  Victor 182, 253
Welcker Casino 9, 19, 48, 140,
          178-182, 201, 231
Welcker Resort 9, 64, 74, 85, 103, 119,
          138
Welcker's bathhouse 138
Welcker's Point 178
Wesa family 48
Wescott, Supervising Inspector 136
Wesner, Fred 198
Westports Steaship Line 166
Whistling Swan 19, 48, 140, 178, 182,
          231
White Gull Inn 40-41, 81, 140, 160,
          178, 182
Whitefish 170
Wiest Plumbing Company 35

Wildwood Boy's Camp 237, 260
Williams, Lewis 241
Williams family 241
Wilms, Rocky 69
Wilson, Helen 223
Wilson, Jim 59
Wilson, Max 59
Wilson & Hendrie 126
Wilson's ice-cream parlor 65
Winter activities 20, 87-88
Wisconsin glacier 1
Wisconsin Idea Theater 254
Wisconsin Public Television 257
Witalison, Charles 59
Woerfel, Hubert 106
Woerfel, Richard 223
Woldt, Herman 60
Women's Club plays 107
Wons, Ruby Hill 165-166
Wood, Grant 254
*Woodmancote* 242, 245
Zachow family 58
Zak, Joseph 59
Zak, Martin 5